Pen and Ink
Drawing
Techniques

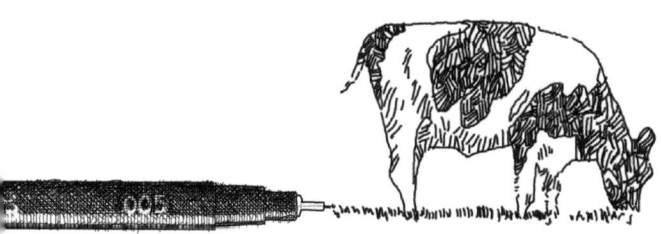

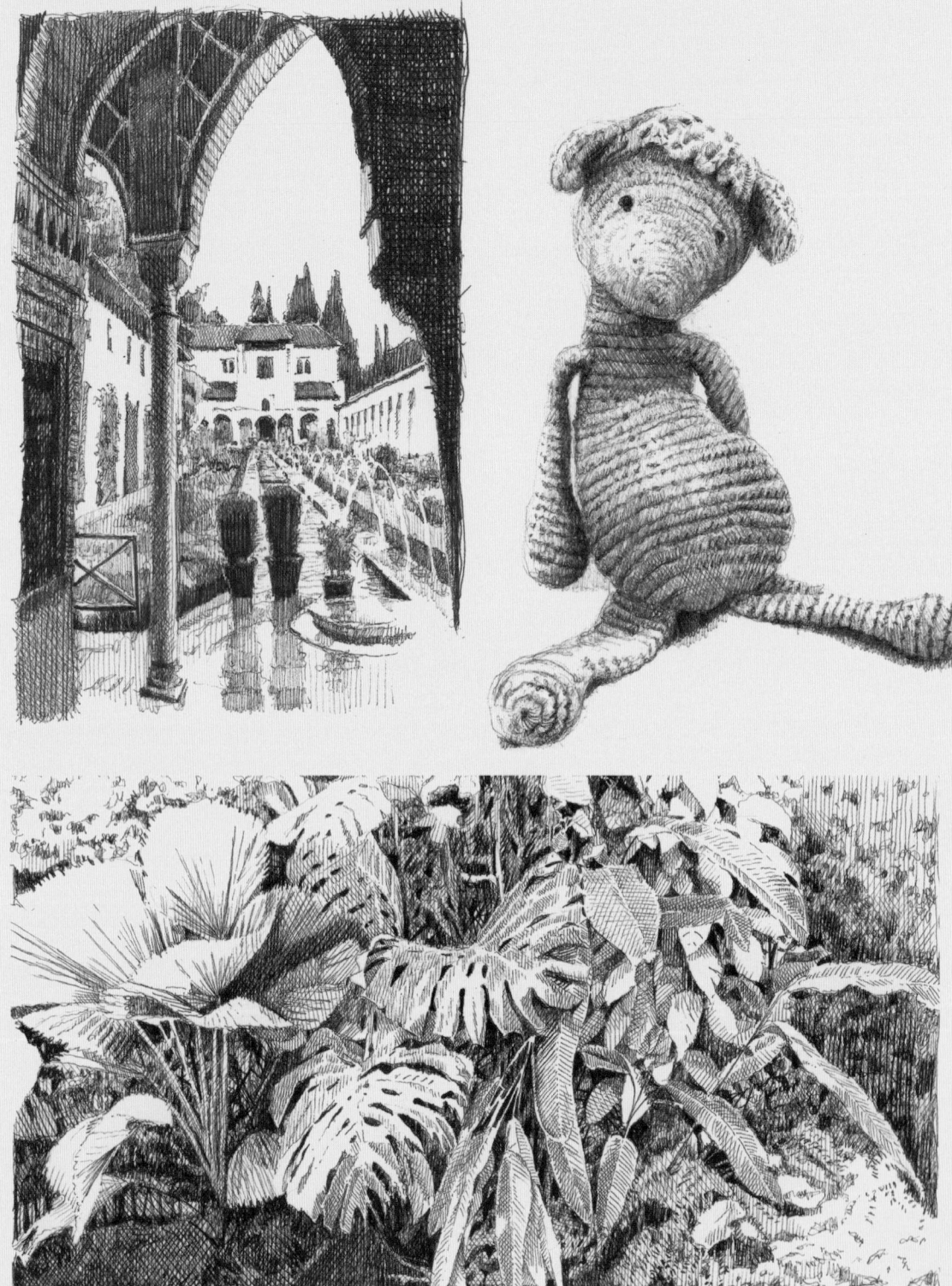

Pen and Ink
Drawing Techniques

STEPS, SUBJECTS & PROMPTS

DAVID MORALES H.

SEARCH PRESS

A QUARTO BOOK

This edition published in 2025 by
Search Press
Wellwood
North Farm Road
Tunbridge Wells
Kent TN2 3DR

ISBN: 978–1–80092-263–1
ebook ISBN: 978-1-80093-262-3

Conceived, edited and designed by
Quarto Publishing, an imprint of
The Quarto Group
1 Triptych Place
London SE1 9SH
www.quarto.com

QUAR: 1173766

Illustrator: David Morales H.
Editor: Charlene Fernandes
Copyeditor: Sarah Hoggett
Managing editor: Emma Harverson
Art director: Martina Calvio
Designer: Hugh Schermuly
Commissioning editor: Jo Lightfoot
Publisher: Lorraine Dickey

Printed in China

Bookmarked Hub
For further ideas and inspiration, and to
join our free online community, visit
www.bookmarkedhub.com

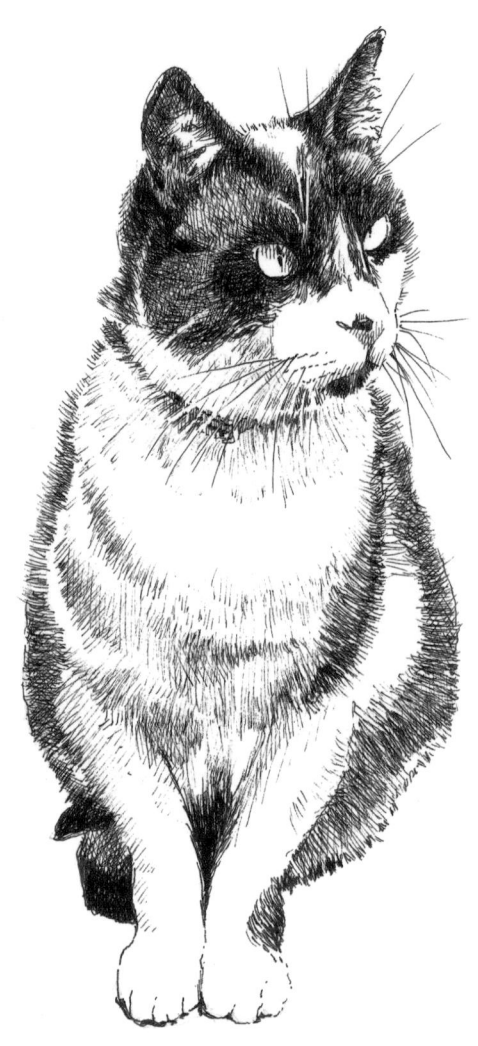

Contents

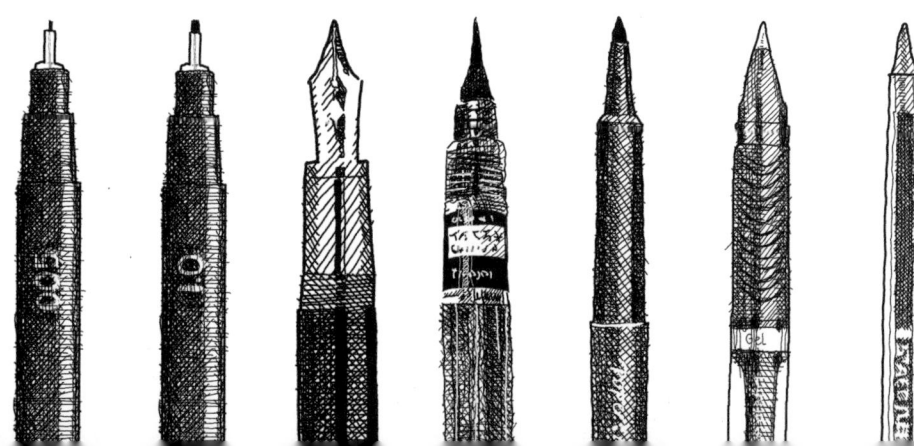

Introduction

Welcome to a journey filled with ink, strokes and creativity. This book is much more than a collection of illustrated pages; it is an intimate compendium of my journey, my passion and my commitment to the art of ink drawing. From the first strokes that outlined my love for this form of artistic expression, to the most refined techniques I have perfected over time, I have written this book with a blend of knowledge and experience and, above all, a fervent desire to share all of this with you.

Before delving into the world of ink, I invite you to traverse the landscapes of my history, explore my gallery of drawings and grasp the essence of what it means to create with this medium, as well as familiarize yourself with the necessary materials to embark on this artistic adventure.

You will discover how to hold the pen with confidence, learn about the different types of lines and master how to achieve tonal values and textures through various pen-and-ink techniques. But this is just the beginning.

We will immerse ourselves in the very essence of the act of drawing: facing the blank paper, observing the world around us with curious eyes, finding inspiration in the most unexpected places, and, fundamentally, learning not to be frustrated in the process

And when you are ready, when you feel the ink flowing through your veins, I will guide you through a series of exercises designed to challenge your skills, expand your creativity and take you beyond your limits.

This book not only seeks to teach you the basic tools of ink drawing, but also to inspire you to explore, to create and to find your own voice in this fascinating artistic universe.

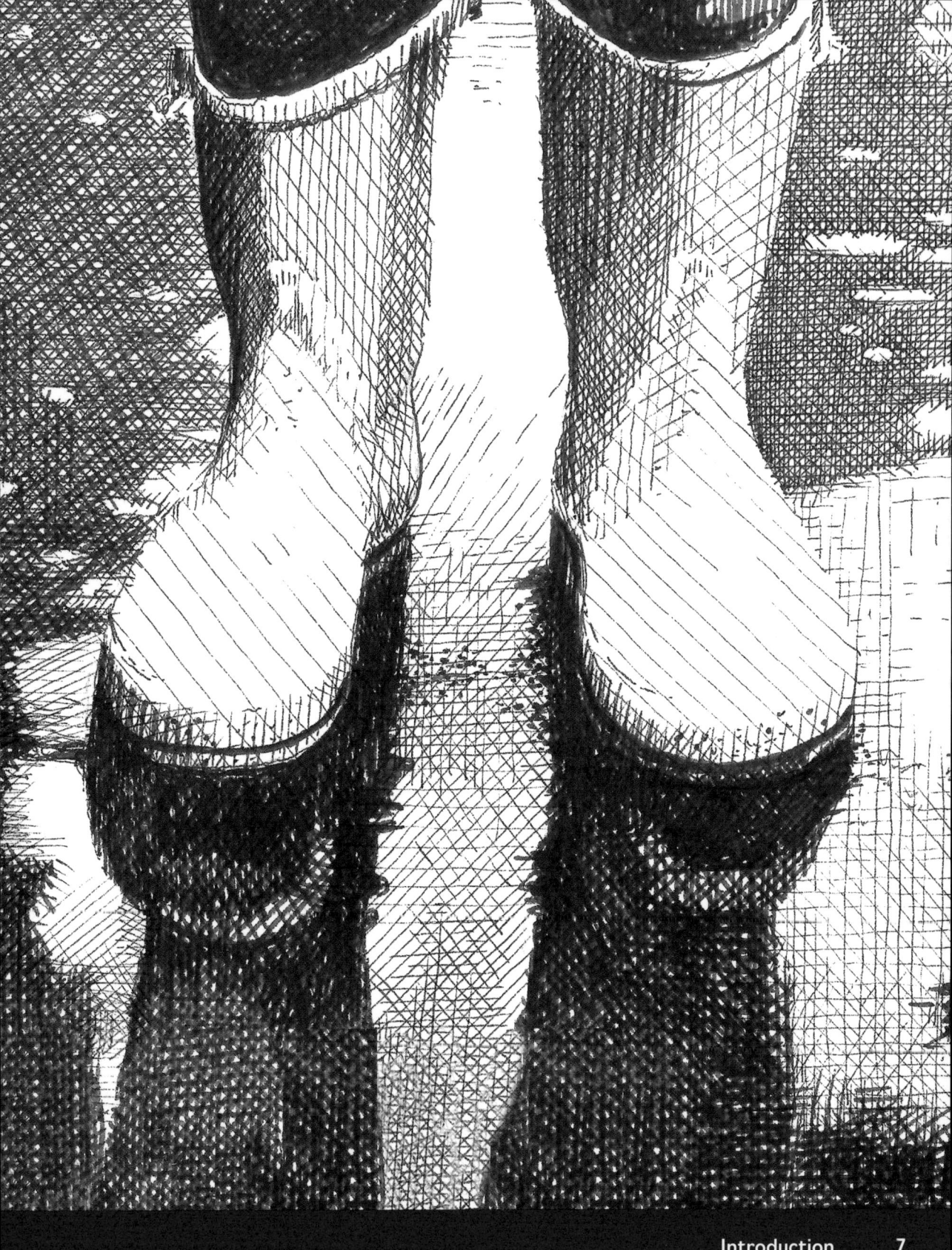

Meet David Morales H.

Like many of you, I have been drawing since I was very young, feeling a restlessness for engaging in any creative activity involving the use of my hands. This need has been a constant throughout much of my life. It was while studying architecture in Bogotá, influenced by so many architects who drew, that I began sketching the buildings that personally interested me. I realized that, through drawing, it is relatively easy to discover and understand the proportions and materiality of architectural structures.

For many years my drawing practice focused on observation and architectural design, but above all, I drew to explain ideas. However, gradually enveloped by work and family responsibilities, I couldn't dedicate as much time to drawing as I would have liked. In 2018, I decided to challenge myself to draw every day for an entire year, partly to make up for lost time and partly to test my ability to stay faithful to the challenge. I called this project 'One Day, One Drawing', and I carried it out for four consecutive years.

Although my preference for pen drawing originated during my years of studying architecture, I quickly realized it would be my ideal ally for daily drawing challenges. The convenience of carrying the essential drawing tools with me at all times led me to simplify the tools in search of the most comfortable carrying option. Thus, I discovered that the simplest way to approach this challenge was to draw on a notebook with a pen, marking the beginning of my exploration and mastery of the pen-and-ink technique.

On the following pages I share drawings from my time as a student, where my interest was focused on architecture, as well as drawings from the 'One Day, One Drawing' project, where my interest extended to everything around me, turning the notebooks into a kind of illustrated diary about my life. This daily documentation in the form of chronological sketches has become the central axis of my work as an artist.

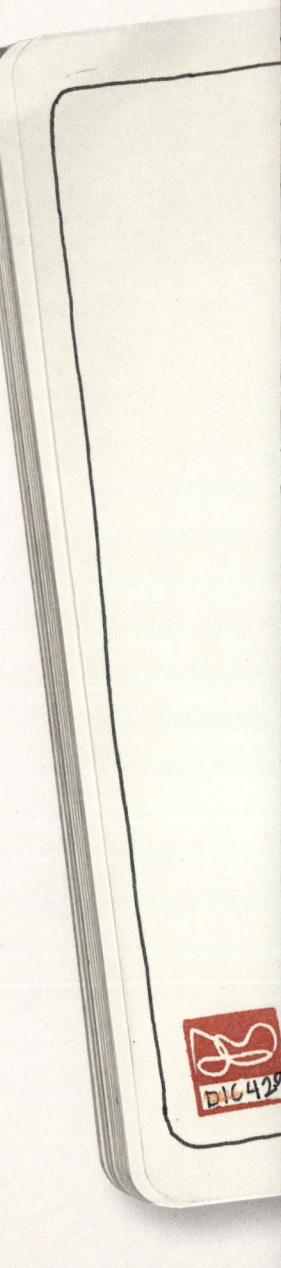

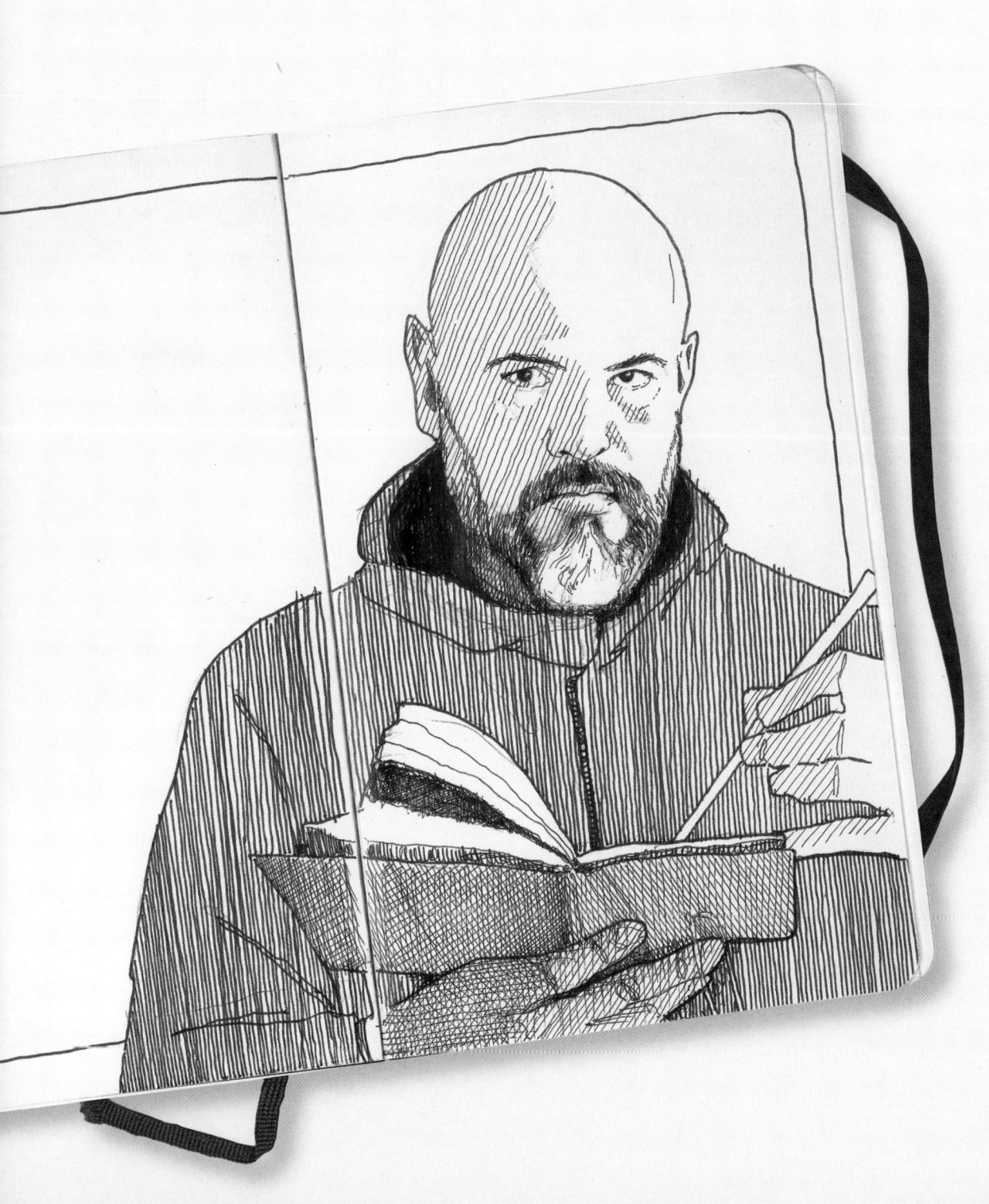

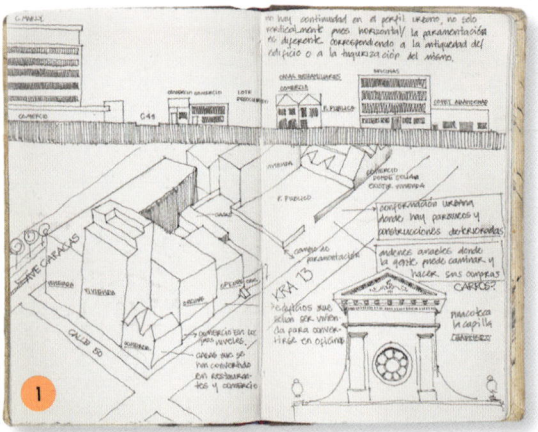

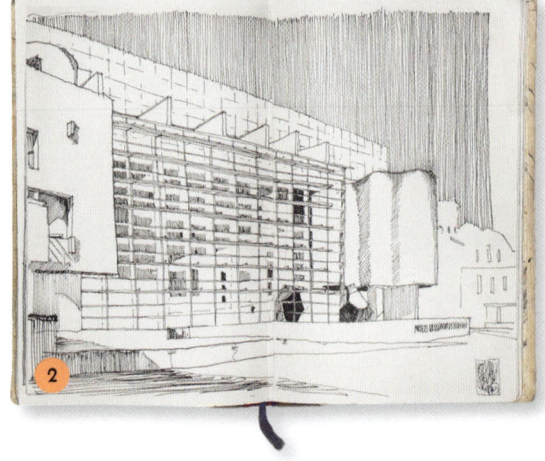

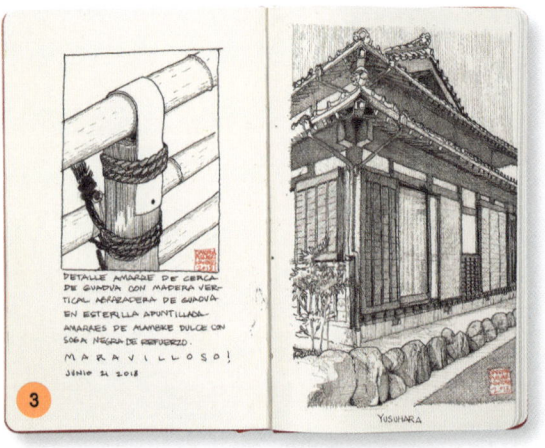

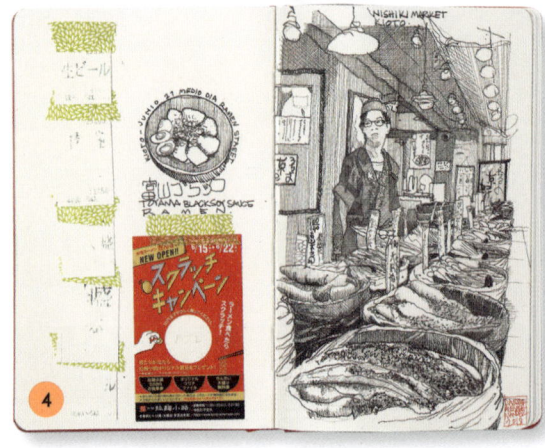

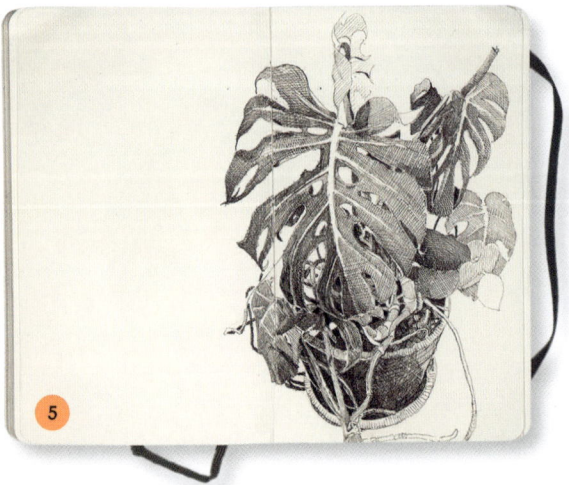

1. Urban observation, Bogotá (1998) While studying architecture, I learned to use drawing as a tool for observation, drawing everything that was relevant to understanding the city.

2. MACBA, Barcelona (2000) During the early years of living in Europe, I drew the most emblematic buildings, those that I had encountered while studying architecture.

3. Bamboo fence detail and wood house, Yusuhara, Japan (2018) Traditional architecture and handcrafted details continue to be a constant source of inspiration when I travel.

4. Nishiki Market, Kyoto, Japan (2018) As well as architecture, unique places and lived experiences feature in my sketchbooks.

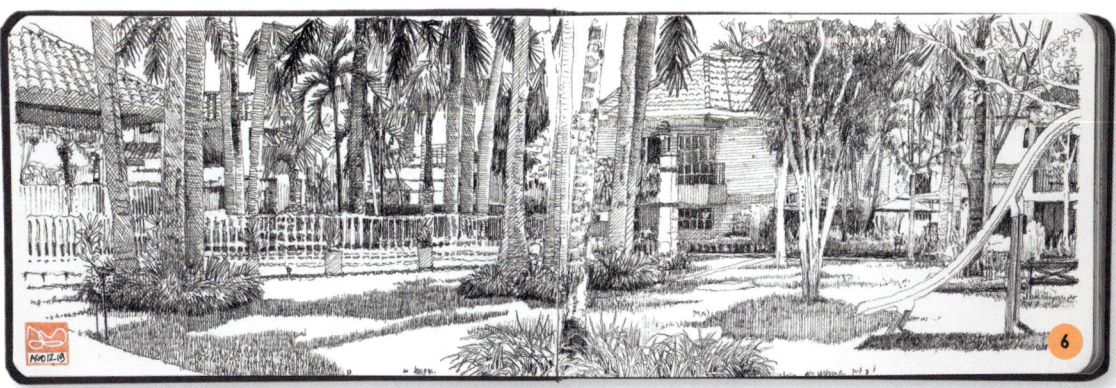

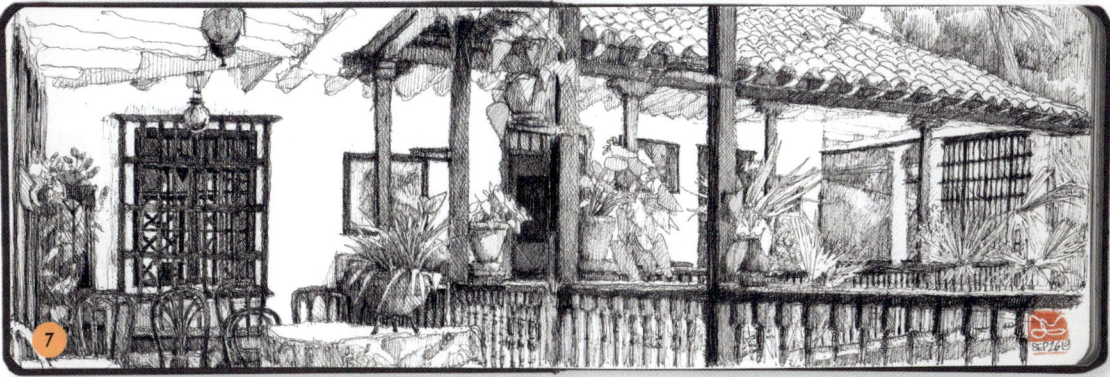

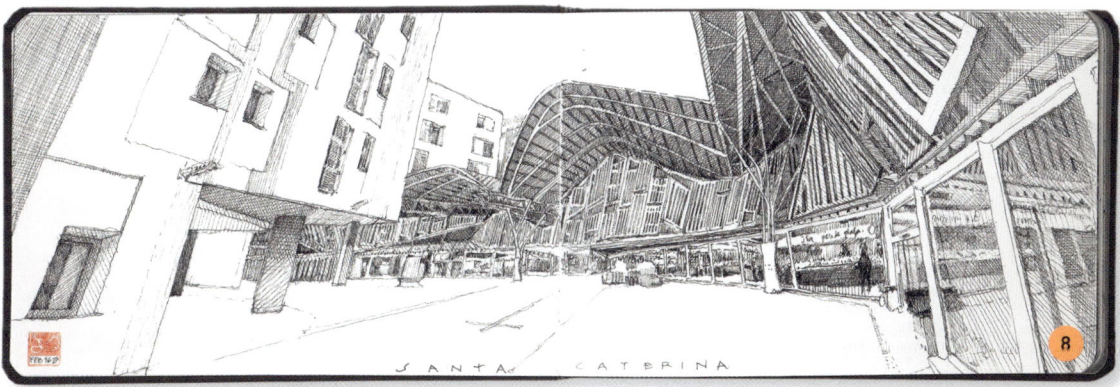

5. Monstera plant, Barcelona (2022) Drawing with hatching allows me to slowly build volumes and helps me practise patience during observation.

6. Palm trees, Colombia (2019) Sometimes the appeal of a place lies simply in having experienced it, such as our neighbourhood while living in Colombia.

7. Colonial house, Colombia (2019) Dedicating time to draw special places, such as the neighbourhood of our house in Colombia, allows me to immortalize these spaces and establish a unique connection with them.

8. Santa Caterina Market, Barcelona (2020) Practice has enabled me to handle projects that include complex geometries.

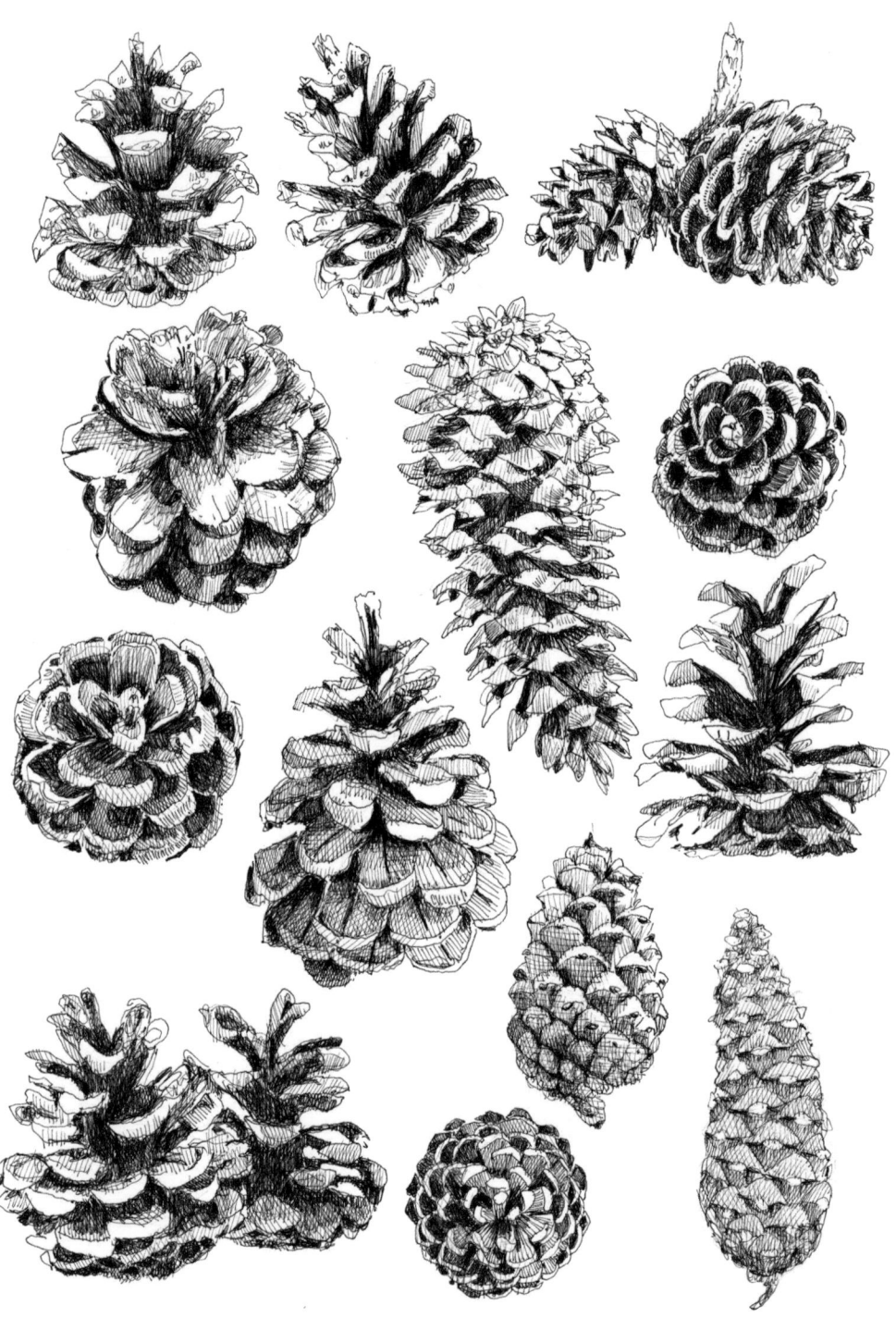

Pine cones (2022) I've always been drawn to the small variations of objects that are part of a collection; through drawing, I can collect countless objects and their variations.

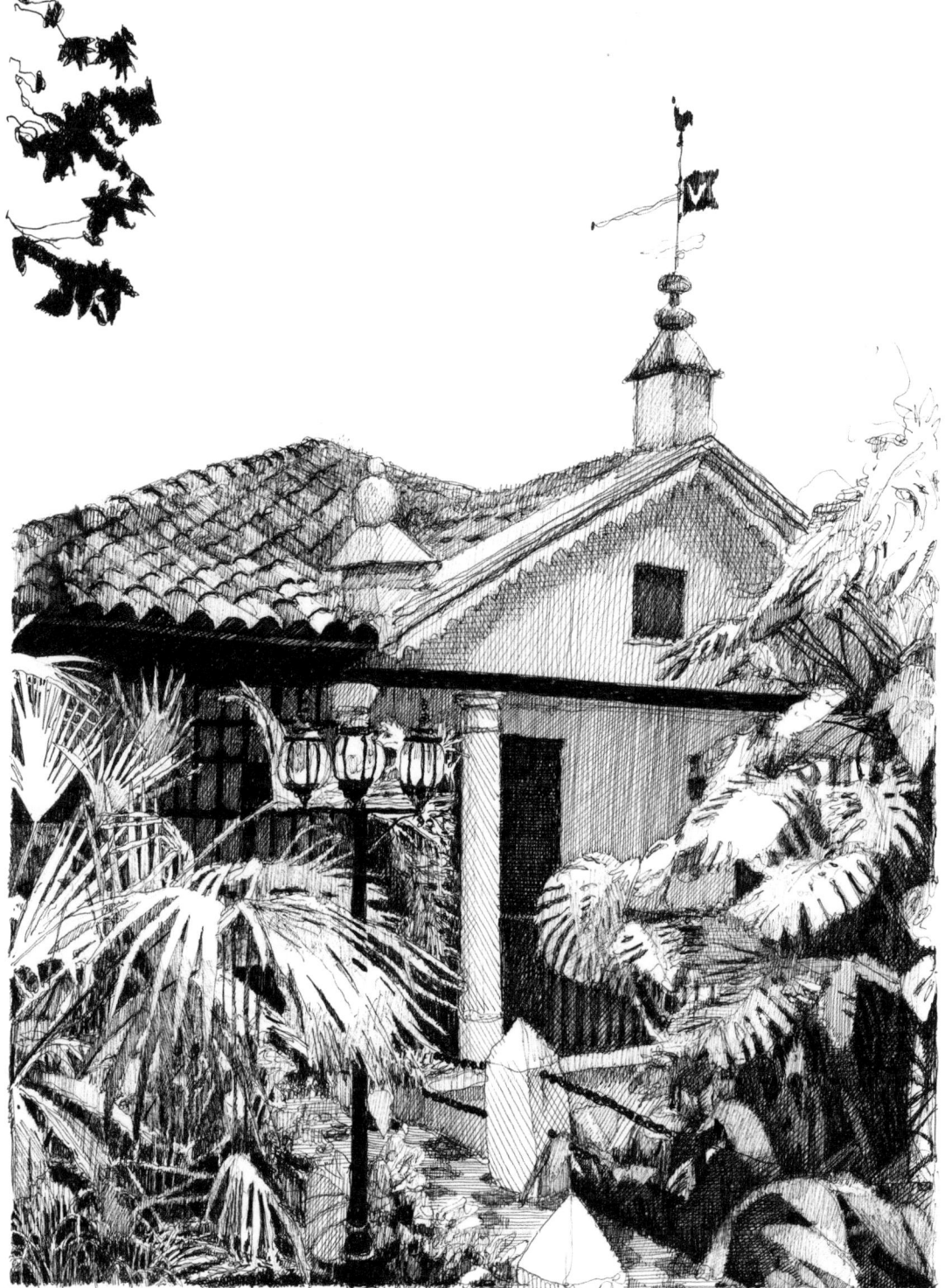

Hacienda El Vergel, Ibagué, Colombia (2019) Over
time, I've found that using pen and ink has led me
closer to exploring light, it being the most accurate
way to depict objects without colour detail.

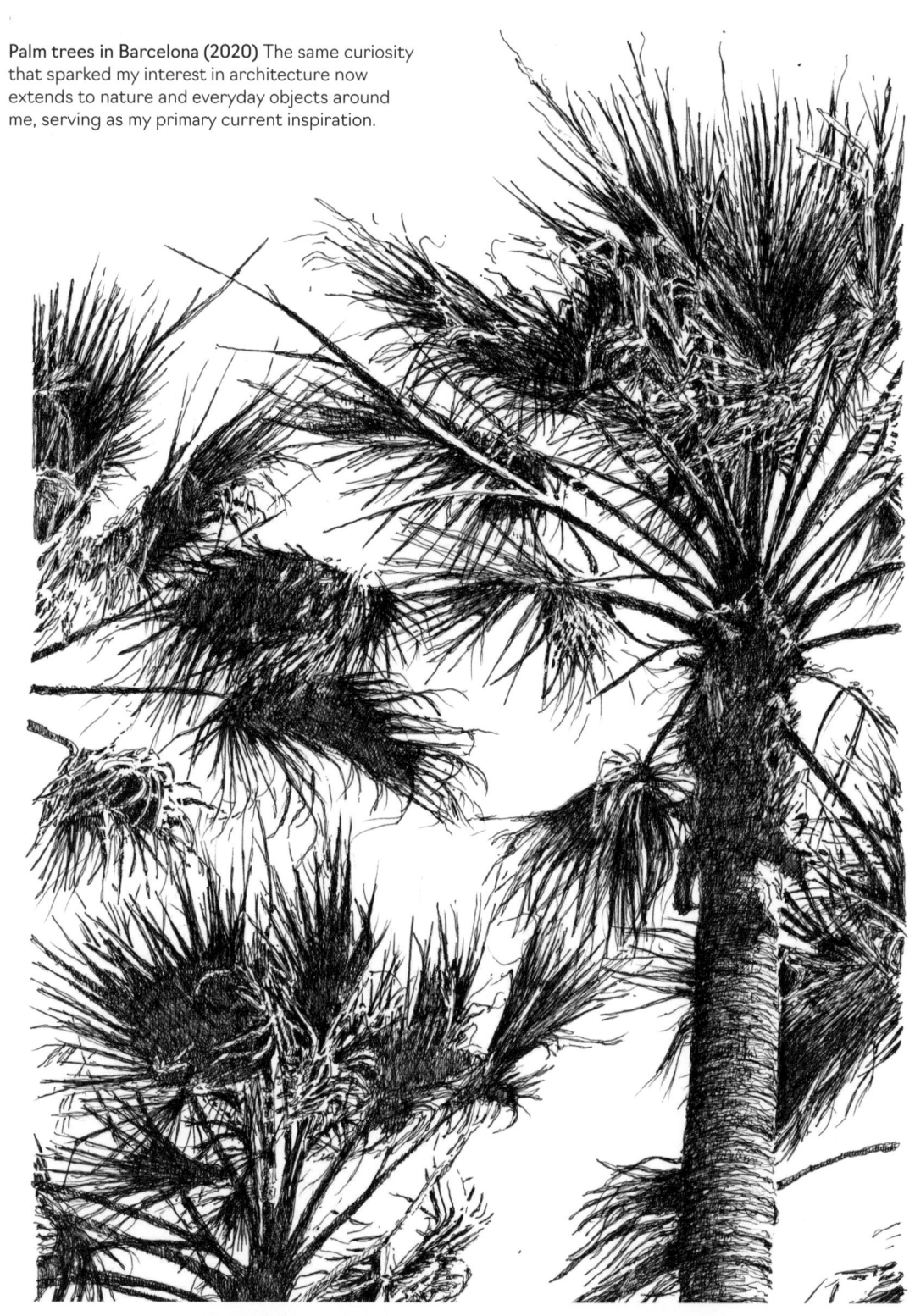

Palm trees in Barcelona (2020) The same curiosity that sparked my interest in architecture now extends to nature and everyday objects around me, serving as my primary current inspiration.

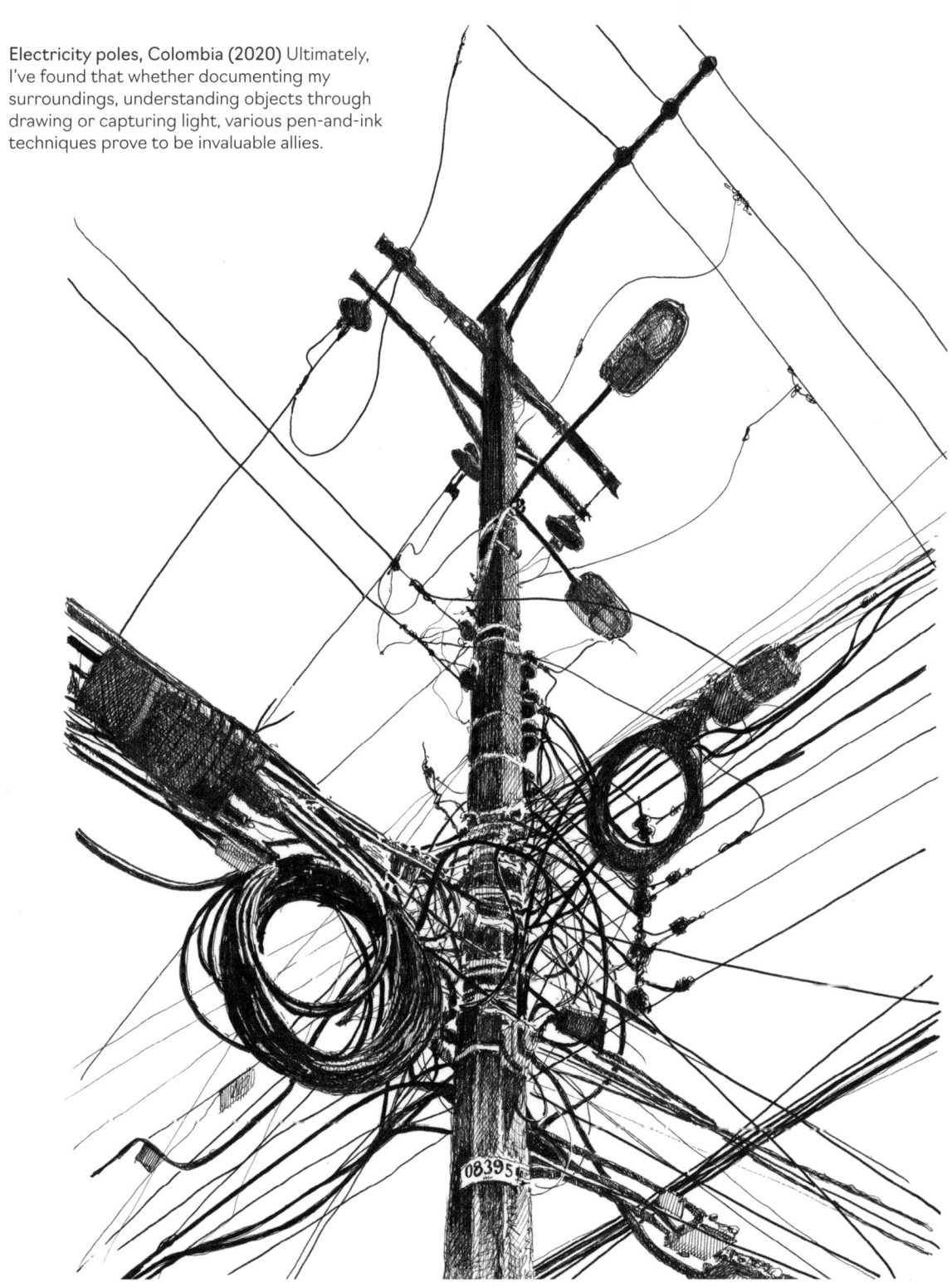

Electricity poles, Colombia (2020) Ultimately, I've found that whether documenting my surroundings, understanding objects through drawing or capturing light, various pen-and-ink techniques prove to be invaluable allies.

SUPPLIES

The materials we use for drawing do not determine our artistic skill, but we cannot ignore the impact they have on the development of our style and technique. The types of pens, the density and flow of the ink, the type of paper used; all these factors play a crucial role in the appearance and quality of the final drawing. For example, a fine-tipped pen allows for precise details and delicate lines, while a wide-tipped pen can produce bold and expressive strokes. Dense and opaque inks can create a dramatic effect, while diluted inks can provide a more subtle and delicate appearance. The paper used can affect how the ink is absorbed and displayed, influencing the clarity and depth of the details.

Artistic skill is built through practice, experimentation and the development of technical and conceptual abilities. However, choosing the right materials can facilitate and enrich this creative process, allowing you to explore new techniques and ways of artistic expression.

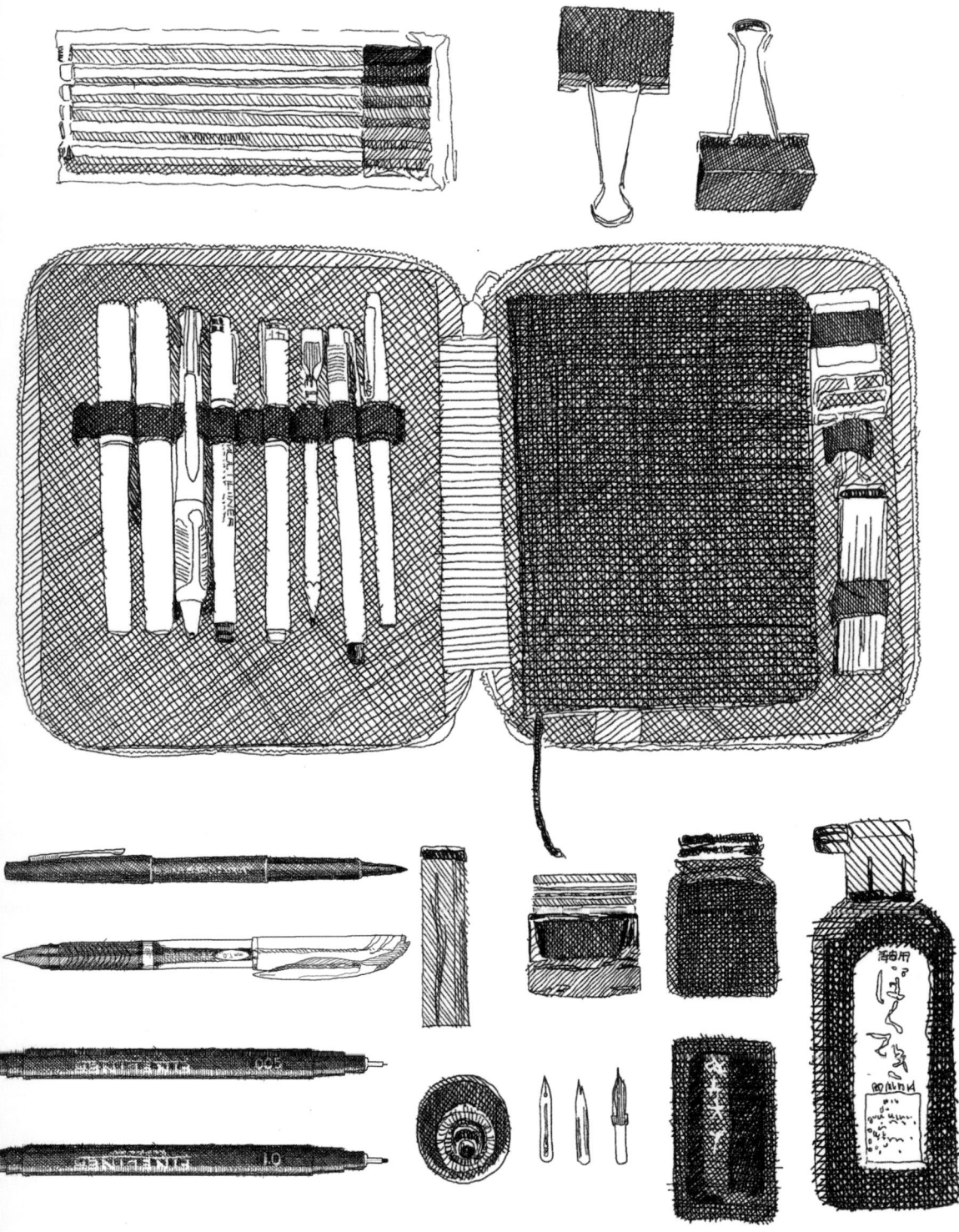

Pens

Choosing the right pen is crucial. Each brand has its own characteristics, and finding the one that best suits your needs and drawing style will make a difference in your artwork. With practice, you'll learn to distinguish between pens and choose the one that allows you to achieve anything from fine, detailed lines to bolder, thicker strokes. This choice will directly influence the final outcome of your work, so take the time to try out different options and find the perfect pen for you.

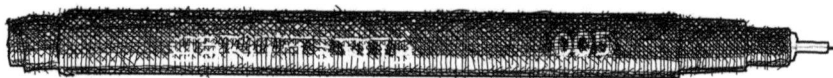

FINELINERS

Fineliners are fine-tipped pens specially designed for drawing precise lines. They have a thin, firm tip that allows for accurate control over the stroke, making them ideal for work that requires accuracy and attention to detail. They come in a variety of tip thicknesses calibrated in millimetres, from extra fine to medium.

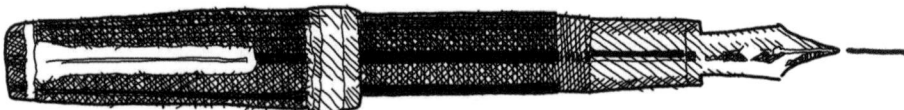

FOUNTAIN PENS

Fountain pens are known for their ability to create varied line widths depending on the pressure applied by the user. They come in a wide range of styles, materials and nib sizes, allowing for customization to suit individual preferences.

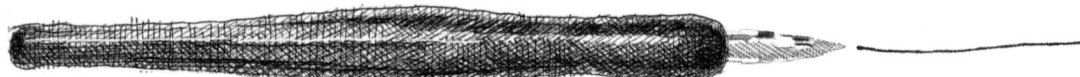

DIPPING PENS

With a dipping pen you have to manually dip the metal nib into ink before each stroke. They come in various nib shapes and sizes, allowing for a range of line thicknesses and styles. Using them requires skill in controlling ink flow. Regular maintenance is essential for optimal performance.

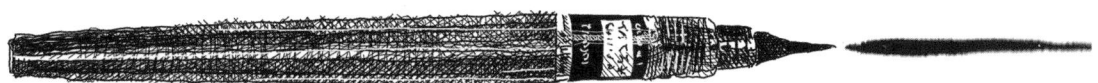

BRUSH PENS

Brush pens combine the convenience of a pen with the expressive qualities of a brush. They are filled with ink and are ready to use without having to be dipped or refilled. They are portable and mess free, making them convenient for on-the-go sketching and drawing.

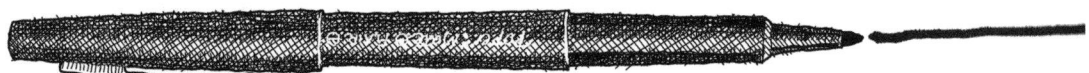

FELT-TIP PENS

With a felt-tip pen you can achieve a consistent line width, making them ideal for bold outlines and filling in areas. These pens come in various tip sizes, offering flexibility for different artistic styles and techniques.

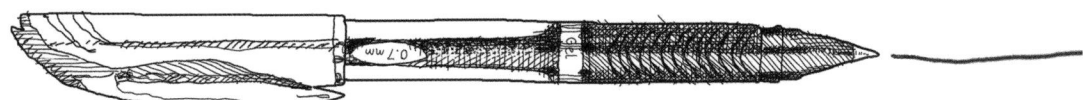

GEL PENS

A gel pen has a rollerball tip that dispenses gel ink onto paper and offers smooth and consistent ink flow. Due to their smoothness and quick-drying ink, gel pens are popular for sketching, outlining and adding details to artwork. They come in a variety of tip sizes, allowing you to achieve different line widths and effects.

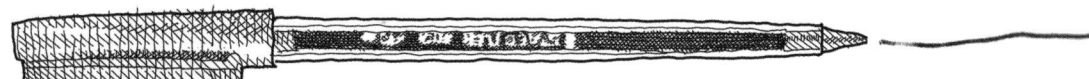

BALLPOINT PENS

A ballpoint pen dispenses ink smoothly as it moves across the paper's surface, producing uniform and precise lines. You can regulate the pressure exerted on the pen, enabling you to achieve both delicate and bold strokes. This not only enhances line work, but is also invaluable for shading techniques, allowing for nuanced and expressive drawings.

Inks

Much like selecting the right pen, your choice of ink significantly impacts your work and is essential in achieving the desired effect in your artistic endeavours. By experimenting with various inks, you can discover which one best complements your technique, preferences and the visual effect you're aiming to achieve. You have a diverse range of options, from traditional inks to more contemporary formulations, each offering its own unique characteristics and possibilities.

DYE-BASED INKS

Dye-based inks contain soluble colourants in a liquid medium, such as water or solvents. Key characteristics of dye-based inks include:

Transparency and colour vibrancy: Dye-based inks are more transparent and offer more vibrant and saturated colours than pigmented inks. This is beneficial for creating striking and expressive colour effects in pen-and-ink art.

Subtle colour blending: Due to their transparency, dye-based inks allow for subtle colour blending. You can overlay inks to create new tones and hues in a delicate manner.

Wash potential: Although dye-based inks may not be as opaque as pigmented inks, they offer a unique potential for ethereal wash techniques in pen-and-ink art.

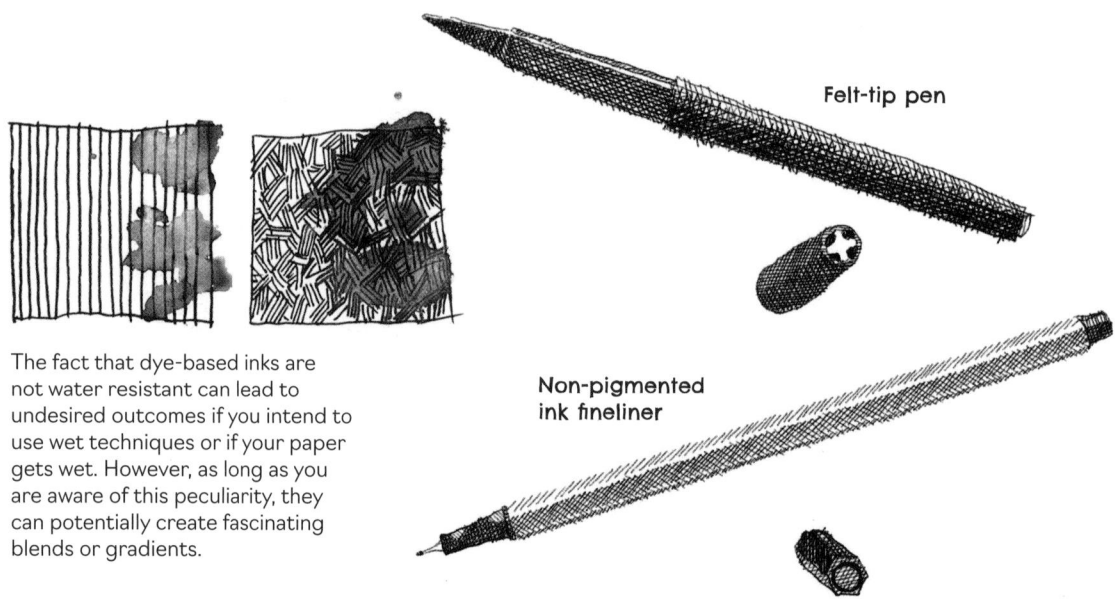

Felt-tip pen

Non-pigmented ink fineliner

The fact that dye-based inks are not water resistant can lead to undesired outcomes if you intend to use wet techniques or if your paper gets wet. However, as long as you are aware of this peculiarity, they can potentially create fascinating blends or gradients.

PIGMENTED INKS

Pigmented inks contain solid pigment particles suspended in a liquid medium. These solid pigments provide coloration to the liquid and remain on the surface of the substrate once the ink dries. Pigmented inks offer several advantages such as opacity, water resistance and durability.

However, when using these inks in fountain pens, it's important to exercise a bit more caution: if pigmented ink dries in the pen's feed or nib, solid pigment particles can clog the ink flow channels, which may affect the pen's performance. Therefore, it's recommended to regularly clean the fountain pen and avoid leaving pigmented ink unused for extended periods to prevent clogging. Some key characteristics of pigmented inks include:

Opacity and colourfastness: Pigmented inks tend to be more opaque and offer greater colourfastness than their dye-based equivalents. This ensures that lines drawn with a pen and pigmented ink are sharper and more durable, with less likelihood of fading over time.

Shading and blending capability: Due to their opacity, pigmented inks are ideal for shading techniques. Layers of ink can be overlapped to create shadows and tonal gradations.

Water resistance: Pigmented inks tend to be water resistant once dry, allowing you to work with them without worrying about smudging or accidental fading.

Price: These inks are more expensive than dye-based inks due to the complexity of the manufacturing process.

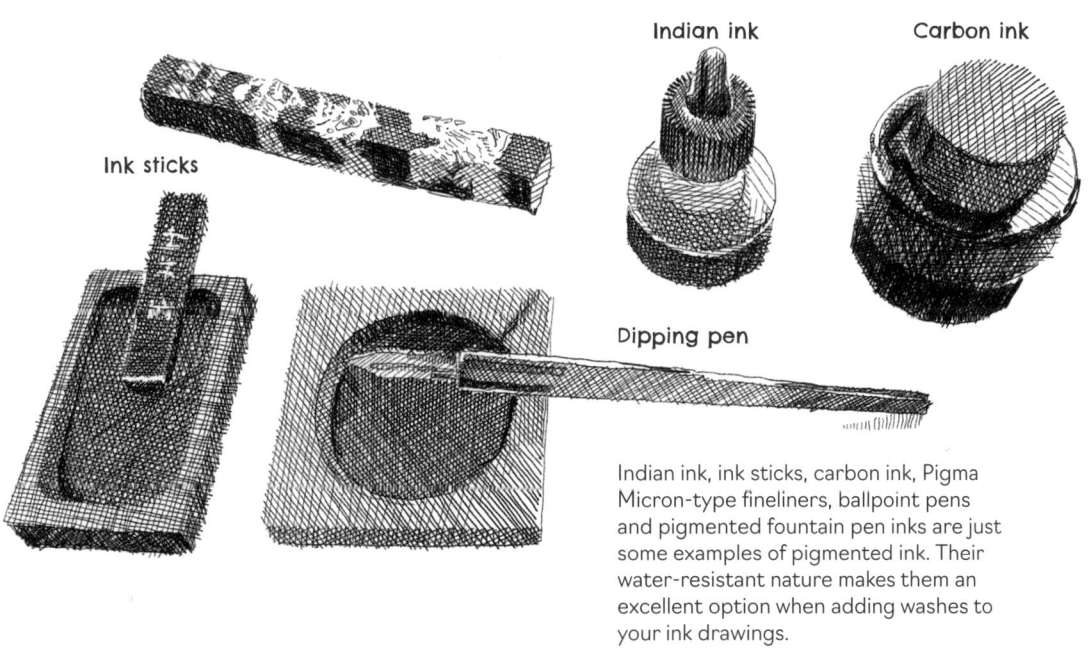

Indian ink

Carbon ink

Ink sticks

Dipping pen

Indian ink, ink sticks, carbon ink, Pigma Micron-type fineliners, ballpoint pens and pigmented fountain pen inks are just some examples of pigmented ink. Their water-resistant nature makes them an excellent option when adding washes to your ink drawings.

Brushes

Brushes can be categorized into two main types: refillable brushes and traditional. The choice between one and the other largely depends on practice and the type of drawing you do.

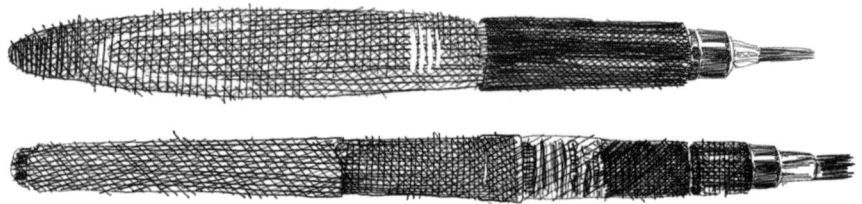

REFILLABLE BRUSHES

The greatest advantage of these types of brushes is the ease they provide in drawing anywhere. They can be loaded with different or diluted inks and are a great help when creating quick shadows.

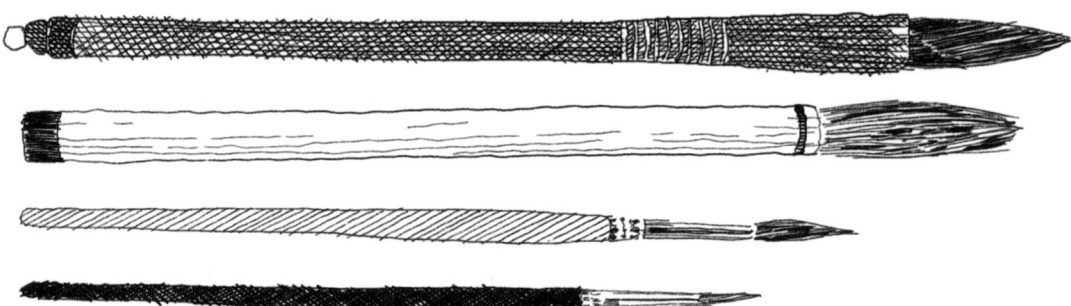

TRADITIONAL BRUSHES

Within the range of traditional brushes there are countless parameters to choose from: types of bristles, lengths, thicknesses, etc. Depending on the quantity and quality of the bristles, these can be loaded with more or less ink, but they always need to be accompanied by a separate ink-loading container. This is why they are more suitable for leisurely work on a table, where you have space to place your tools.

Paper

Papers, far from being simple supports, constitute a vast universe to be discovered, and your choice of paper is important for a satisfying experience. Look for good absorption that allows you to maintain a constant workflow, along with a texture that suits the type of drawing you are doing and pen you are using.

The weight of the paper is a consideration when working with pen and ink. Papers intended for this purpose typically start at a weight of 80 grams per square metre (gsm). This type of paper is ideal for quick sketches, especially those that do not require heavy filling, as ink can easily seep through.

The optimal papers are between 100 and 200gsm. Within this range, the paper has the ability to absorb ink evenly, ensuring that it does not bleed through the sheet.

Above 200gsm and the paper is robust enough to use ink as a wet technique. At this weight washes and other techniques requiring a higher liquid load can be employed without compromising the paper.

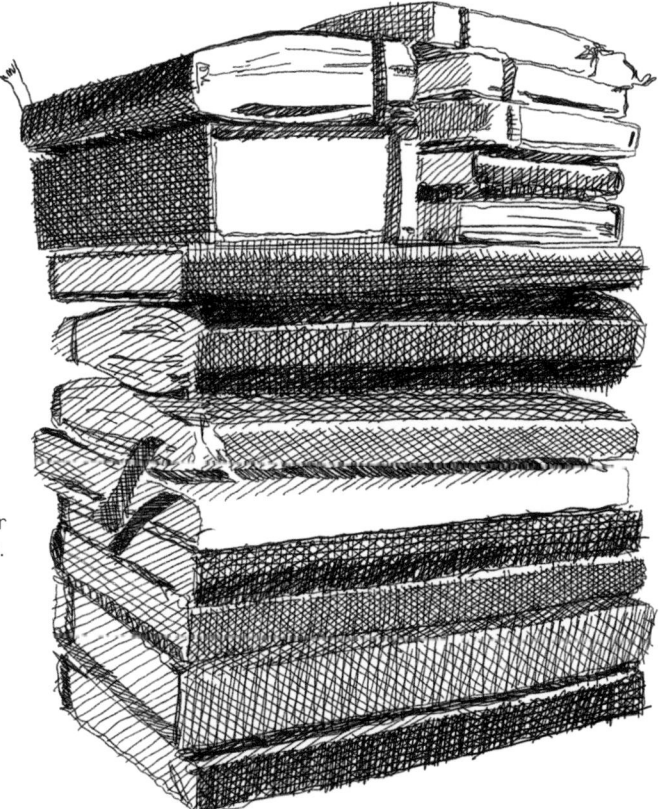

When choosing a sketchbook, think not only about the type and weight of the paper but also about the presentation and format. Personally, I pay special attention to the sketchbook's ability to open completely flat. This is invaluable as it allows for work without the inconvenience of the seam between pages, facilitating double-page creation and ensuring a smooth and unobstructed drawing experience.

Other tools

From supports and gadgets to cases and additional tools, the world of drawing offers an array of equipment that can either enhance or complicate your artistic process. In this section, I'll highlight some of the tools I frequently utilize in my pen-and-ink work.

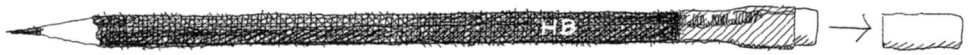

PENCILS AND ERASERS

When it comes to choosing a pencil for my initial sketches in ink, I primarily focus on the hardness of the graphite. I prefer a pencil with a firm but not overly hard lead, which equates to an HB rating. It's worth noting that under some brands, the HB designation may vary in name. The crucial aspect is that it's a pencil of medium hardness. As for erasers – the softer, the better, as they ensure that you won't damage the paper when using them.

You can buy pencils that allow you to change erasers, thus combining these two elements into a single tool, reducing the number of utensils you need to carry with you.

DRAWING CHAIR

Often, when drawing away from a table or studio, finding a suitable place to sit that provides the necessary view can be challenging. For many artists, drawing while standing is not a viable option. That's why a folding chair specifically designed for drawing can be a valuable addition to your basic drawing kit.

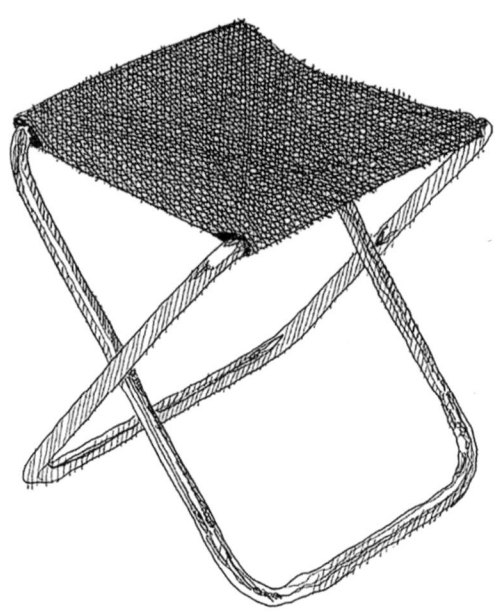

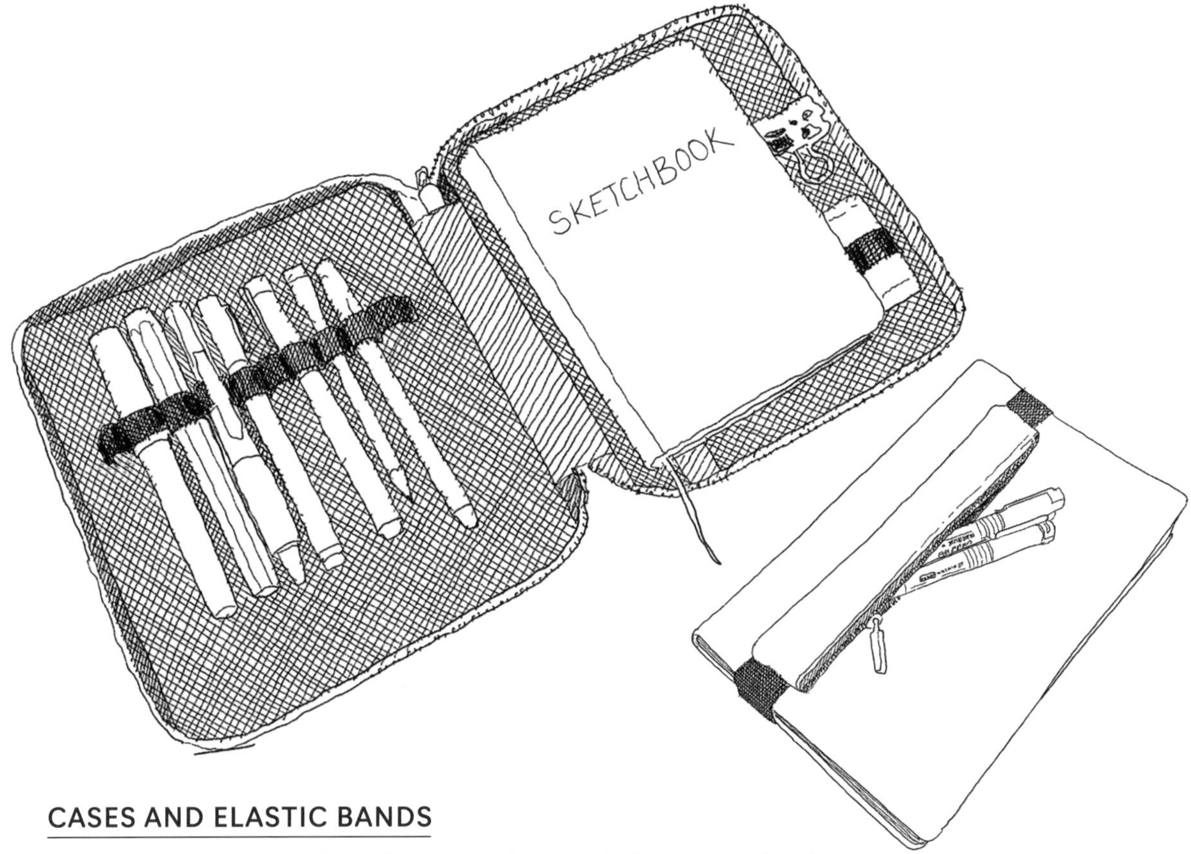

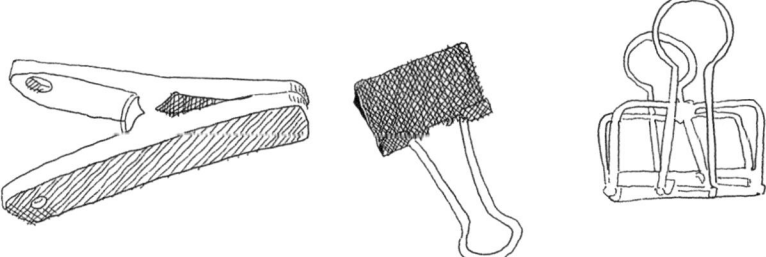

CASES AND ELASTIC BANDS

Your goal should be to always have everything needed to draw on hand, regardless of location. In this regard, cases become a constant necessity. Some cases can hold both the sketchbook and additional materials, while others are designed to attach to the sketchbook. The former allows for carrying more items, while the latter are lighter and take up less space.

CLIPS

Whether you're drawing on a table or outdoors, one or two clips can be very useful for holding the sheets you're working on.

TECHNIQUES

This chapter serves as a practical guide to pen-and-ink techniques. We'll begin by discussing how to hold your pen for effective strokes, then delve into essential techniques using a range of drawing tools. We'll cover hatching, cross hatching, contour hatching, stippling, tick hatching, woven hatching and scribbling, uncovering how each technique produces unique effects. We'll explore the importance of giving weight to your lines and varying pressure, and using tonal values and textures to breathe life into your works. We'll also analyze some common errors, and I'll share my preferences with you.

In addition, you'll find a series of practical exercises combining the various techniques to consolidate your mastery of the art of pen and ink.

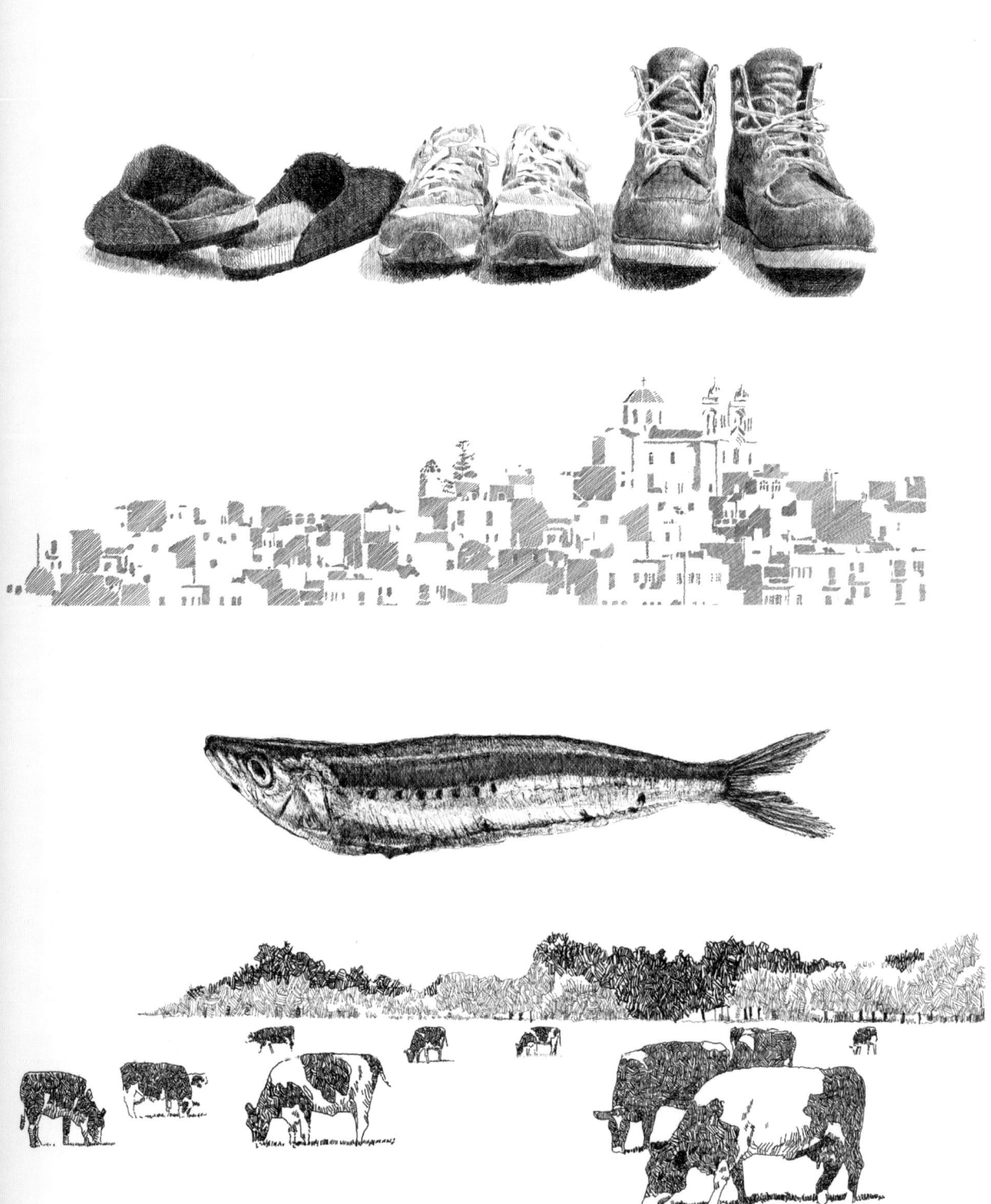

Holding your pen

The way you hold your pen when drawing is a personal expression of your relationship with art. There is no single correct way to do it, as each of us adapts our hand and strokes based on how we naturally grip the instrument.

GRIP

Don't limit yourself to a single grip. Experiment with different positions until you find one that offers you the greatest comfort and freedom of movement.

1. A relaxed grip, holding the pen away from the nib, can give your strokes a sense of fluidity and freedom, allowing for a more personal expression in your artwork.

2. For smaller details, adjust your grip slightly and bring your fingers closer to the tip. This can make your lines more precise in delicate areas of your drawing.

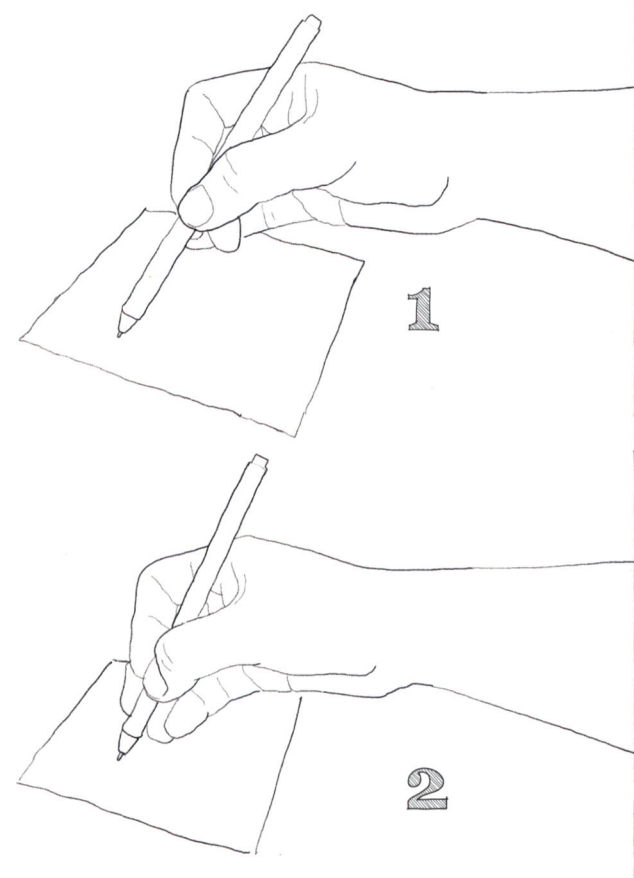

PERSONAL PREFERENCE

In my case, through practice, I have discovered that holding the pen away from the tip in a relaxed manner gives me more freedom in my strokes. This less tense grip also has a tangible impact on my comfort and physical well-being when drawing. Reducing pressure on my hand and wrist allows me to undertake longer sessions without the fatigue or muscle tension that can come from gripping the pen tightly.

The loose grip technique also gives me better control over my line thickness and variation, making it easier to transition between

PHYSICAL COMFORT AND SURFACES

When holding a pen, your physical comfort can make a big difference to your creative process. Adopting a more relaxed grip and maximizing support points for your hand not only enhances your experience but also directly impacts on your productivity.

It's essential to recognize the difference between drawing outdoors, where you may have little support for your sketchbook and hand, and drawing on a stable surface, such as a table. Drawing in the street may offer few support points, making your hand less stable. Sitting comfortably at a table and resting both arms on it, on the other hand, provides a solid foundation that improves both your control and your precision.

Being aware of the limitations of your physical environment and adapting accordingly is crucial. Physical comfort thus becomes an indispensable ally to enhance your artistic expression, whether it's in the hustle and bustle of the street or the tranquillity of your workspace.

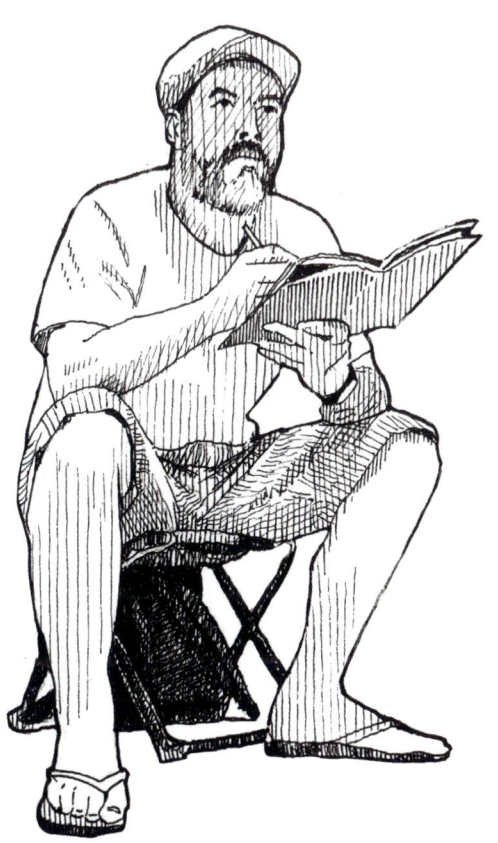

strokes. Nevertheless, in finer details, I slightly adjust my grip and bring my fingers closer to the tip of the pen to create a more precise line.

Ultimately, holding the pen loosely is not just a technique but also an invitation to explore a new type of artistic expression. It serves as a reminder that our relationship with our tools is as crucial as the technique itself, and can open up a whole new world of creative possibilities.

Types of line

In pen-and-ink art, line drawing in a variety of lengths and styles is an essential skill. There are three fundamental types of line that adapt to diverse artistic needs and expressions. From shorter lines executed with the finesse of the fingers, to longer lines drawn with the power of the elbow, each type differs not only in length but also in the part of the arm used as a base and the required point of support.

FINGER LINES

Finger lines are short strokes that range from 0 to 5cm (0 to 2in) in length. This measurement corresponds to the natural range of motion of our fingers when holding the pen. To extend and make this type of stroke more flexible, hold the pen in a more relaxed manner.

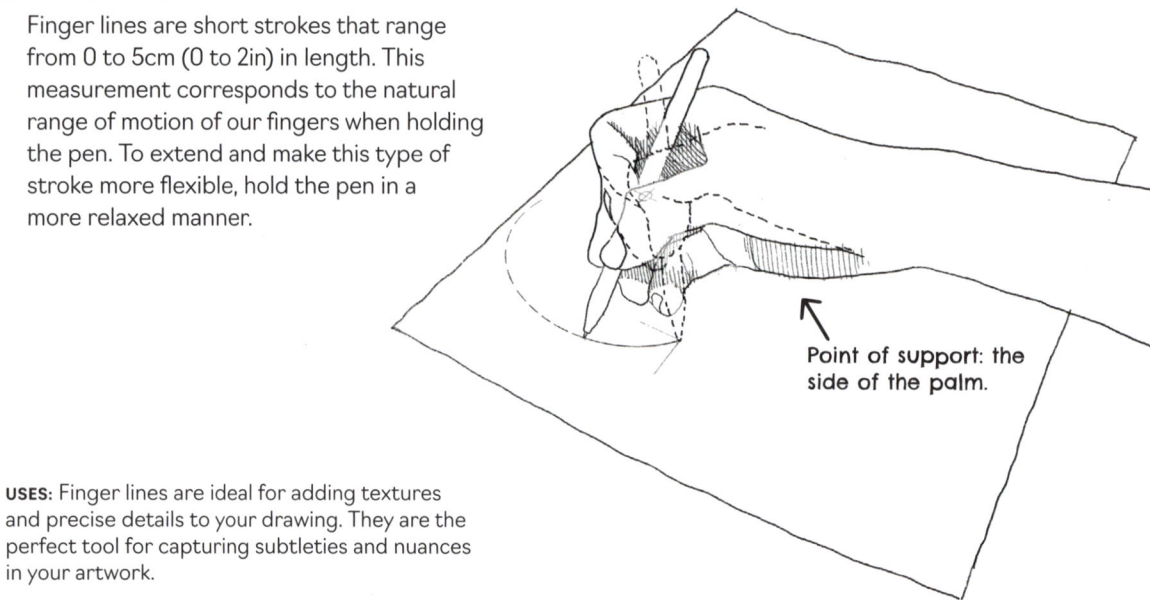

Point of support: the side of the palm.

USES: Finger lines are ideal for adding textures and precise details to your drawing. They are the perfect tool for capturing subtleties and nuances in your artwork.

WHY SHOULD YOU LEARN THE THREE TYPES OF LINE?

Understanding and practising these different types of line not only enhances your technical skills but also enables you to convey a wide range of details and emotions in your artworks. While it's natural for drawing unfamiliar types of line to feel tiring, thinking about multiple points of support for your hand and controlling your breathing are effective ways of minimizing this and extending your practice sessions. By honing your proficiency in these three types of

WRIST LINES

These lines are slightly longer, ranging from approximately 5 to 20cm (2 to 8in). To execute them, use the wrist as a pivot point to move the pen from one position to another. The preferred point of support is typically the forearm, since the hand needs to separate from the paper to allow wrist movement.

SHOULDER LINES

Shoulder lines are the longest strokes you can make. They use the entire arm as a base, making them ideal for strokes on a large scale. Their most common application is in creating contours in larger-sized drawings.

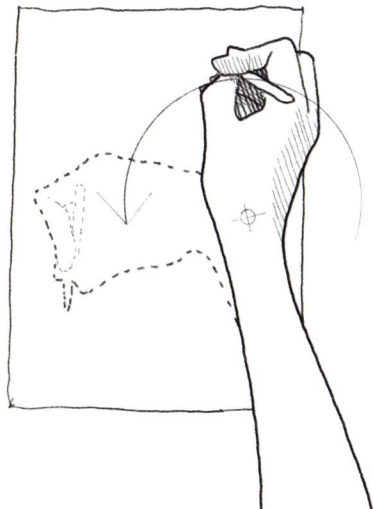

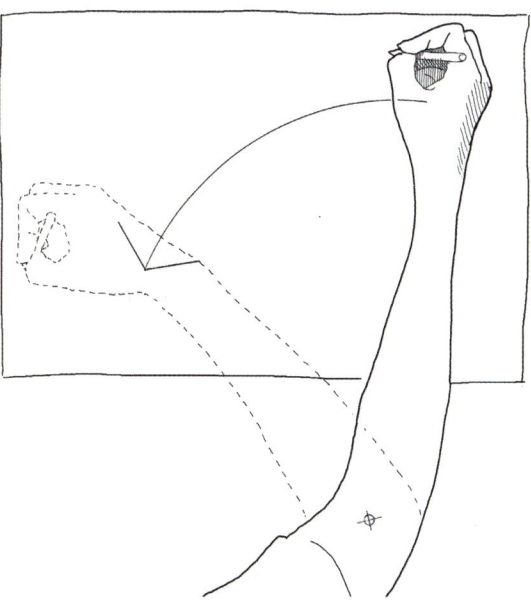

USES: Wrist lines are essential for defining the contours of your drawing. They are also valuable for creating tones and values in your artwork, adding depth and form to your compositions.

USES: Shoulder lines give breadth and fluidity to your strokes, making them crucial for defining contours in large-scale drawings. They are the primary tool when precision and continuity are required in larger works.

line you can unlock the door to a vast world of creative possibilities and consolidate your ability to capture the unique vision that each artist carries within.

Outlines: straight lines

Straight lines are continuous and uniform strokes that connect two points in a single direction. They lack curves or angles, maintaining a constant trajectory. Straight lines are crucial for defining contours, edges and geometric structures. They can vary in length, thickness and orientation and are used to convey different visual elements, from the simplicity of a clear outline to the complexity of patterns such as hatching.

SOLID LINES

Continuous lines are used to define the outer edges of objects.

DASHED LINES

Composed of short segments and spaces in between, dashed lines create a visual effect that may suggest smooth edges or hidden lines.

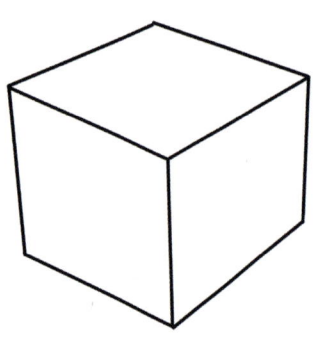

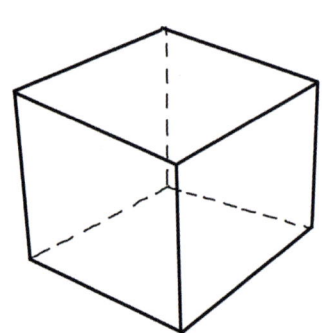

CONSIDERATIONS

- Adopt a comfortable position and ensure good arm control for smooth and precise movements.

- For a uniform appearance, aim to draw the line in a continuous motion rather than in short segments.

- Focus on a target point at the end of your intended line. Keep your eyes on this end point as you draw, rather than on the tip of your pen or pencil. This will help guide your hand and maintain the straight line.

- Control the pressure of the drawing tool for consistent lines. Adjust the pressure based on the intended stroke.

- Continuously observe the stroke and the end point of the line; adjust if necessary.

HATCHING

These parallel lines are used to represent shadows, textures or tones in various directions and densities.

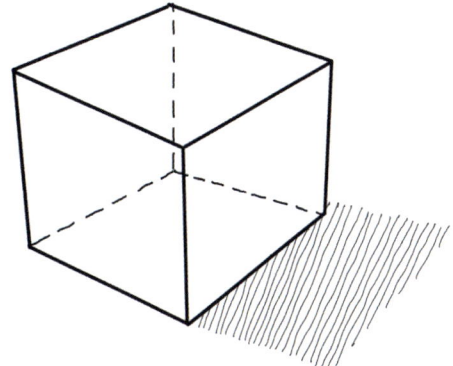

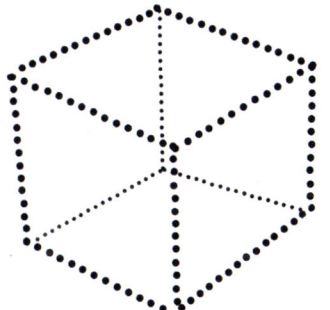

DOTTED LINES

Dotted lines can be used to draw contours more subtly or to highlight objects distinctively and delicately.

- Try to maintain a constant rhythm when drawing lines. Consistency in speed will contribute to line uniformity and avoid unnecessary variations.

- Experiment with different line thicknesses to add dynamism and emphasis to your drawing. You can achieve this by adjusting the amount of pressure you apply to the drawing tool.

- Use straight lines of varying lengths and orientations to create textures. By grouping lines, you can achieve different visual effects

- Work on maintaining the stability of your hand to avoid tremors.

Outlines: curved lines

Curved lines are strokes that follow a smooth and nonlinear trajectory, constantly changing direction. Unlike straight lines, curved lines exhibit undulations or arcs along their path. Curved lines are essential for representing organic shapes, softening contours and creating a sense of movement or fluidity. They can vary in amplitude, radius and direction, ranging from the simplicity of an arc to the energy of a spiral line.

ARCS

An arc is a curved line that represents a smooth portion of a circle. This stroke, characterized by its smoothness, is used to convey a seamless and harmonious transition between two points.

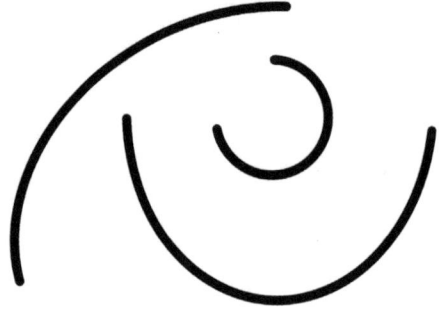

WAVY LINES

Wavy lines are curved strokes that mimic the undulating pattern of waves. They are particularly valuable for conveying soft and flowing textures. Moreover, they are instrumental in creating a visual effect that implies continuous and fluid motion.

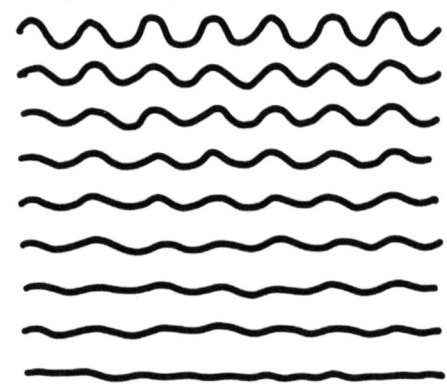

MEANDERING LINES

Meandering lines are gently curved strokes that follow an unpredictable path. They create a sense of winding pathways or watercourses, infusing the composition with a natural and organic feel. These lines add a touch of spontaneity, mimicking the irregular patterns of nature.

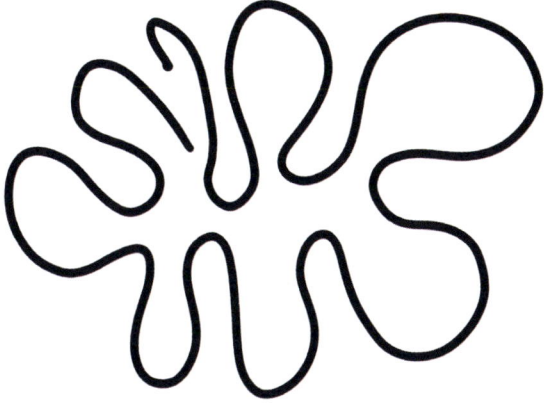

SPIRALS

Spiral lines are curved strokes that revolve around a central point, forming a spiral shape, employed to create dynamic visual effects or highlight specific areas.

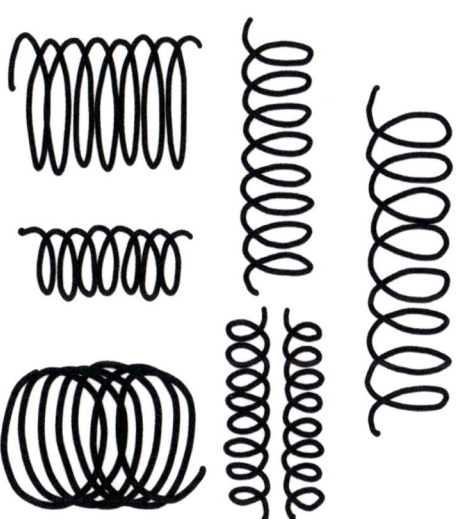

CONSIDERATIONS

- Adopt a continuous and smooth motion when drawing curved lines. Avoid abrupt movements for more natural curves.

- Keep your wrist flexible to allow turns and curved movements without stiffness, facilitating the creation of more organic curves.

- Identify the imaginary centre of rotation and adjust your movement accordingly.

- Use reference points or visual markers to help maintain a coherent shape when drawing longer curved lines.

- Remember that, just as with straight lines, regular practice will significantly improve your ability to draw curved lines with precision and style.

Hatching

Hatching involves drawing parallel lines to create shadows and depth. Adjusting the spacing (density) and the width (pressure) of the line can deliver subtle shading and striking contrasts. Hatching can also be used to outline contours.

THIS PAGE Consistency in placing your strokes is important to create an image such as this one. Note how the strokes follow the same direction, giving the illustration a clean look and easily identifiable outlines.

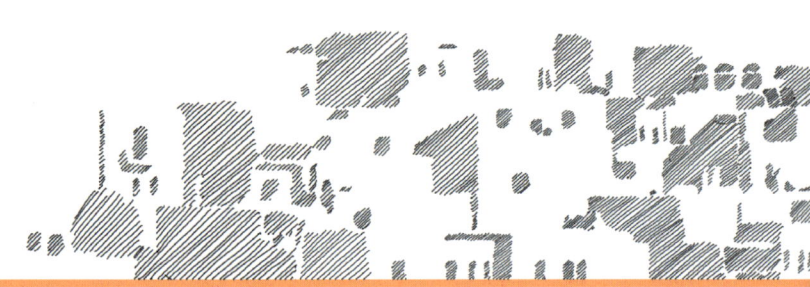

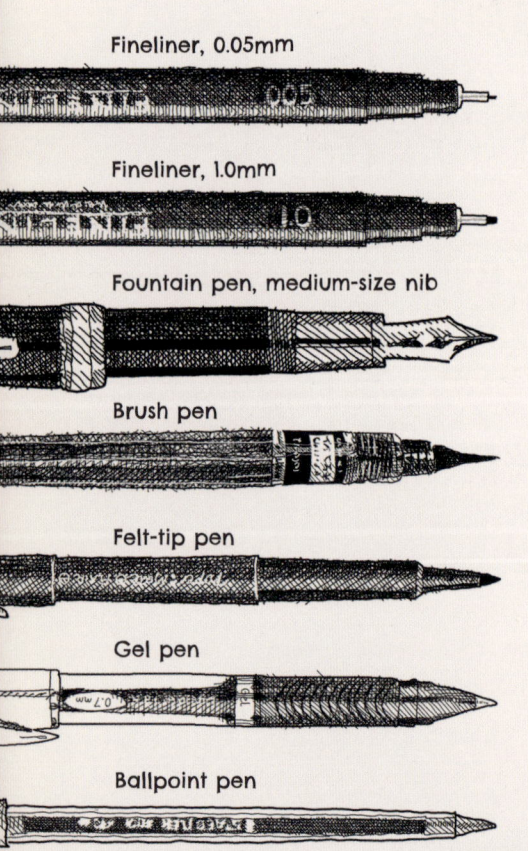

Fineliner, 0.05mm

Fineliner, 1.0mm

Fountain pen, medium-size nib

Brush pen

Felt-tip pen

Gel pen

Ballpoint pen

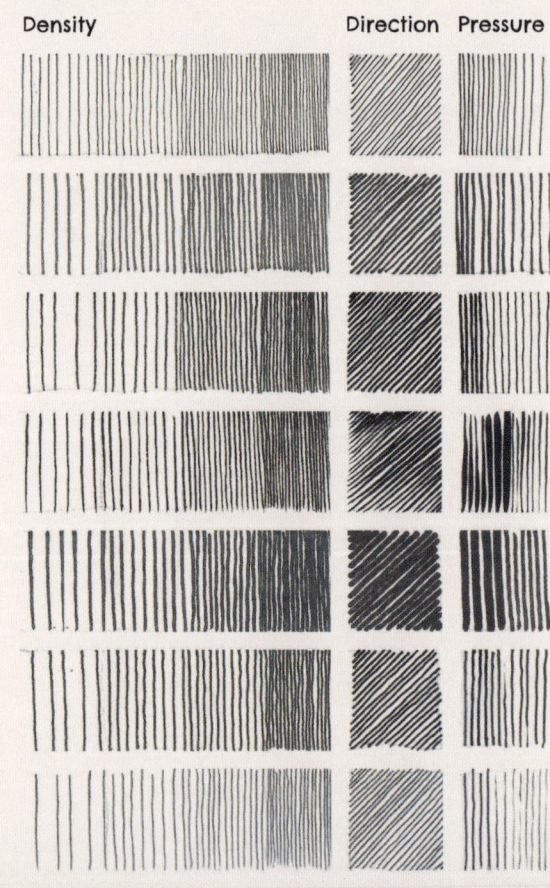

Density   Direction   Pressure

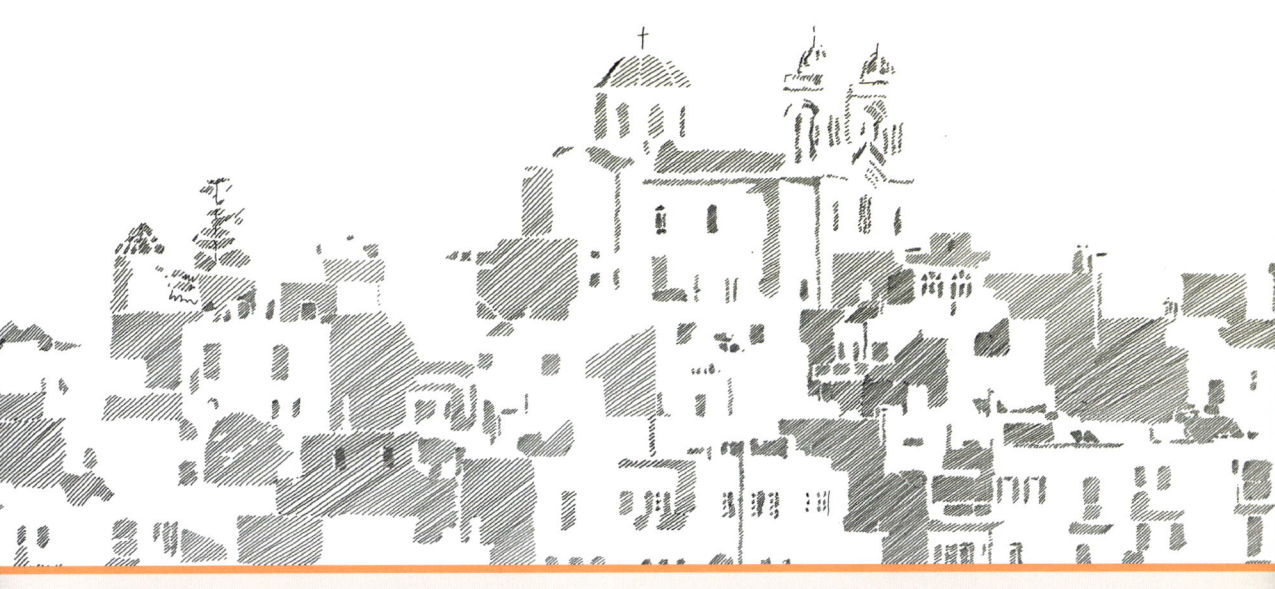

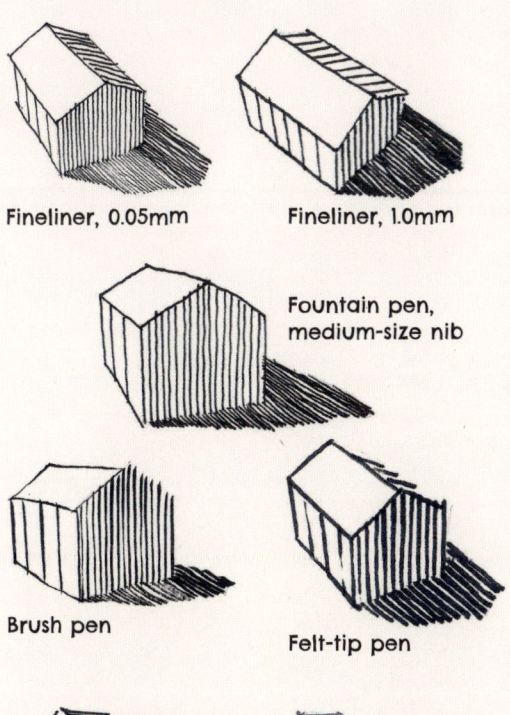

Fineliner, 0.05mm

Fineliner, 1.0mm

Fountain pen,
medium-size nib

Brush pen

Felt-tip pen

Gel pen

Ballpoint pen

MY PREFERENCE

Typically, when shading in a single direction, I do it vertically. It's the line direction that comes most naturally to me without having to move the paper. However, when drawing architecture, I find diagonal lines to be ideal. They help prevent the lines from blending with the subject outlines, ensuring a cleaner and more defined representation.

COMMON MISTAKE

Inconsistency in line density: It is crucial to maintain a consistent line density in areas that should exhibit similar shading. Sudden variations in the number of lines can lead to unexpected and undesirable effects in shading, creating areas that appear darker or lighter than intended.

PRACTICE

Draw lines in a single direction to define contours and details in a simple drawing. This not only enhances your hatching skills but also improves your ability to outline shapes effectively.

Cross hatching

Cross hatching entails producing a sequence of intersecting parallel lines. Typically, the lines are drawn at an angle to each other, and you can alter their density, thickness and direction.

THIS PAGE The cross-hatched nest is created with a fineliner to achieve multiple stroke directions in the shadowed areas. Note how the depth of the nest is conveyed by increasing the pressure and density of the strokes, in contrast with the negative space of the eggs, which creates focus on the subject.

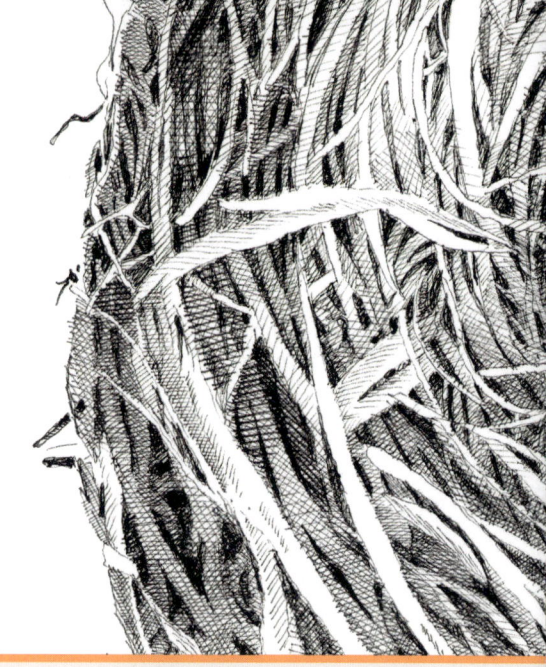

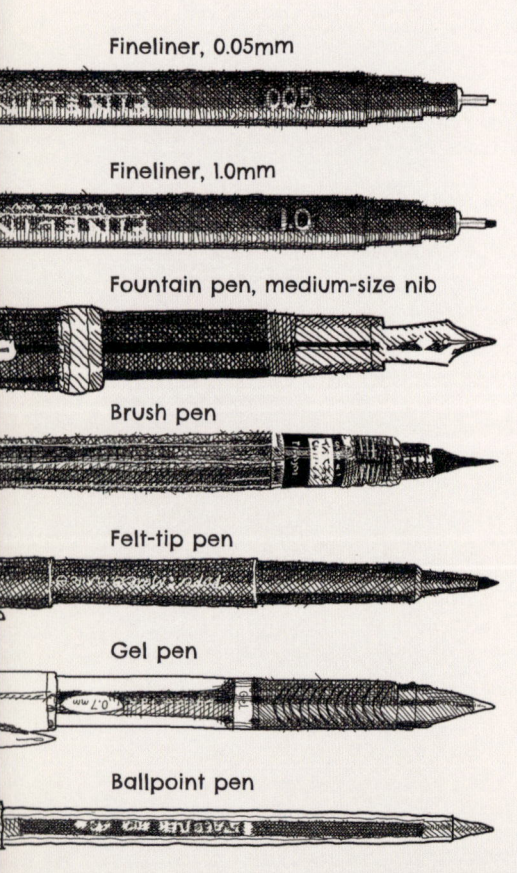

Fineliner, 0.05mm

Fineliner, 1.0mm

Fountain pen, medium-size nib

Brush pen

Felt-tip pen

Gel pen

Ballpoint pen

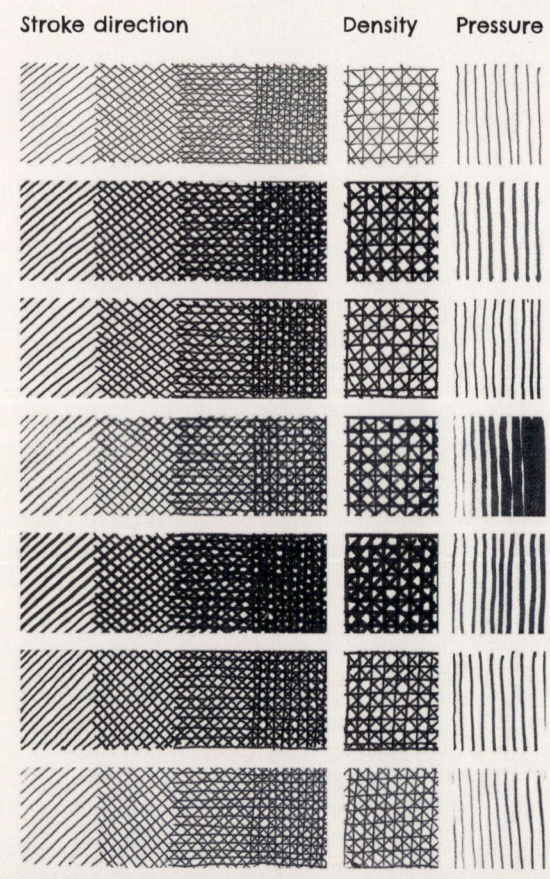

Stroke direction   Density   Pressure

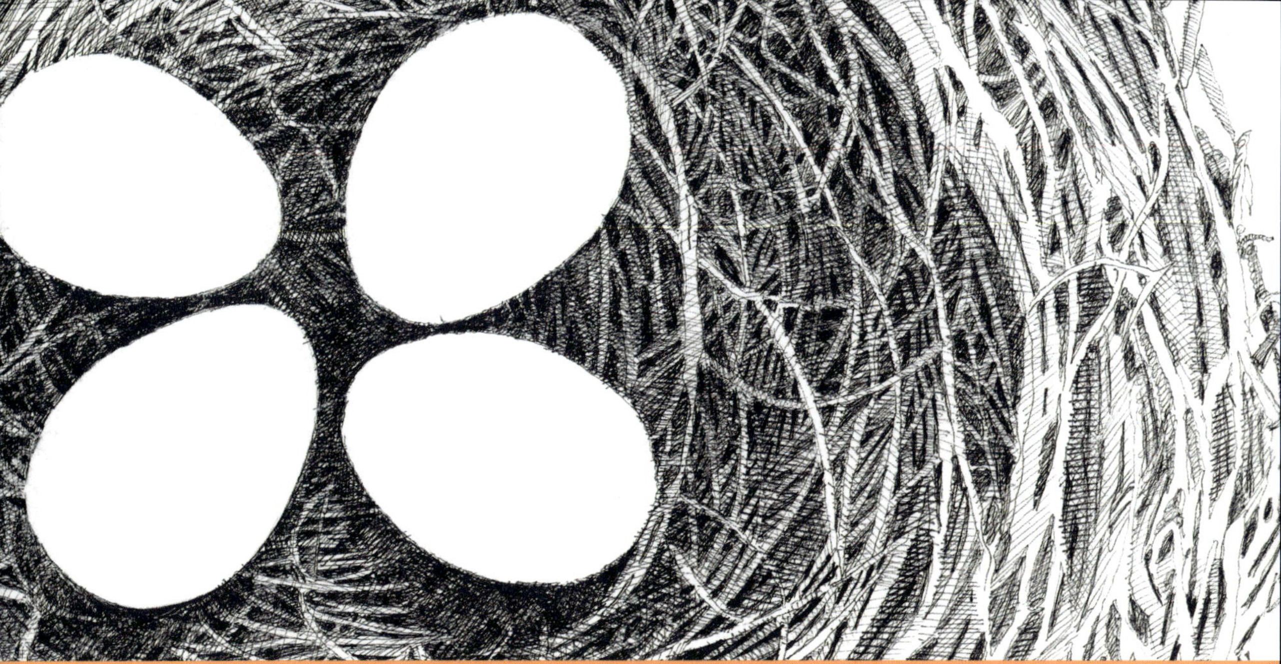

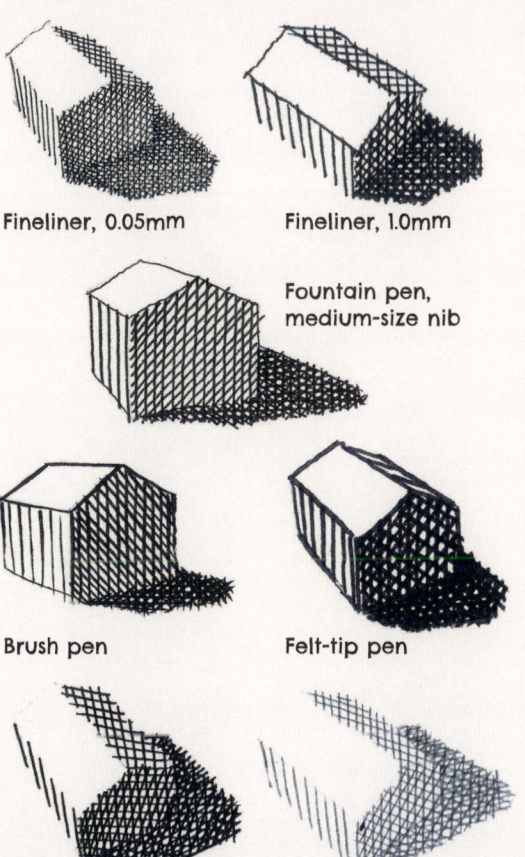

MY PREFERENCE

I use a 0.05mm fineliner for cross hatching. The thin lines provide a greater range of values, allowing a wider variety of tones when I sketch.

COMMON MISTAKE

Inconsistent spacing between hatch lines: This can make the hatching appear sloppy and unprofessional. Keeping the spacing between lines consistent creates a more even, polished look.

PRACTICE

Draw straight lines on a sheet of paper, using your arm and wrist to make the motion. Keep your lines parallel and of consistent length and spacing.

Focus on your breathing and relax your hand as you draw. Tension and stress can cause your lines to be shaky or uneven, so try to stay calm and centred.

Fineliner, 0.05mm

Fineliner, 1.0mm

Fountain pen, medium-size nib

Brush pen

Felt-tip pen

Gel pen

Ballpoint pen

Contour hatching

Contour hatching focuses on creating lines that follow the contours of objects, highlighting both shadows and edges. This technique adds dynamism and detail to the image, emphasizing the three-dimensional structure of the subject.

THIS PAGE A portrait is the perfect subject on which to practise contour hatching, as there are many hollows, ridges and shapes in this one image.

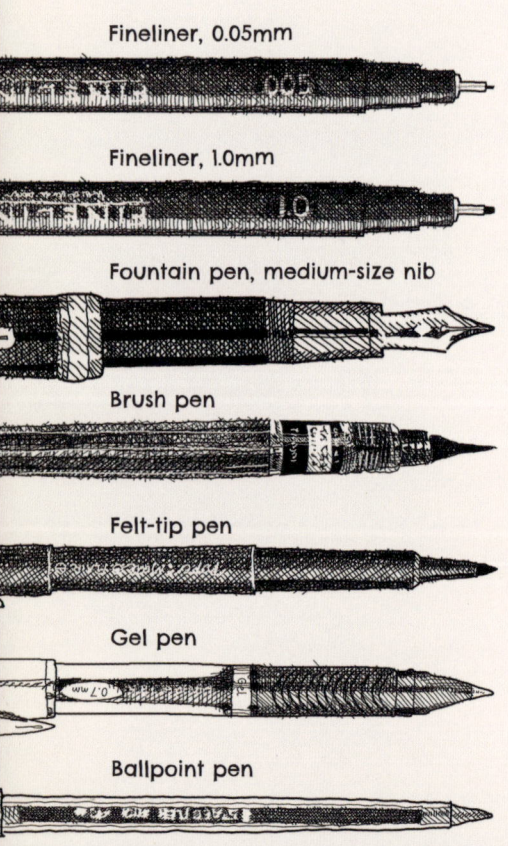

Fineliner, 0.05mm

Fineliner, 1.0mm

Fountain pen, medium-size nib

Brush pen

Felt-tip pen

Gel pen

Ballpoint pen

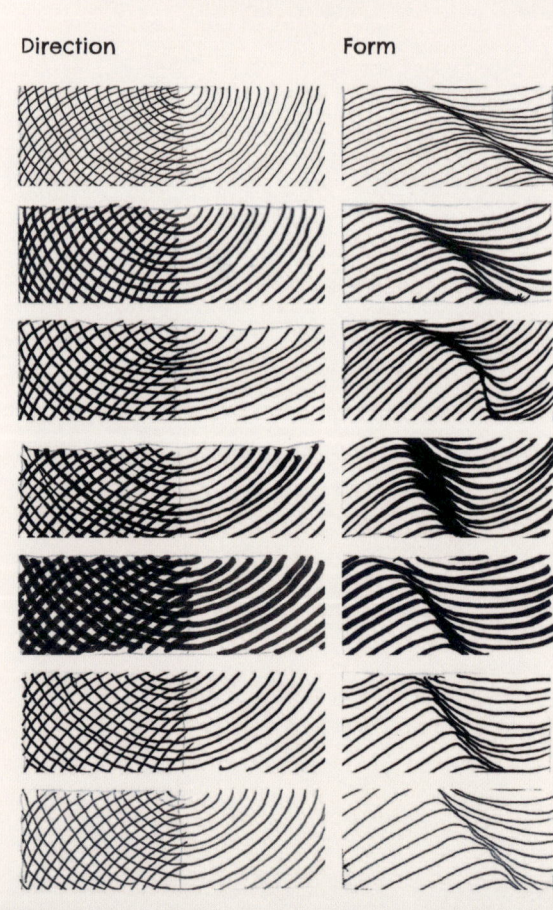

Direction

Form

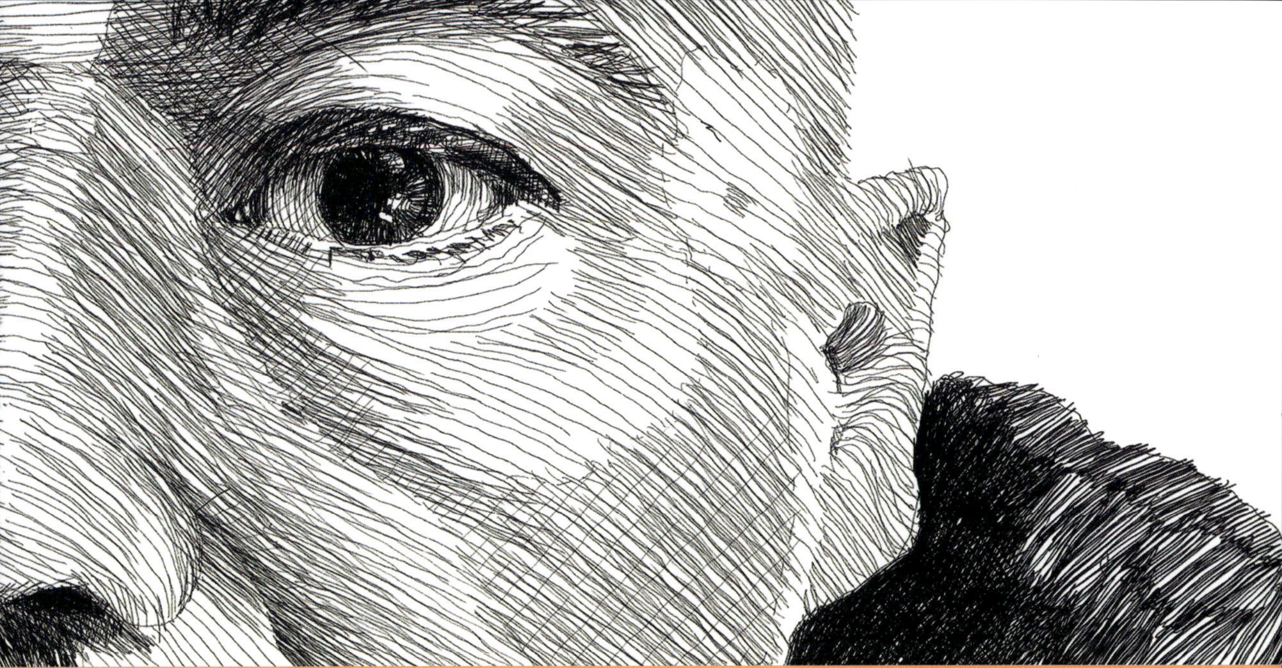

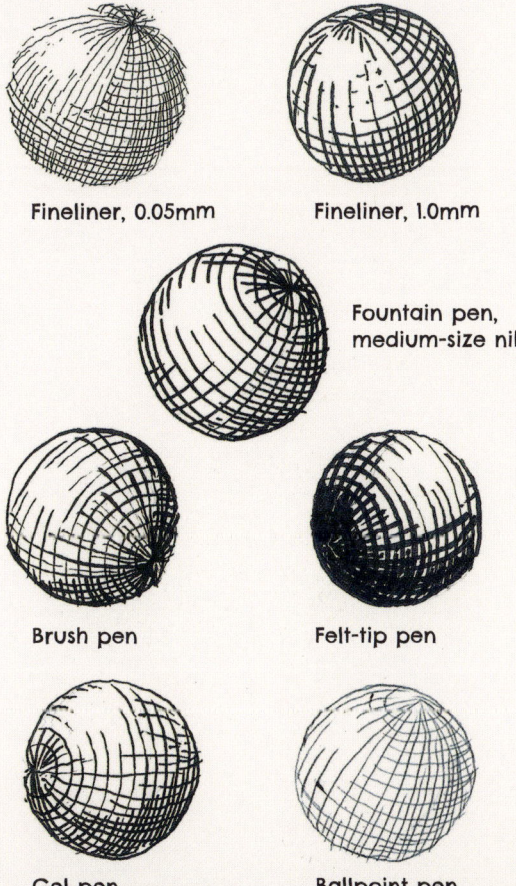

Fineliner, 0.05mm

Fineliner, 1.0mm

Fountain pen,
medium-size nib

Brush pen

Felt-tip pen

Gel pen

Ballpoint pen

MY PREFERENCE

To avoid getting lost in the complexity of this technique, I like to sketch some guidelines in pencil indicating the shape the lines should follow. Afterwards, I draw the lines in ink in between these guidelines.

COMMON MISTAKES

Failing to closely follow the contours: This can result in shading that does not conform properly to the form, leading to a distorted representation.

Applying too many shading lines: This, along with making the shading lines overly dense, can saturate the drawing, making it challenging to identify the contours and thereby losing crucial details.

PRACTICE

Draw straight lines on a sheet of paper. Draw a globe map, emphasizing parallel and meridian lines with special attention. Observe how these lines define the shape of the sphere.

Stippling

Stippling involves creating shadows and textures by applying small ink dots at different pressures and distances. Instead of continuous lines, this method uses variation in the size (pressure), proximity (density) and order (pattern) of the dots to achieve tonal effects and details.

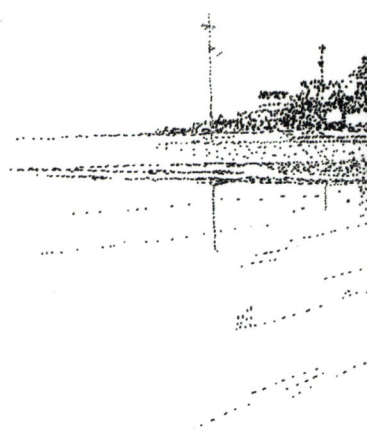

THIS PAGE Stippling is used to good effect in this illustration of a Japanese village. The spacing and density of the dots are employed to create hierarchies within the drawing. Thus, the elements towards the edges and the more subtle ones are sketched with more dispersed stippling, while the geometries in the centre are detailed with a higher density of dots.

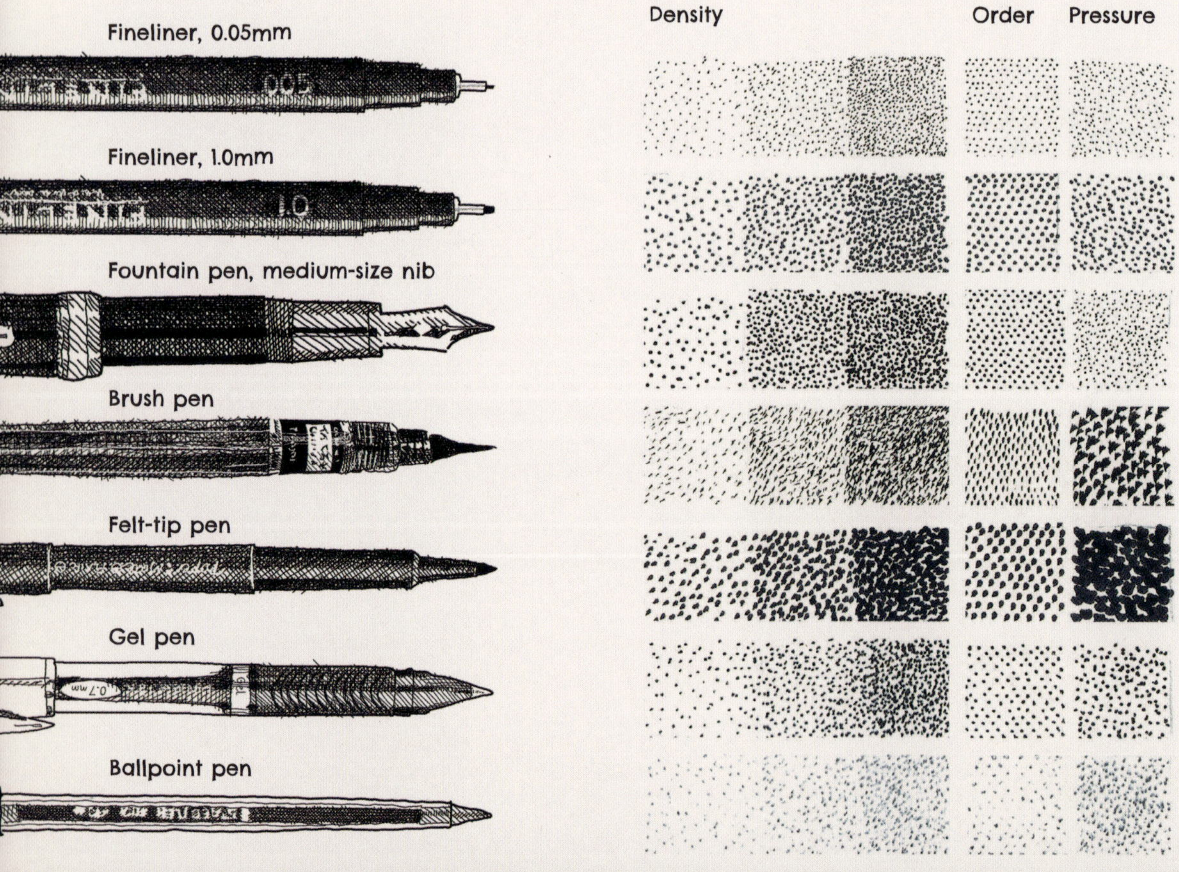

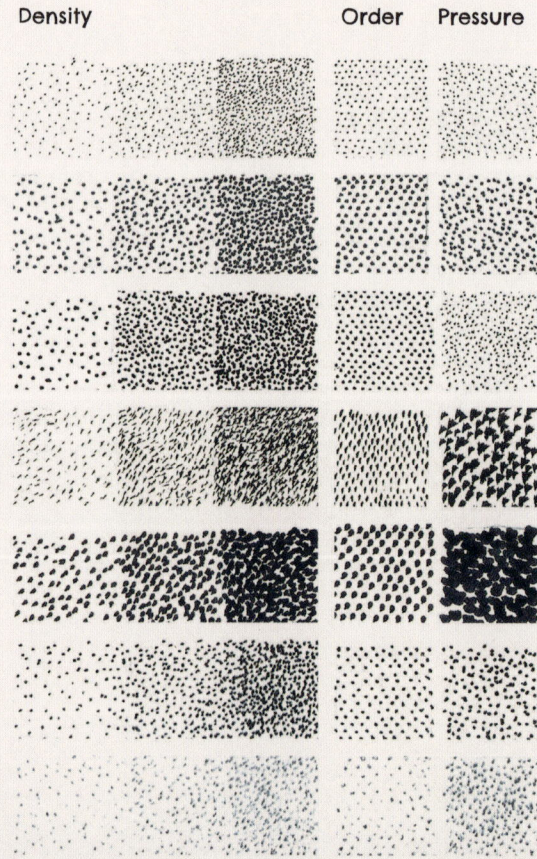

Fineliner, 0.05mm

Fineliner, 1.0mm

Fountain pen, medium-size nib

Brush pen

Felt-tip pen

Gel pen

Ballpoint pen

Density

Order

Pressure

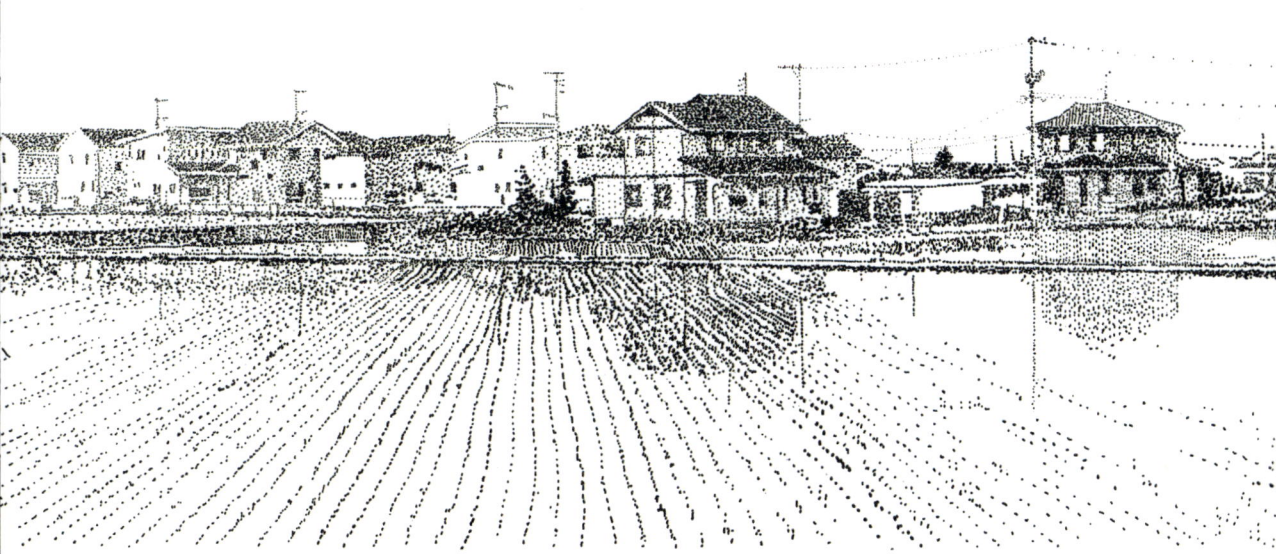

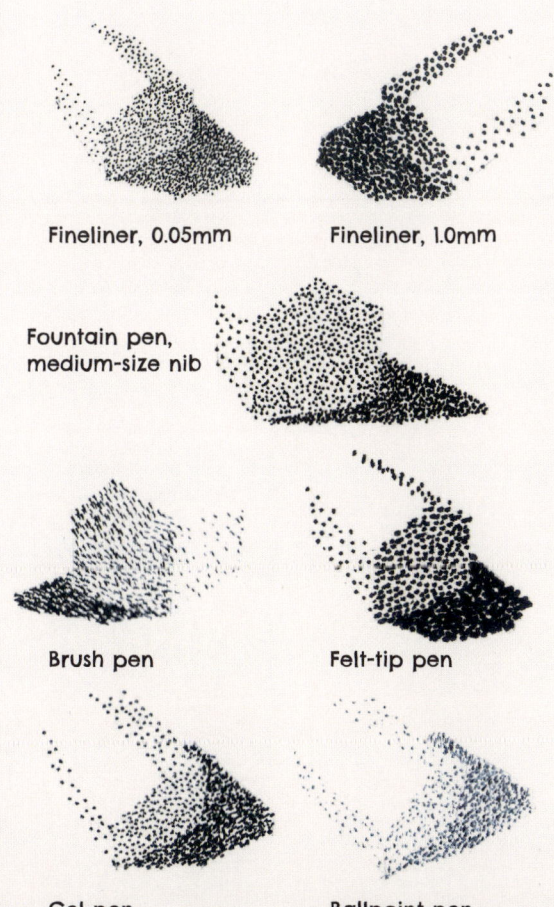

Fineliner, 0.05mm

Fineliner, 1.0mm

Fountain pen, medium-size nib

Brush pen

Felt-tip pen

Gel pen

Ballpoint pen

MY PREFERENCE

Given that stippling can be a time-consuming process, I avoid frustration by applying the dots in an organized manner. Typically, I choose between two approaches: starting from the outermost edges and progressing towards the interior of the forms, or following imaginary lines formed by the dots as I draw them.

COMMON MISTAKE

Impatience: The stippling technique demands patience. Impatience may lead you to hastily apply the dots, compromising the precision and quality of your work.

PRACTICE

Create a tonal chart by varying the density of dots to generate gradations.

Practise clearly outlining the contours and boundaries of simple shapes using stippling.

Cross hatching + stippling

STEP BY STEP: COFFEE CUP

Combining stippling, for precise tonal values in lighter areas, with cross hatching, for quick dark tones, creates efficient and detailed drawings, achieving an ideal balance between speed and visual richness.

1. BASIC PENCIL LINES

Begin by gently sketching the outline of the cup with a pencil, subtly marking the tonal areas. Feel free to omit details such as the spoon if you prefer.

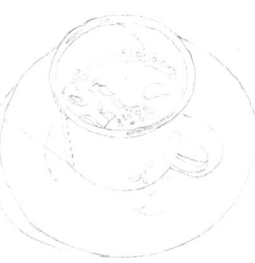

2. SPOT THE SHADOWS

With a 0.2mm fineliner or similar, start by filling the shadows on the porcelain; this will highlight the darker areas and help define mid-tones and highlights.

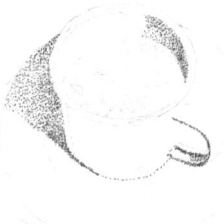

3. MID-TONES

Fill in the other areas patiently, paying attention to tonal variations. Take advantage of the slow nature of this technique to focus on the details.

Maintain a consistent control of your speed when applying dots to prevent them from turning into unwanted lines or shapes.

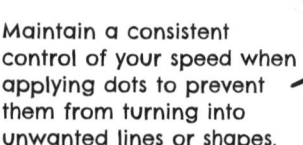

4. ADJUST VALUE RELATIONS

With the saucer and cup established, work on the cast shadows and adjust the light-dark relationship across the entire composition. Add dots in empty spaces to fine-tune the tone as needed.

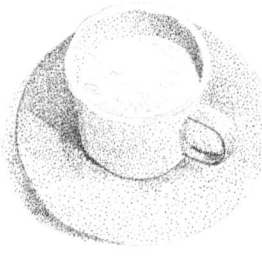

5. CROSS HATCHING

For the coffee, utilize all four directions of cross-hatching lines. Begin with the first two layers in the pre-defined darker areas. Avoid outlining the drawing – instead, let the difference between values define the volumes.

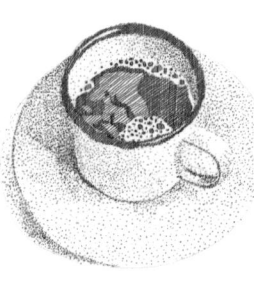

6. MORE CROSS HATCHING

Apply a third layer across the entire area, excluding the foam that is the lightest area of the coffee. Then apply the final layer of cross hatching, covering the entire surface.

Avoid drawing the outlines; you will achieve better results.

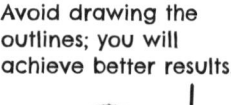

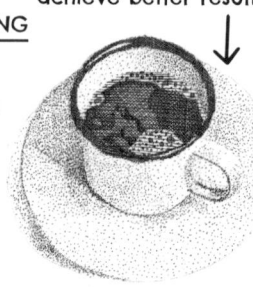

7. ADJUSTING VALUES

Finish by adding additional dots to the darker areas to adjust the values and create more contrast in your drawing.

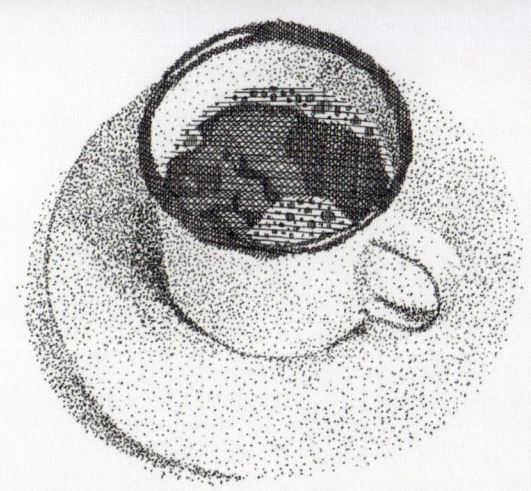

SEE ALSO
Cross hatching, page 38
Stippling, page 42

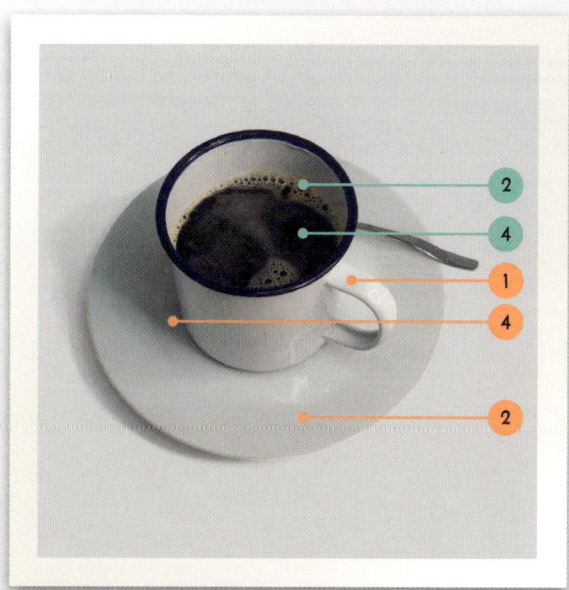

VALUES

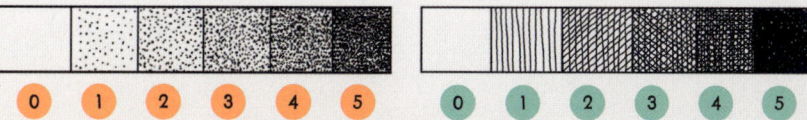

Tick hatching

Tick hatching creates tonal variations using small parallel lines that can be joined or separated as needed. This technique is particularly effective when drawing at a certain speed, allowing for adjustments in line density to achieve tonal variations.

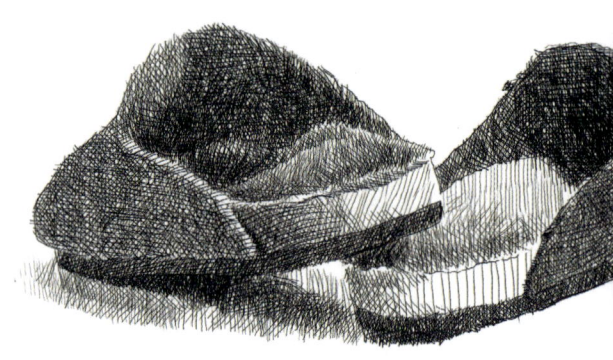

THIS PAGE Tick hatching creates texture across these footwear options. By increasing the density and number of directions, a sense of depth is created for the shadows beneath the shoes.

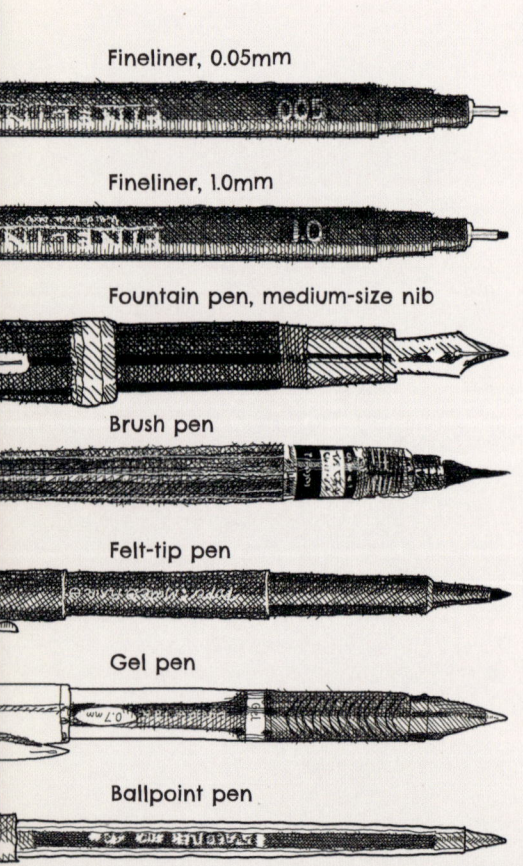

Fineliner, 0.05mm

Fineliner, 1.0mm

Fountain pen, medium-size nib

Brush pen

Felt-tip pen

Gel pen

Ballpoint pen

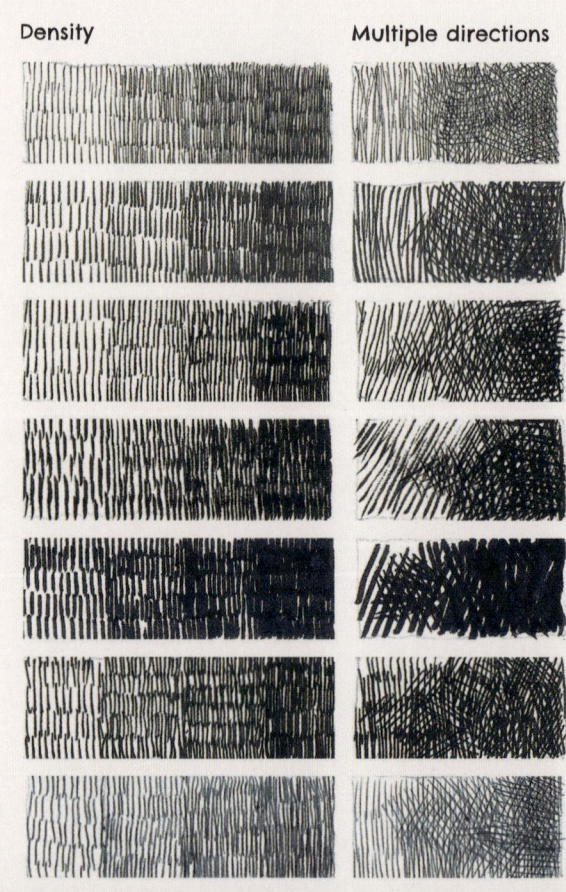

Density

Multiple directions

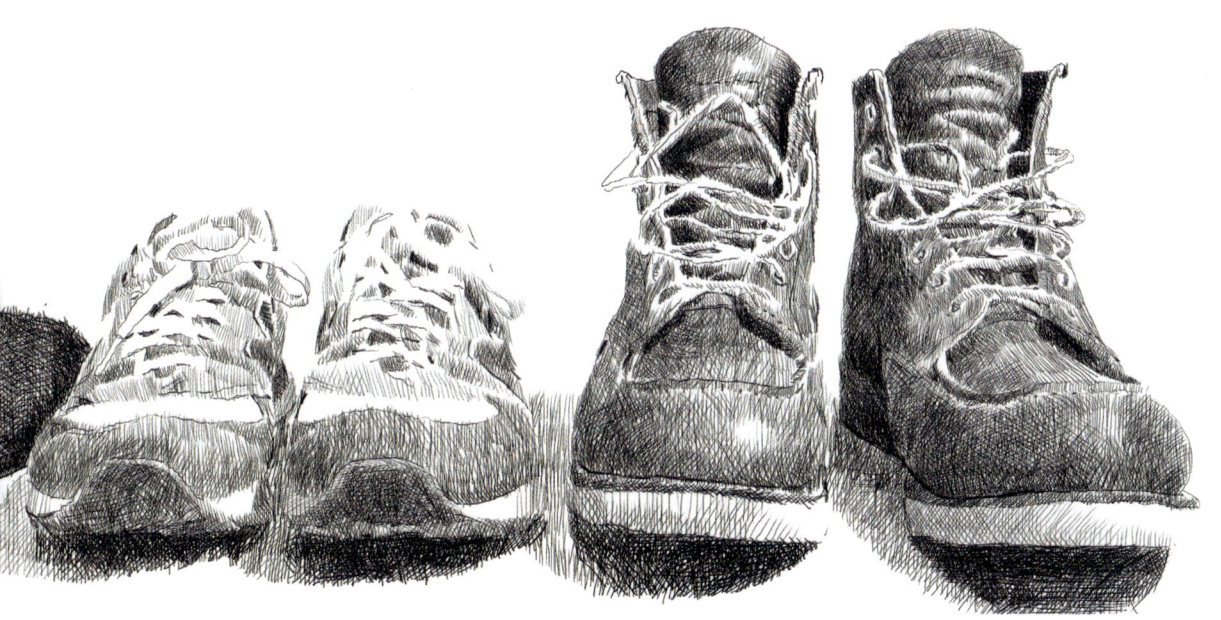

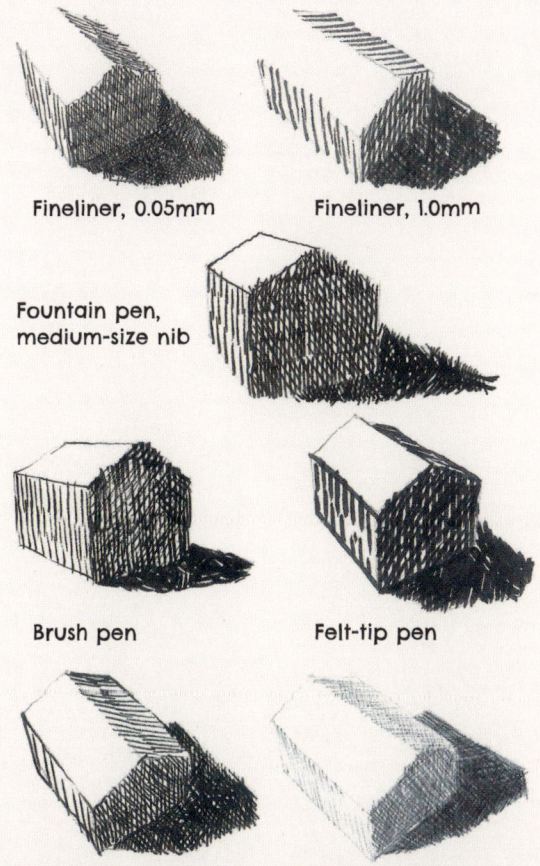

Fineliner, 0.05mm

Fineliner, 1.0mm

Fountain pen,
medium-size nib

Brush pen

Felt-tip pen

Gel pen

Ballpoint pen

MY PREFERENCE

I prefer using fine nibs, which allow me to expand the range of tonal values in the drawing. Although there is a risk of damaging the tips, as this technique encourages quick strokes, I prefer to be careful because the results are worth it.

COMMON MISTAKES

Failing to maintain a consistent line length: This can impact the coherence of the shading.

Not considering the speed: The speed at which you apply the ticks can influence the appearance and uniformity of the shading.

PRACTICE

Produce the same tone with variations in your stroke speed to understand how this influences the appearance of shading.

Practise applying these strokes in small areas without going beyond the outline, to enhance your precision.

Weighting lines

This term refers to varying the line thickness to highlight specific elements in the drawing. This create depth and guide the viewer's attention. The variation in thickness contributes to a sense of weight and dimension within the composition.

THIS PAGE The use of thick lines to highlight the body of the houses is a way of adding depth to the image and showing how they are inset from the roof.

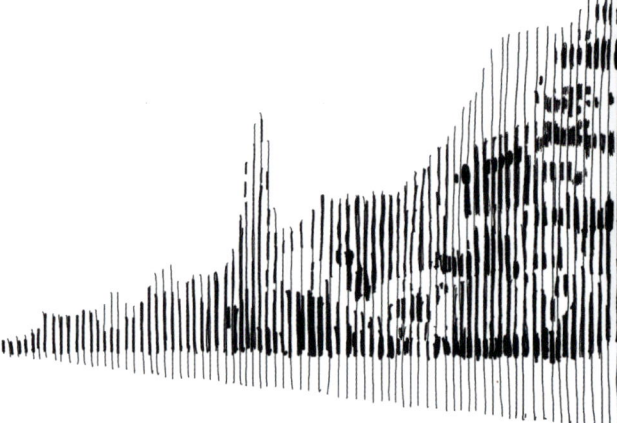

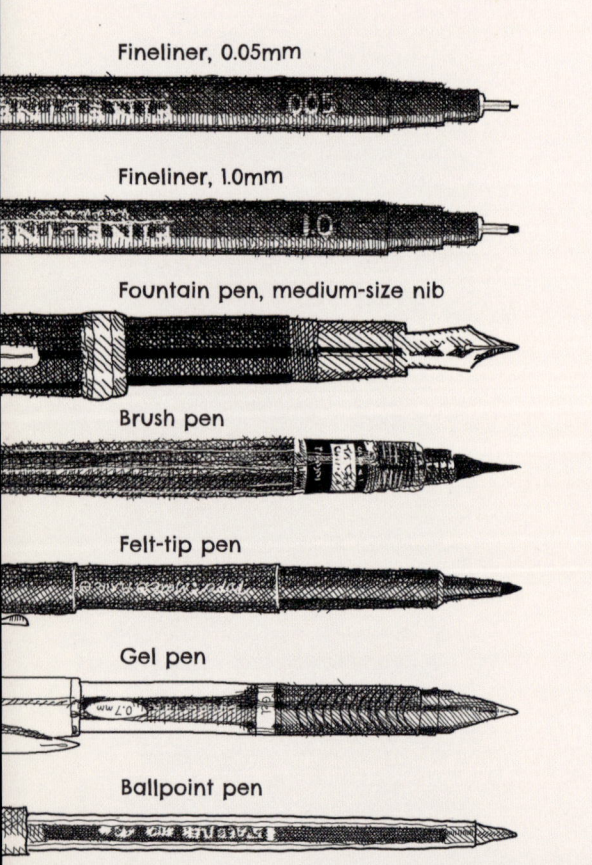

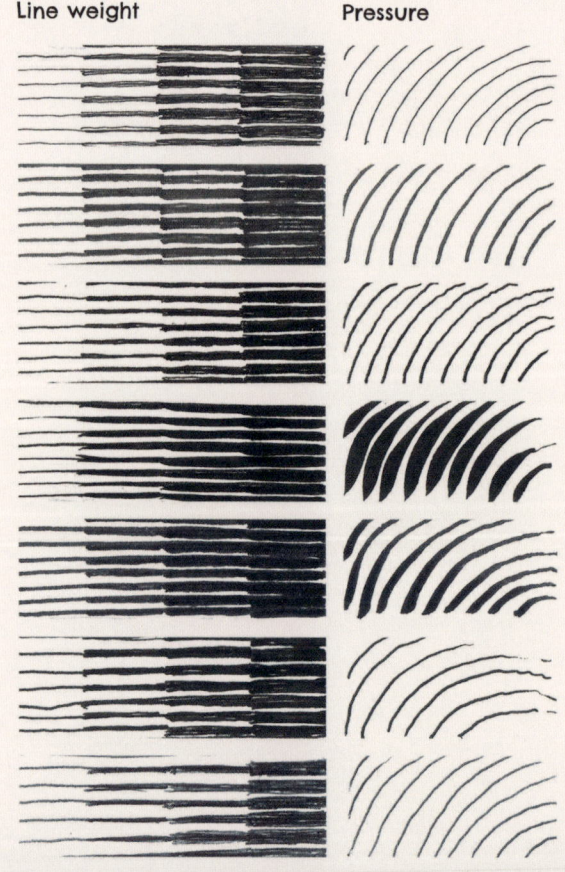

Fineliner, 0.05mm

Fineliner, 1.0mm

Fountain pen, medium-size nib

Brush pen

Felt-tip pen

Gel pen

Ballpoint pen

Line weight

Pressure

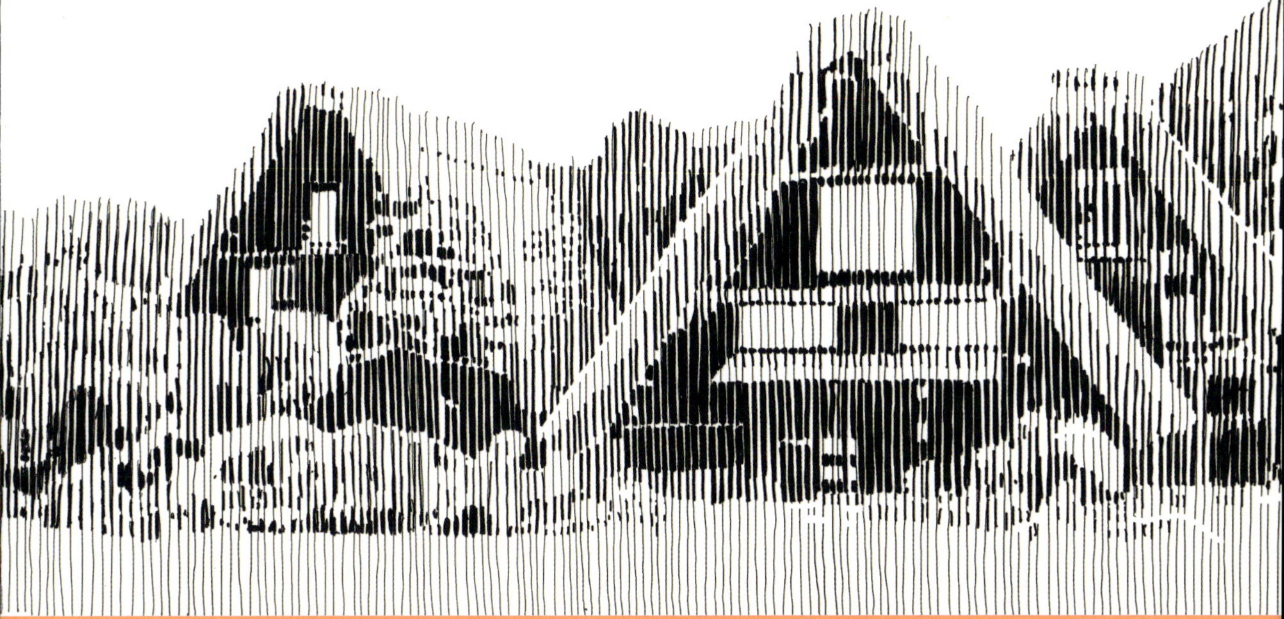

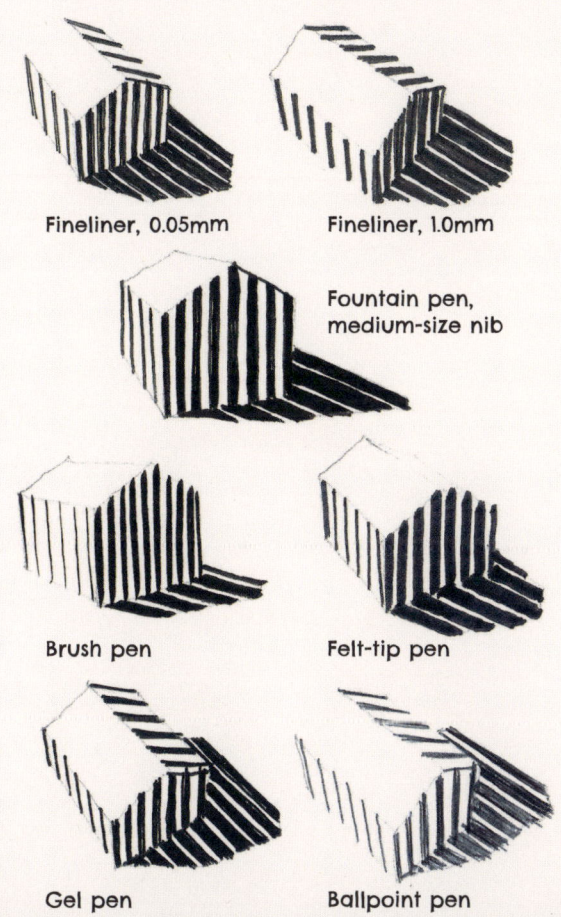

Fineliner, 0.05mm

Fineliner, 1.0mm

Fountain pen, medium-size nib

Brush pen

Felt-tip pen

Gel pen

Ballpoint pen

MY PREFERENCE

I don't usually use this technique as the primary foundation in my drawings, as it requires some planning and doesn't come to me spontaneously. However, I often employ it to highlight figures or compositionally frame the drawing. By thickening the lines in certain parts of the composition I can quickly and effectively bring attention to them.

COMMON MISTAKES

Exaggerating the thickness of lines: Doing this without visual reasoning can have a negative impact on the overall aesthetic and cohesiveness of the drawing.

Applying lines that are excessively thick: If you do this to less important details, you can divert attention from the main subject and disrupt the visual balance.

PRACTICE

Sketch simple patterns and employ thicker lines on specific elements to give them importance.

Weighting lines + contour hatching

STEP BY STEP: ONION

This combination allows for clear and precise control of volumetrics and tonal values. While contour hatching gives a three-dimensional effect by indicating the volume of the object, weighting lines can be employed to accentuate different values in the drawing and specific details.

1. BASIC PENCIL LINES

Draw basic lines, paying attention to the contour and the relationship between the different layers of the onion. You can also briefly sketch the roots.

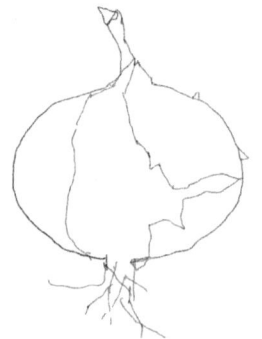

2. CONTOUR GUIDES

Subtly indicate the direction of the onion fibres to serve as a guide when drawing the ink lines. Also, outline the different tonal areas.

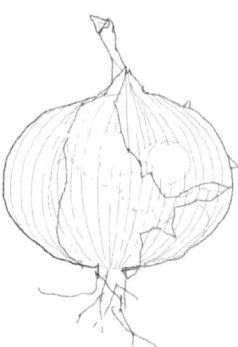

3. FIRST HATCHING LAYER

Using a 0.05mm or similar marker, outline the contour lines throughout the volume, avoiding the indicated areas of greater illumination.

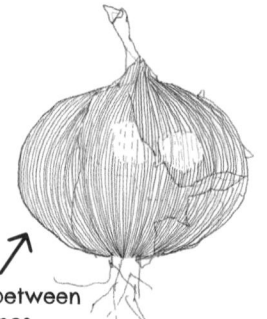

Draw ink lines between the reference lines while maintaining the same direction.

4. SECOND HATCHING LAYER

With the same marker, intensify the darker areas corresponding to the shadow on the right and bottom, while continuing to avoid the lighter values. It's now time to draw the outline of the roots.

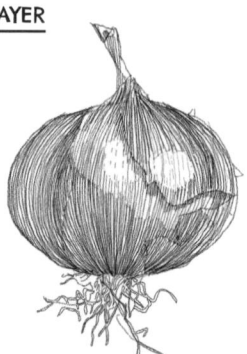

5. THIRD HATCHING LAYER

For this layer, use a thicker marker and go over the previously drawn lines within the darker values.

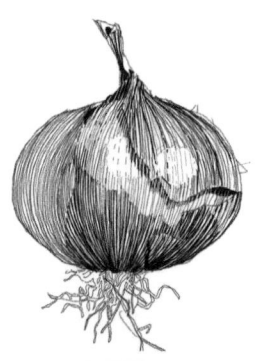

6. FOURTH HATCHING LAYER

Emphasize the lines as needed, always following the direction of the pencil lines, until you achieve the desired values.

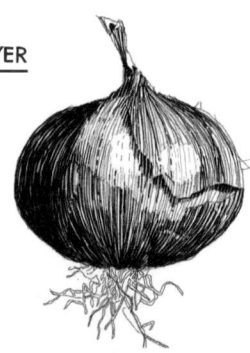

7. DETAILS

Finally, dedicate some thick lines to small details, such as the roots or small pieces of skin sticking out from the sides, and outline the shadows, highlighting the change in layers of the onion.

SEE ALSO
Weighting lines, page 48
Contour hatching, page 40

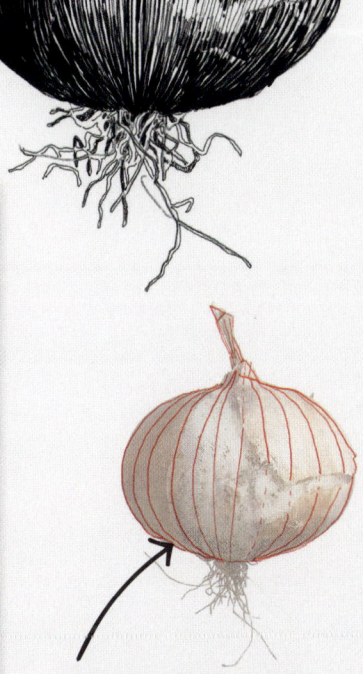

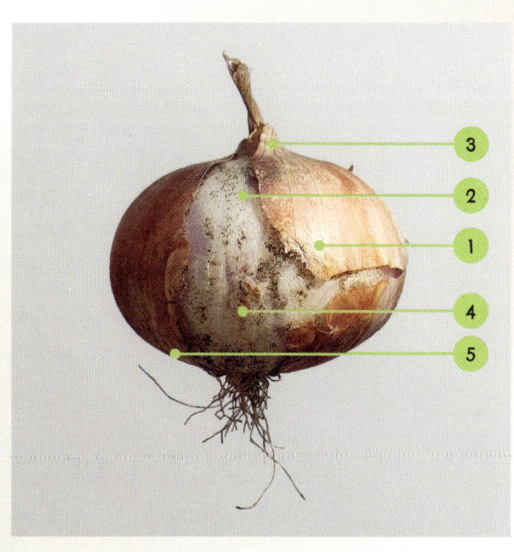

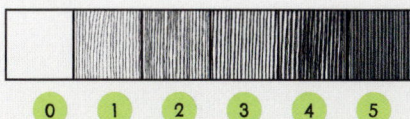

The onion fibres enable us to easily follow the direction of the contour hatching lines.

VALUES

| 0 | 1 | 2 | 3 | 4 | 5 |

Woven hatching

This is a technique that involves weaving lines over and under each other to create shading and texture, resulting in a woven-like pattern that adds depth and dimension to the artwork.

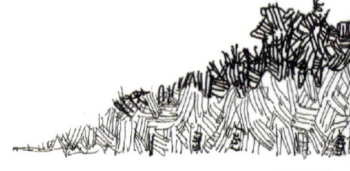
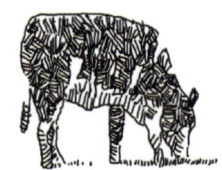
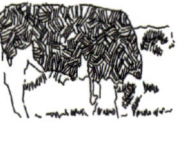
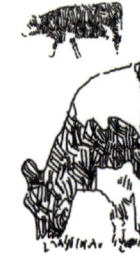

THIS PAGE Woven hatching beautifully captures the patterning on these Friesian cows, easily discernible on the subjects in the foreground. In the background, the direction, stroke length and speed are altered between the rows of trees to show the depth of the woodland.

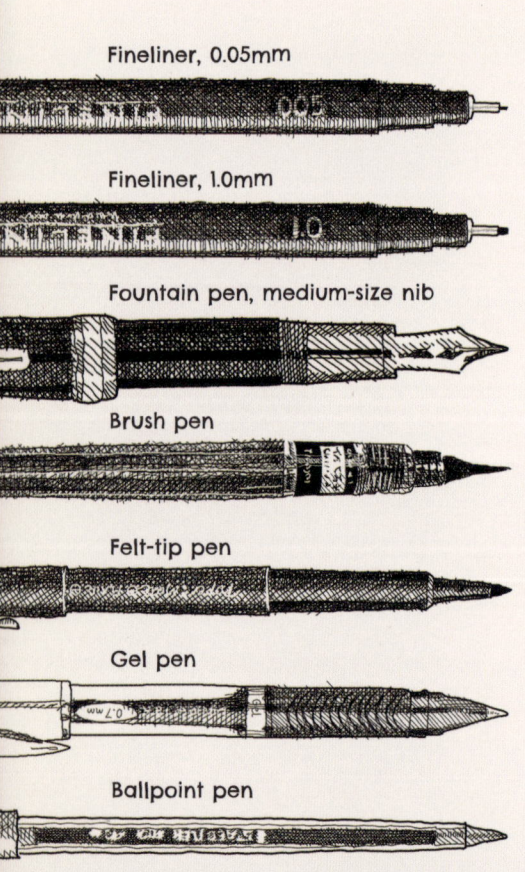

Fineliner, 0.05mm

Fineliner, 1.0mm

Fountain pen, medium-size nib

Brush pen

Felt-tip pen

Gel pen

Ballpoint pen

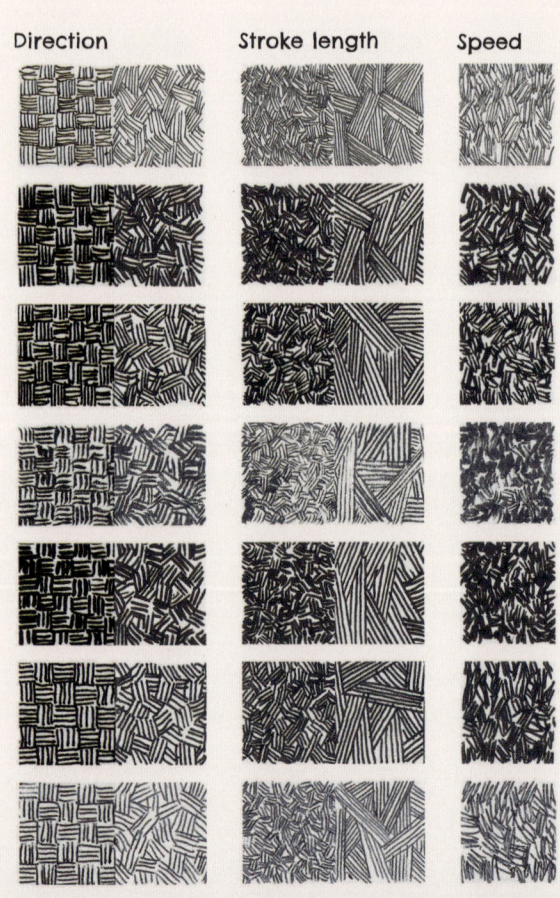

Direction Stroke length Speed

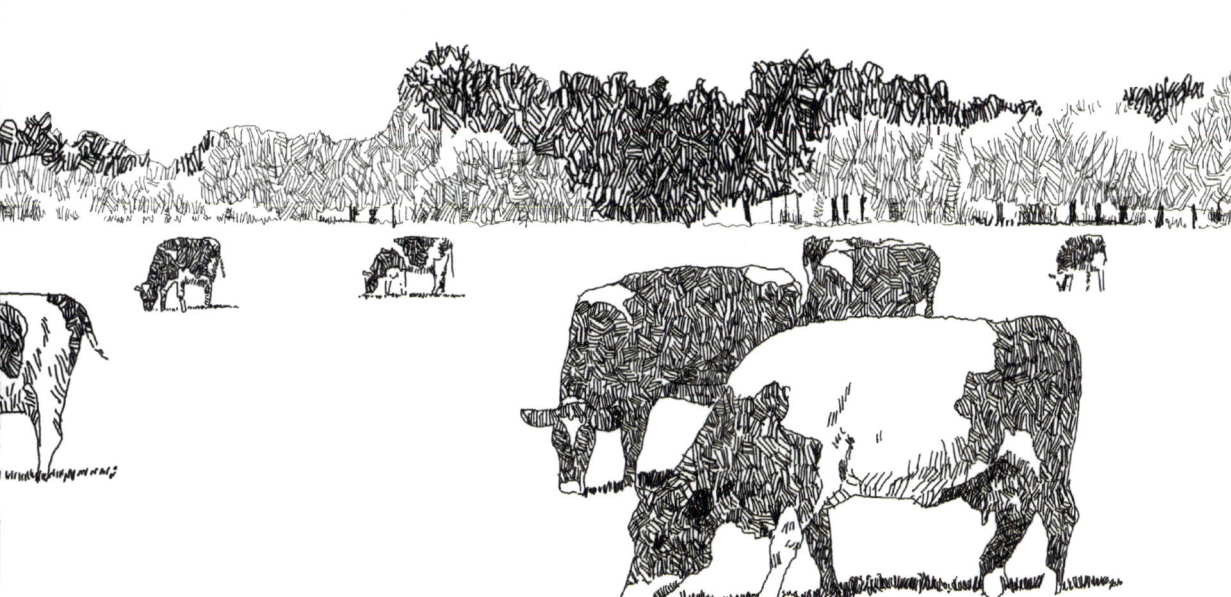

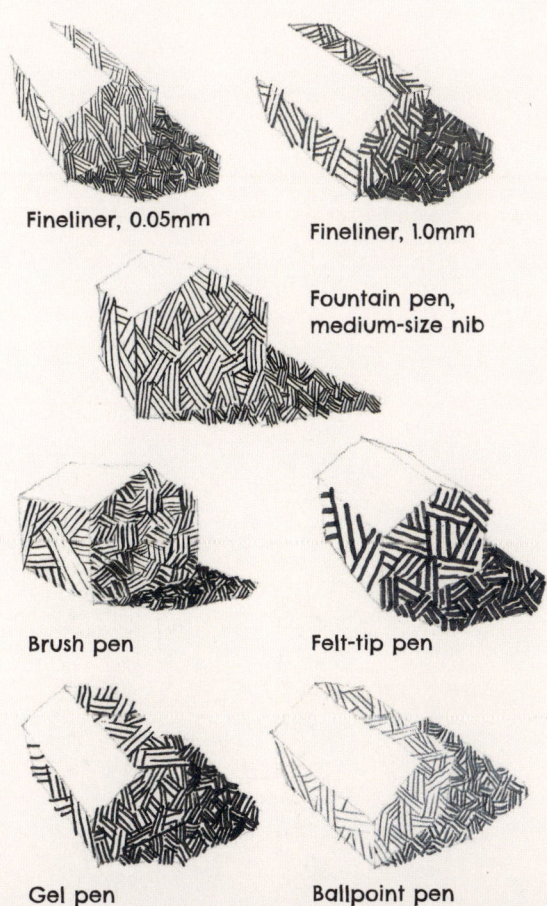

Fineliner, 0.05mm

Fineliner, 1.0mm

Fountain pen, medium-size nib

Brush pen

Felt-tip pen

Gel pen

Ballpoint pen

MY PREFERENCE

I prefer to use flexible nibs for the woven hatching technique as they enable me to vary the line thickness by pressure, making it easier to achieve the necessary values.

COMMON MISTAKES

Inconsistency in spacing can generate undesired contrasts and affect visual coherence; moreover, it can make the drawing appear disorganized.

Overworking an area: Spending too much time on one part or going over it repeatedly can result in smudging or unintended marks on the drawing.

PRACTICE

Draw a series of squares or rectangles and fill them in with the woven hatching technique, varying the spacing between the lines to create different values from light to dark. This exercise will help you develop control over the pen and ink and improve your ability to create gradations of tone.

Scribbling

This technique involves quick and disorderly strokes, criss-crossing in a chaotic manner to create textures and shadows. Instead of controlled lines, this spontaneous and free approach adds vitality and dynamism, capturing movement and individual expressiveness.

THIS PAGE Scribbling is especially effective in this illustration of a sardine because its disordered and spontaneous nature adds a naturalness to the drawing and allows for quick variations in the shades of the shiny scales.

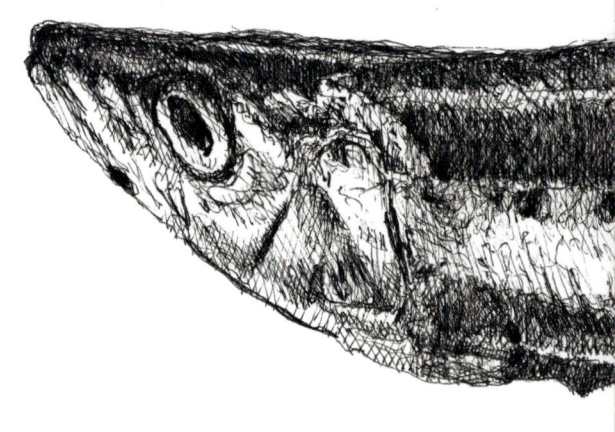

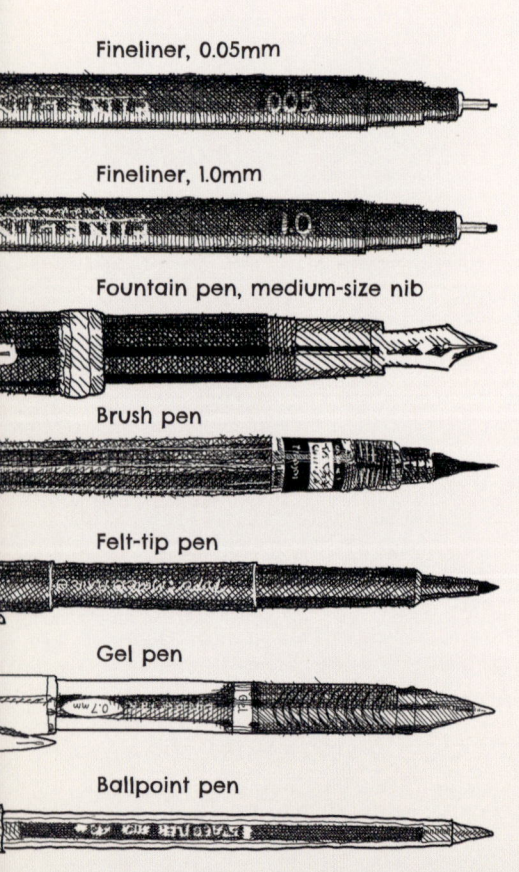

Fineliner, 0.05mm

Fineliner, 1.0mm

Fountain pen, medium-size nib

Brush pen

Felt-tip pen

Gel pen

Ballpoint pen

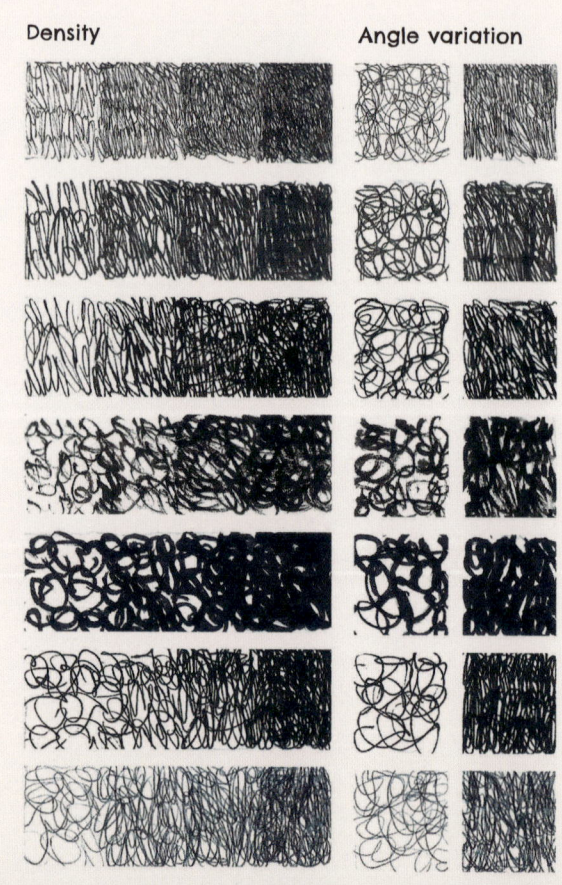

Density

Angle variation

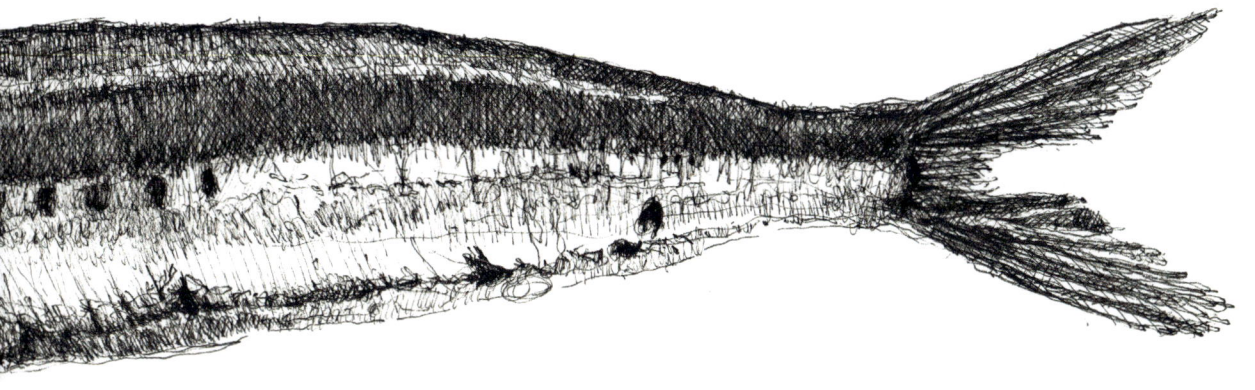

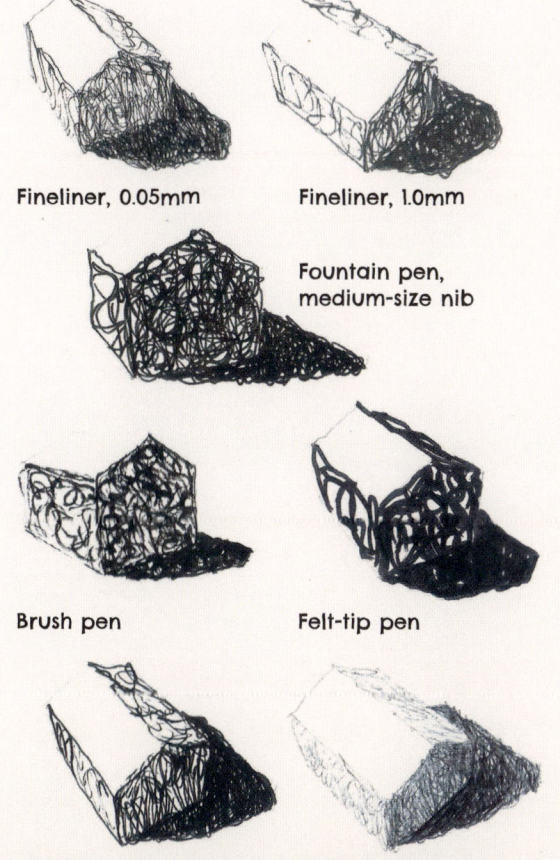

Fineliner, 0.05mm

Fineliner, 1.0mm

Fountain pen,
medium-size nib

Brush pen

Felt-tip pen

Gel pen

Ballpoint pen

MY PREFERENCE

I love the character that this kind of stroke imparts to the drawing; I frequently use it when aiming to create a sense of spontaneity and usually apply it over cross hatching, particularly in darker values, to soften the typical rigidity of the grid, especially when drawing nature.

COMMON MISTAKES

Applying scribbling inconsistently: This can create visual discordance.

Changing the speed: If defined contours are needed, changing your speed of application can result in lack of control.

PRACTICE

Generate simple geometric shapes using controlled scribbling to refine precision and consistency.
    Apply scribbling in layers, starting with light strokes and progressively increasing the intensity to produce shading effects.

Varying pressure

Variation in pressure plays a fundamental role when using pen and ink. By adjusting the pressure on the drawing tool you can achieve precise control over the thickness and intensity of the lines. Mastering this makes it easier to create visual hierarchies, textures and nuances in shading.

THIS PAGE The more distant trees are depicted with subtle and delicate lines, while those closer are drawn by applying more pressure to produce a more defined stroke, thus creating an atmospheric sense of distance.

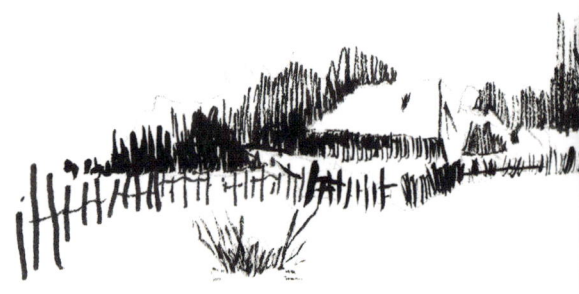

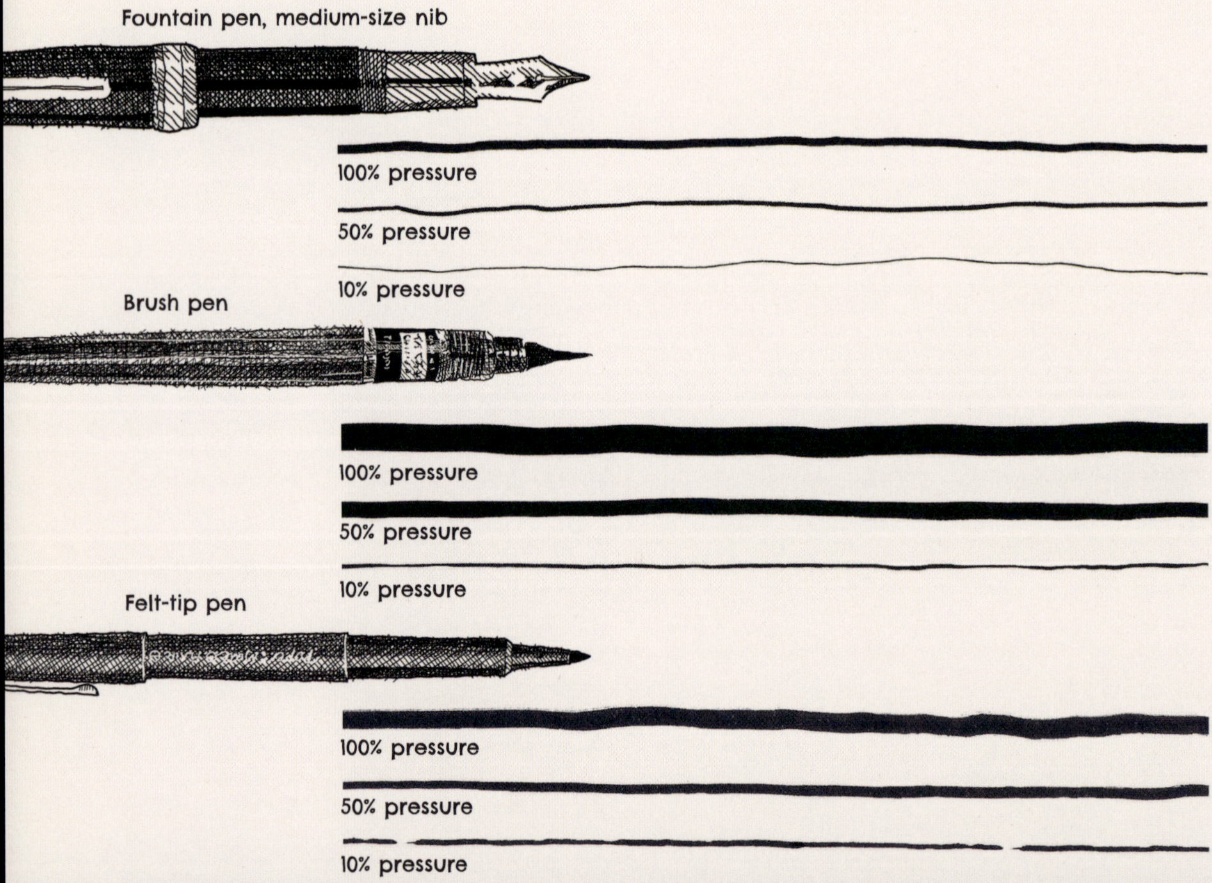

Fountain pen, medium-size nib

100% pressure

50% pressure

10% pressure

Brush pen

100% pressure

50% pressure

10% pressure

Felt-tip pen

100% pressure

50% pressure

10% pressure

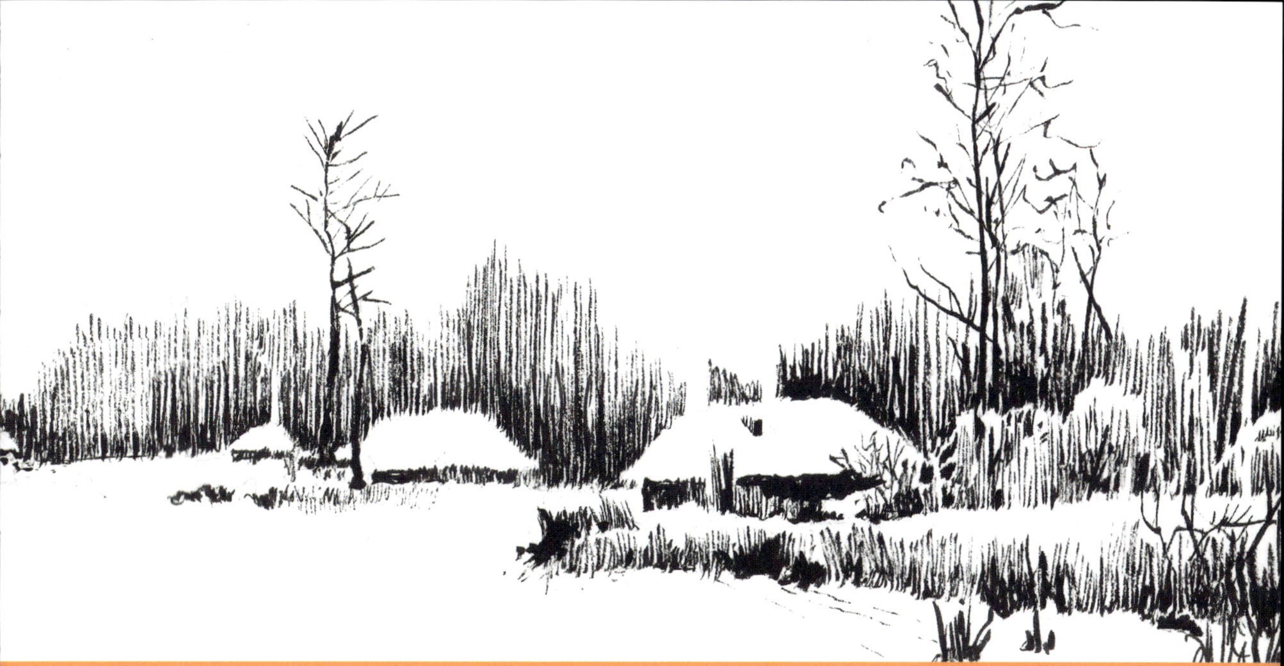

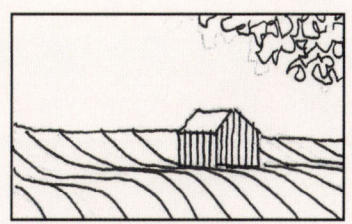
In this first drawing, all lines have the same intensity and no hierarchy is created.

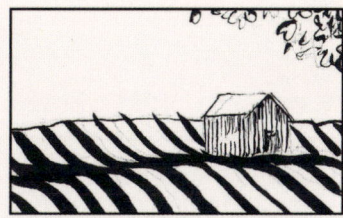
By thickening the lines of the ground, attention is drawn to this element, making it the central focus of the drawing.

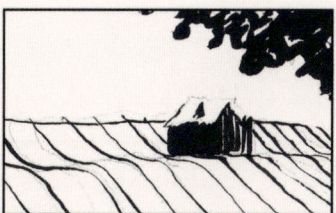
Alternatively, if you thicken the lines of the foreground house and tree, you can create a sense of depth that was not present before.

COMMON MISTAKES

Using the incorrect line thickness: Tools such as calibrated markers have a fixed line thickness with limited responsiveness to pressure variations, while others, such as brushes, are much more susceptible to such changes. Recognizing these differences and applying pressure variation in accordance with each tool's capabilities is crucial to achieving the desired result.

Inconsistent pressure: Caused by fatigue or carelessness, inconsistent pressure can result in abrupt and unpredictable line thickness variations. Consistently applying a uniform pressure in similar lines is crucial for a cohesive appearance. Avoiding unexpected changes in pressure enhances the drawing's overall smoothness and aesthetic harmony.

PRACTICE

Create a series of lines with calibrated markers of various thicknesses. Using a brush pen, replicate each line by applying the pressure necessary to match the thickness of the marker lines. This exercise will strengthen your ability to adjust pressure according to the requirements of the drawing.

Cross hatching + scribbling

STEP BY STEP: PINE CONE

By combining cross hatching and scribbling you can achieve dynamic and expressive artwork. Cross hatching provides values, while scribbling adds fluidity and breaks up stiffness in parallel strokes for a more natural effect.

1. BASIC PENCIL LINES

Sketch simple pencil lines to ensure the correct proportions and relationships between the cone scales. Outline the lighter and darker areas for easy hatching later.

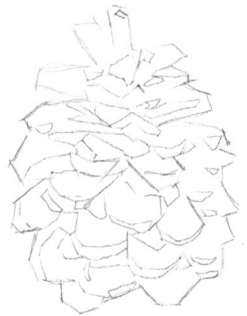

2. INK OUTLINE

Using an 0.2mm fineliner pen (or similar), outline the pine cone shape and scales that you previously sketched in pencil. Be sure to make confident, fluid strokes.

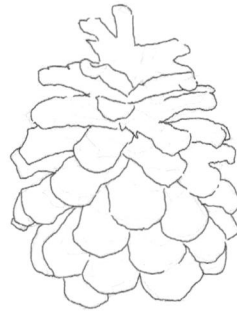

3. FIRST HATCHING LAYER

Begin by using your preferred hatching direction. For instance, if vertical lines are easier for you, start with those. Hatch the area you previously sketched in pencil that corresponds to the darkest value.

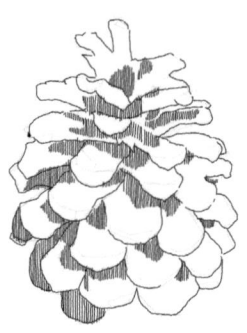

4. SECOND HATCHING LAYER

Begin developing the mid-tones of the pine cone by adding another layer of hatching marks at a 45-degree angle to the previous layer. This layer should cover most of the cone, but avoid the lighter areas to maintain contrast.

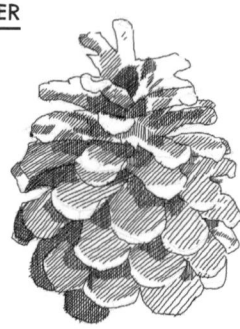

5. THIRD HATCHING LAYER

To create a distinction between mid-tone values, apply a new layer of hatching in the opposite direction to the previous layer, altering the density of the lines in the darker areas of the pine cone.

You can use a thicker nib to achieve darker values.

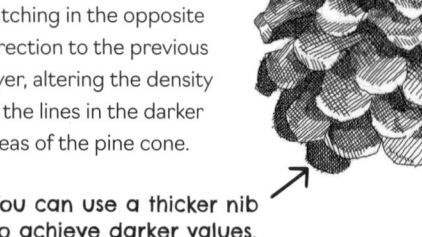

6. FOURTH HATCHING LAYER

Contrast is essential for creating volume in your drawing. By applying a final layer of hatching in the opposite direction to the first layer, you can accentuate the darkest values and some of the mid-tones, and achieve the desired contrast and dimension.

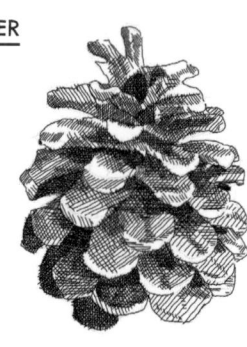

7. SCRIBBLING FINAL LAYER

To create the texture and markings
of the pine cone's scales, you can
now utilize the scribbling technique.
However, it is important to use this
technique judiciously to avoid
overworking the different values
in your drawing.

SEE ALSO
Cross hatching, page 38
Scribbling, page 54

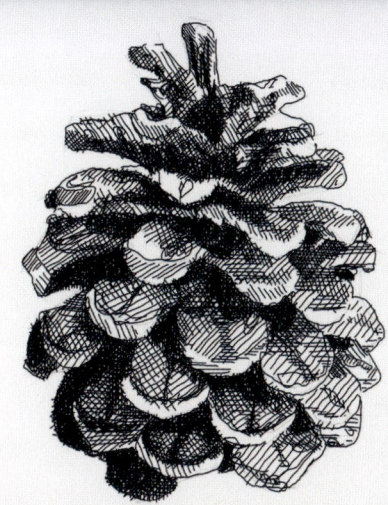

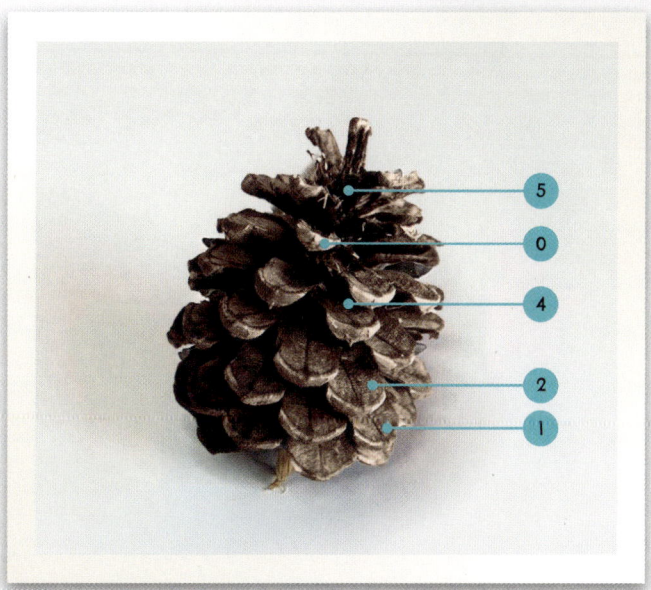

VALUES

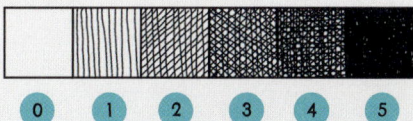

Understanding values

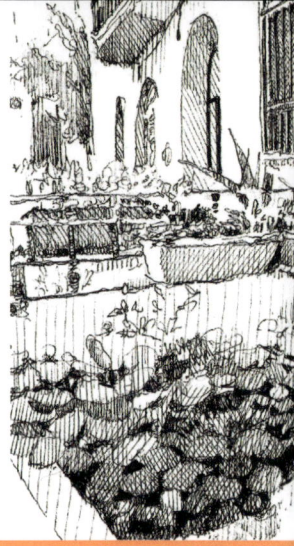

The term 'values' (or 'tone') refers to the relative lightness or darkness of different areas within an artwork. In pen-and-ink drawing, values are created by varying the density of lines. The use of values is crucial in creating depth and form to create a three-dimensional image.

THIS PAGE The different values on the plants suggest not only the variations in colour but also the shaded areas underneath them. Likewise, the dark window recesses indicate that they are in shadow, unlike the sunlit building facade.

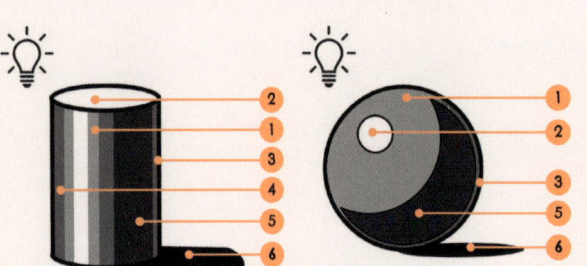

UNDERSTANDING LIGHT AND SHADOW

1. Medium light
2. Maximum light
3. Reflection
4. Medium shadow
5. Maximum shadow
6. Cast shadow

EXPERIMENT WITH VALUE SCALES FOR DIFFERENT RESULTS

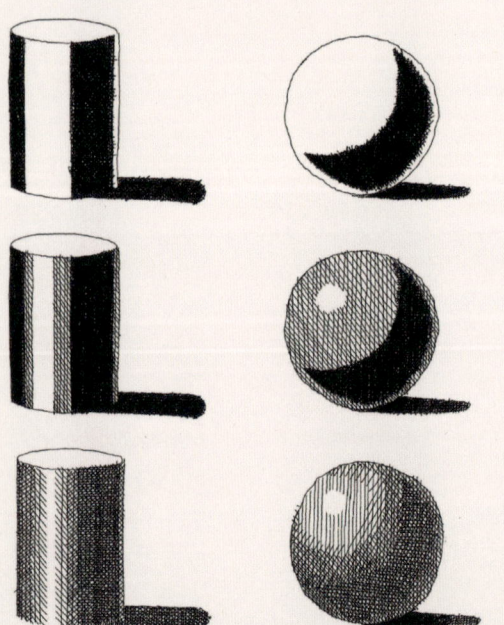

High contrast, two-step values

Medium contrast, three-step values

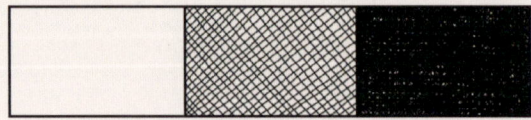

Soft contrast, six-step values

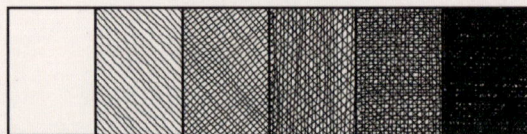

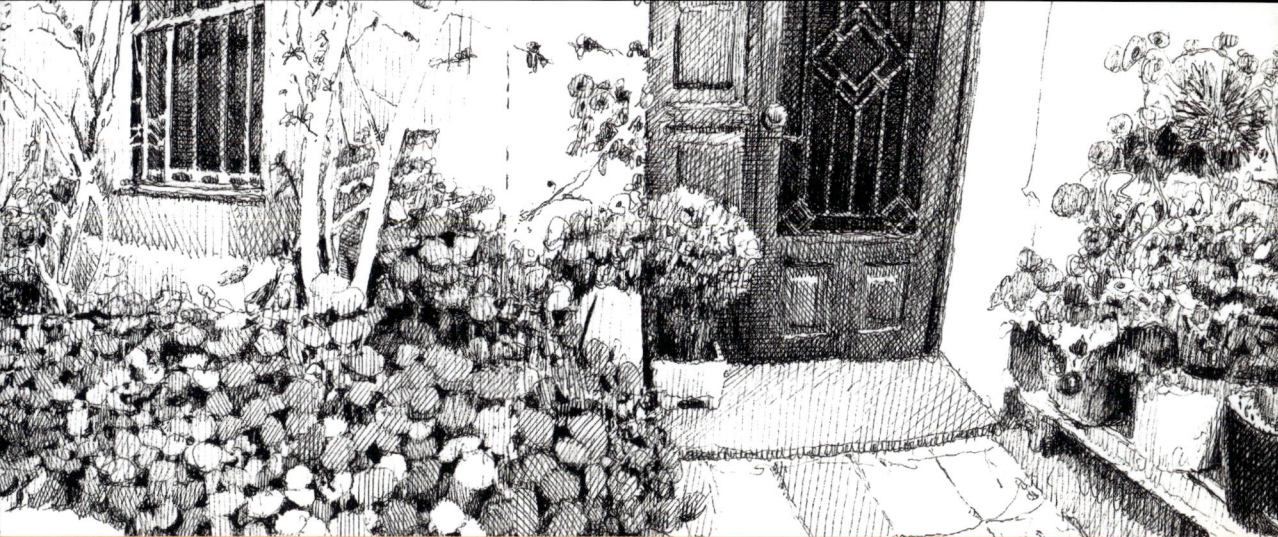

DIFFERENT TECHNIQUES, SAME FUNDAMENTAL CONCEPT

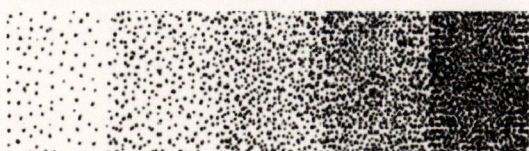

Stippling

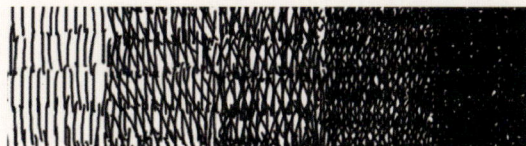

Tick hatching

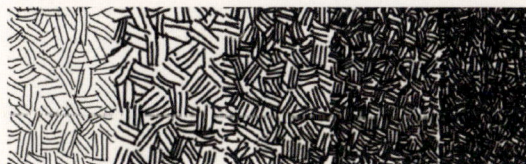

Woven hatching

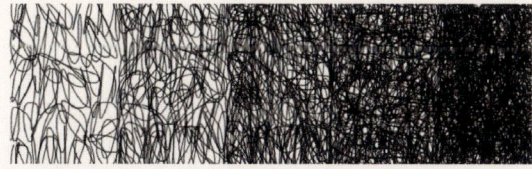

Scribbling

COMMON MISTAKES

A number of mistakes can be made when attempting to draw values, many of which can only be identified through practice. There are two main mistakes that I would like to point out.

Overworking the drawing: When trying to create a range of values, it can be easy to get carried away with adding more and more lines. This can result in a drawing that looks busy or muddy, with no clear sense of light and shadow.

Not leaving enough white space: White space is just as important as the lines themselves. Not leaving enough white space can make the drawing look confusing, so be sure to leave appropriate white space to create contrast and enhance the overall impact of the artwork.

PRACTICE

Select a simple object, such as a piece of fruit or a cup, and place it under a single light source to create shadows and highlights. Then use different techniques to create a range of values that depict the form of the object. Also experiment with leaving areas of white space to create contrast.

Weighting lines + hatching

STEP BY STEP: CACTUS POT

By combining these two techniques you can efficiently establish visual hierarchies, distinguishing volumes and tonalities quickly. This combination is perfect for quick sketches that do not require extensive details or complexity.

1. BASIC PENCIL LINES

With a pencil, lightly sketch the lines, outlining the geometric shapes and the different values created by shadows.

You can use an H or HB pencil. ↗

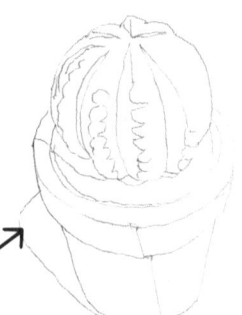

2. CONTOUR GUIDES

Use a brush pen or a thick fineliner to outline the external geometric shapes.

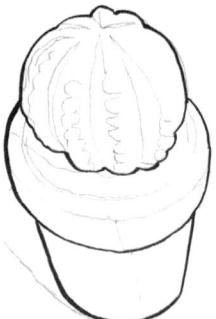

3. FIRST HATCHING LAYER

With a 0.05mm fineliner or a similar pen, draw the internal outlines and the boundaries of the shadows. It's crucial that the two pens you use have a noticeable difference in thickness.

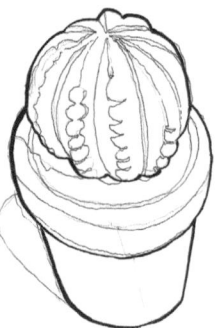

4. SECOND HATCHING LAYER

Apply a dense hatching for the darkest values, such as the shadows cast by the cactus and the pot.

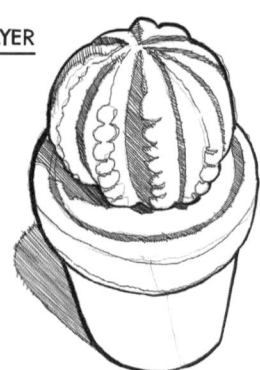

5. THIRD HATCHING LAYER

Once the shadows are filled, add the mid-tones, taking care to leave white spaces to highlight the lighter values. It is crucial to leave these areas ink-free to create highlights.

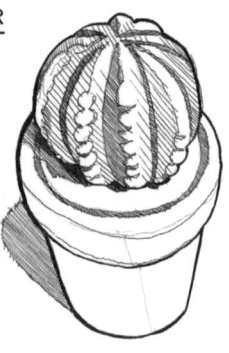

6. FOURTH HATCHING LAYER

Repeat the same process for the pot.

You can use different-sized nibs for hatching. ↗

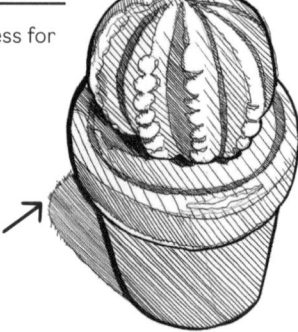

7. DETAILS

Finally, using the brush pen again, go over the darkest values. This way, you will achieve greater contrast, enhancing the depth of the drawing.

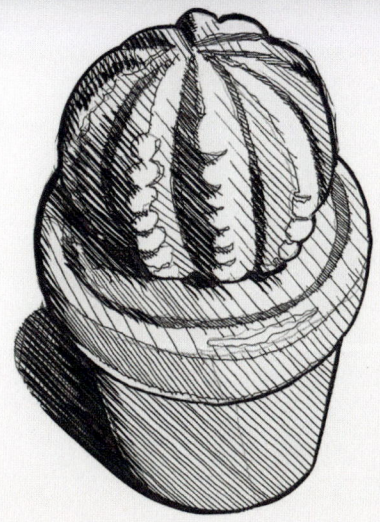

SEE ALSO

Hatching, page 36
Weighting lines, page 48

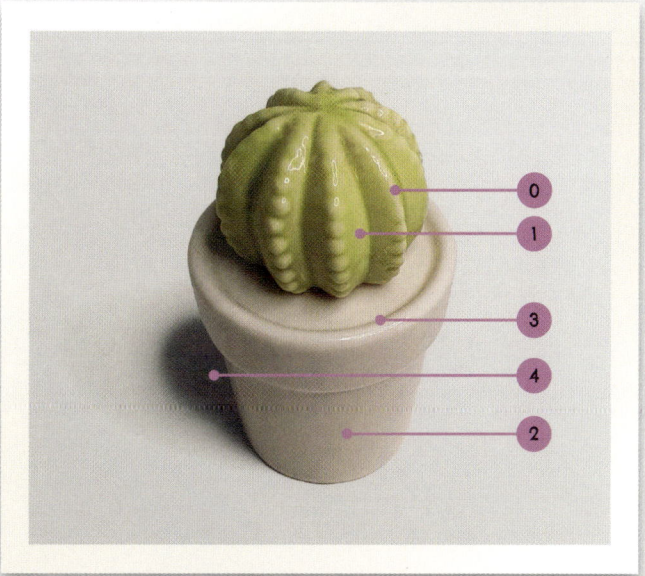

VALUES

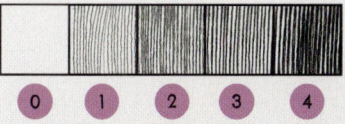

0   1   2   3   4

Textures

At times, drawing each individual object in a scene becomes impractical due to distance, size or a preference. In such situations you can turn to textures to add visual appeal and tactility to the drawing. Textures enable the viewer to establish a more intimate connection with the illustration and interpret its nature and character.

THIS PAGE. Note how many different textures are employed in this image, from sharp, spiky lines for the foreground branches to tight cross hatching on the roof tiles.

There are countless ways to represent textures and, with practice, each artist develops their own techniques. The visual result of these textures depends on various factors, such as the technique used, the tool employed and the speed with which the marks are applied. In this section I would like to share with you the process that I typically use to create textured patterns.

Let's imagine for a moment that we are going to apply different textures to a sphere. While this is unlikely in reality, it will serve to explain step by step the process of creating textures.

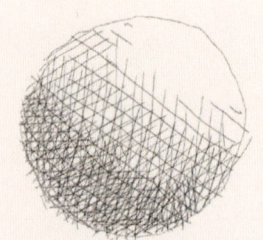

ABSTRACTION OF THE TEXTURE

The first step is to analyze the strokes that make up the desired texture. Observe if they are long, short, sinuous, vertical, horizontal or if they form any pattern. Try to discover their peculiarities.

Let's take, for example, the image of a brick wall. A brick wall is made up of vertical and horizontal short lines.

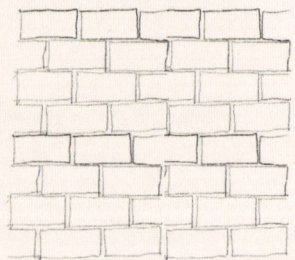

APPLICATION OF ABSTRACTION

Apply the abstraction to the figure, following its shape. Note how the lines are now more curved. In some cases the shape will be blurred, as there are textures that, due to their size or nature, do not fully follow or cover the form, such as long hair or grass.

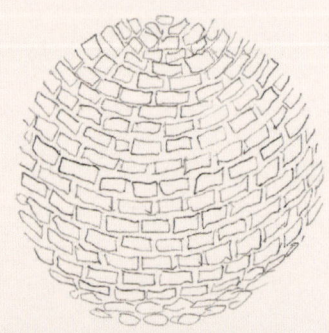

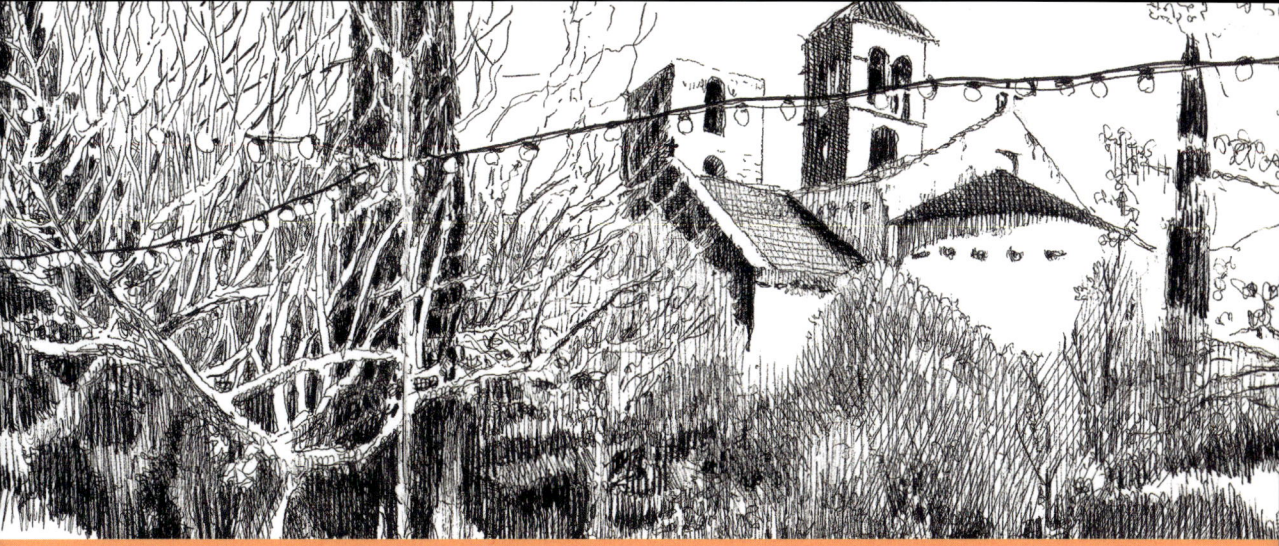

ADDITION OF DETAILS

Now it's time to incorporate details into your texture. Depending on the subject, you can introduce contrast, spots or other elements that give your texture a more natural or organic appearance. Certain techniques adapt more easily to certain textures but, in general, you can create these details using any technique.

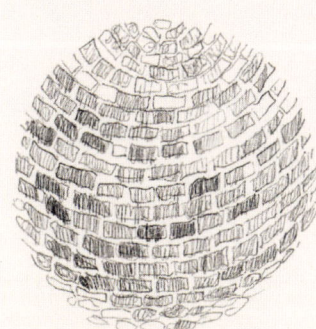

ADDITION OF SPECIFIC SHADOWS

Finally, add the specific shadows of the sphere. These shadows, along with the particularities of the texture, convey enough information for the observer to be able to understand the nature and volume of the object.

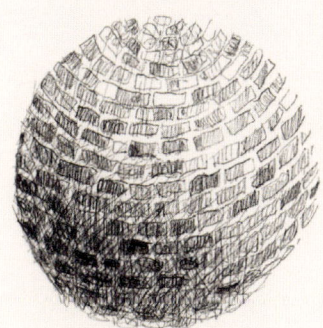

DEFINITION OF SIZE

It is crucial to define the size at which you will draw the reference. The further away and the smaller the drawing, the less definition and detail the texture will have. Overemphasizing a distant texture can disrupt the sense of scale.

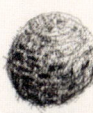

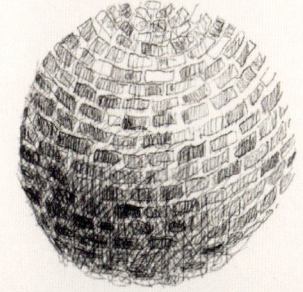

WOOD

Focus on the knots and the vertical, sinuous direction of the trunk to create the wood texture. Use these elements as a starting point to craft a realistic texture.

WATER

Observe the water's horizontal movement and the waves, creating distinct shadows and highlights. This highlights the water's liquid nature, especially the gentle sway of the waves.

GRASS

Represent grass with lines of varying length based on grass type. Include shadows from irregularities in the terrain and density of the grass for dimension and realism.

STONE

We can draw an infinite number of shapes and types of stones. Apart from their shape, observe the joints between them; in this case, they are darker and give volume and clarity to the texture.

Abstraction

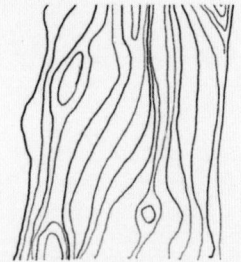 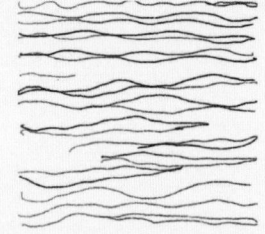 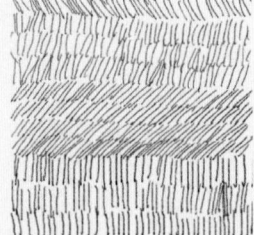 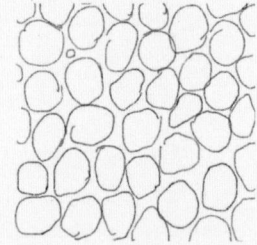

Texture

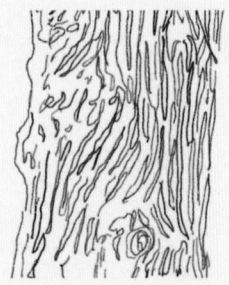 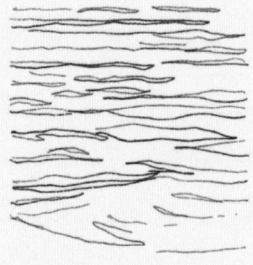 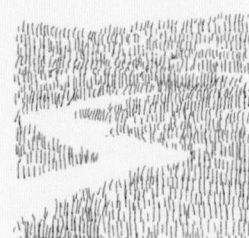 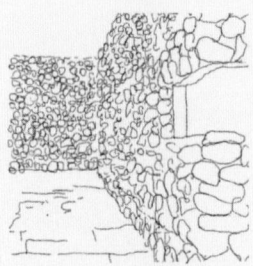

Texture + shadows

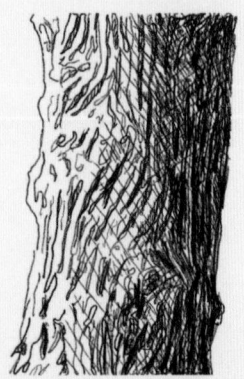 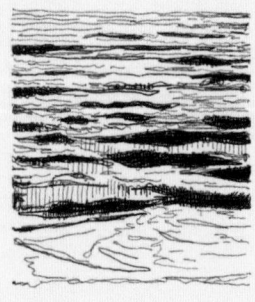 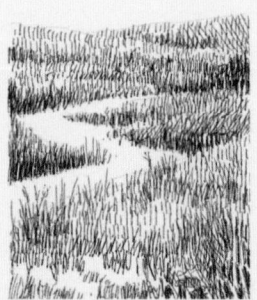 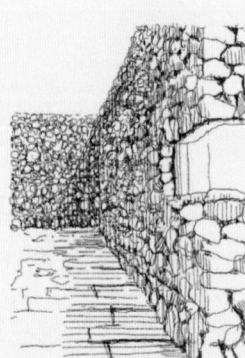

HAIR/FUR

This is perhaps one of the most complex textures to create, as it follows a different direction for each hair type. By observing these details you can achieve very specific hair textures.

FEATHERS

Feathers, like hair, follow a specific direction, but they also follow a pattern that changes in size and rhythm depending on the case.

COMMON MISTAKES

Overemphasizing details: Focusing too much on intricate details within the texture can lead to a loss of overall cohesion and visual balance.

Neglecting scale and proportion: Applying textures without considering their appropriate scale in relation to the overall composition can result in inconsistencies and distortions.

Using inappropriate tools: Choose a pen or brush that allows you to make the kind of marks you need for the texture in question.

Lack of variation: Not incorporating a variety of textures within a composition can result in a flat and visually uninteresting drawing.

Inconsistent line weight: Utilizing uneven or inconsistent line weights when creating textures that don't require it can result in an unbalanced and fragmented appearance.

Ignoring the light source: Neglecting to consider the direction and intensity of light can lead to shading that is unrealistic for the textures.

Lack of patience: Rushing the process of creating textures can compromise the overall quality of the drawing.

Overcomplicating patterns: Incorporating excessively complex patterns within textures can overwhelm the viewer and detract from the drawing's appeal.

PRACTICE

Based on the examples on this page, choose an object that catches your interest, simplify and abstract its texture using basic lines, then apply that texture to the chosen object. Try adjusting the scale until you achieve a satisfactory result.

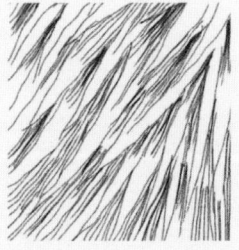
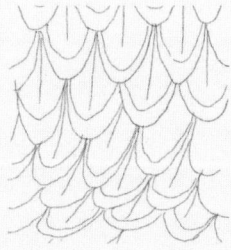
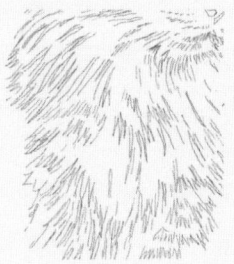
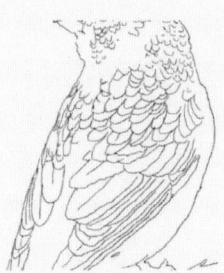
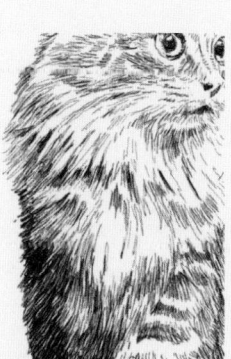
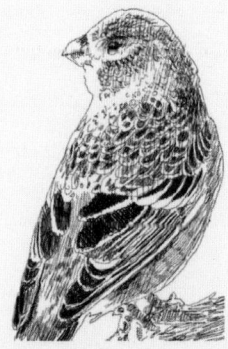

Adding colour

Talking about colour could fill an entire book, but in this case we'll focus on colour as a visual companion to your drawings. This powerful compositional tool allows you to direct attention towards specific elements or details, even altering the overall perception of the drawing.

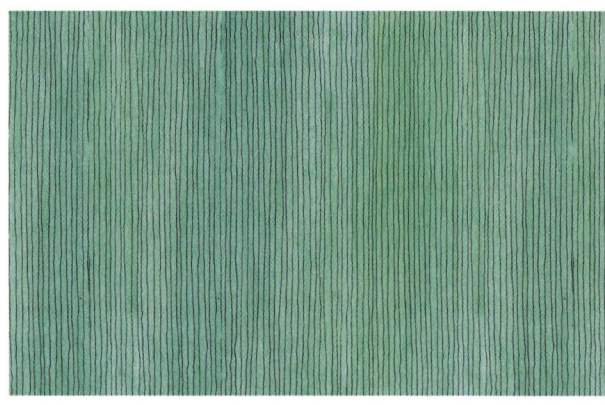

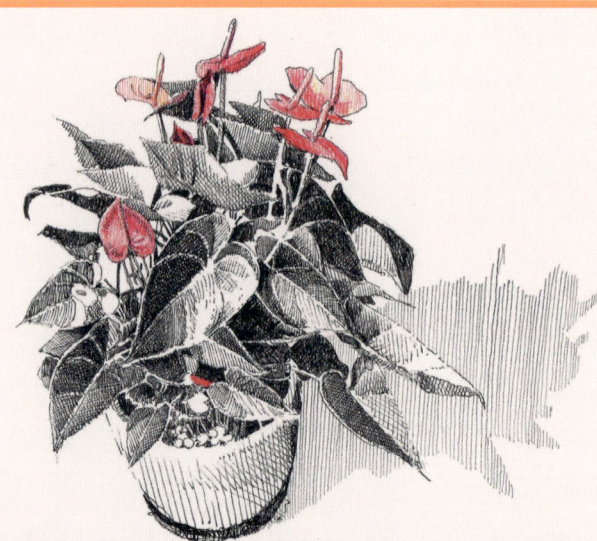

Colour in a specific area of the drawing

When you introduce colour to a specific area of a drawing you create a visual focal point. The viewer's eyes are naturally drawn to coloured areas amid a black-and-white environment.

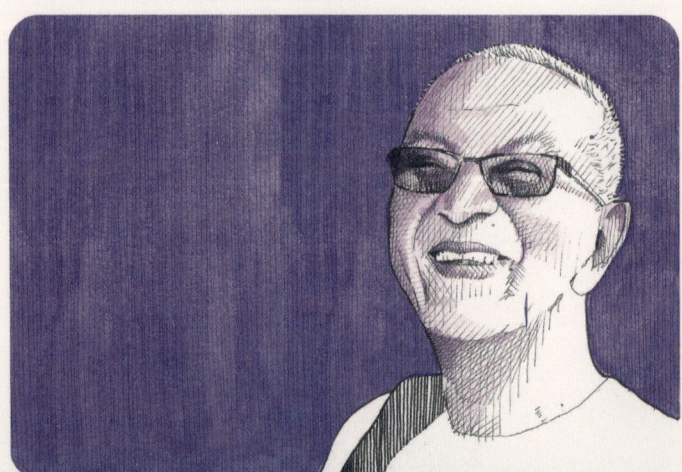

Use of colour as a background

By employing colour as a background you highlight the figures drawn in black and white, leveraging the association of the white paper with the illumination on the figure. Adjusting the intensity and tonality of the background can effectively enhance the shapes and details.

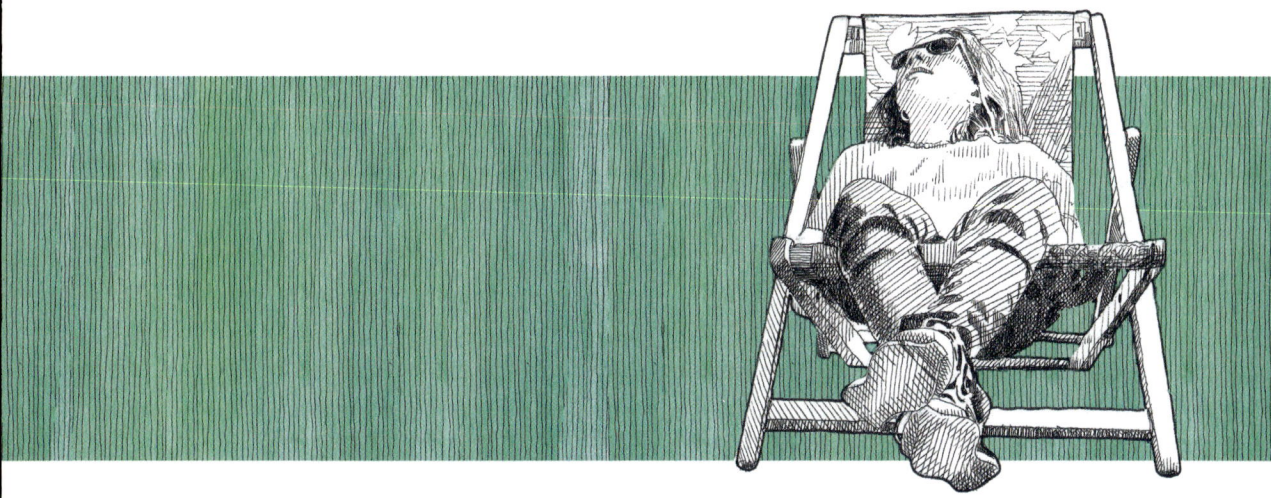

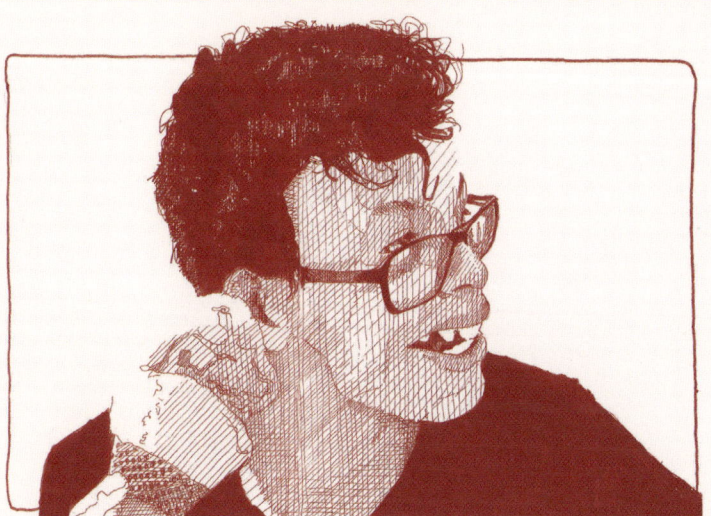

Use of a single colour for all strokes

When you opt for a single colour for all strokes in a drawing, you imbue the work with intention. Depending on the chosen tone and saturation, you can convey various emotions, from serenity to intensity. Vary the density and thickness of the strokes to guide the viewer's attention.

Use of different colours

When deciding to use different colours, you add new information to your drawing, providing details about the materiality and nature of the object that are impossible to convey exclusively in black and white.

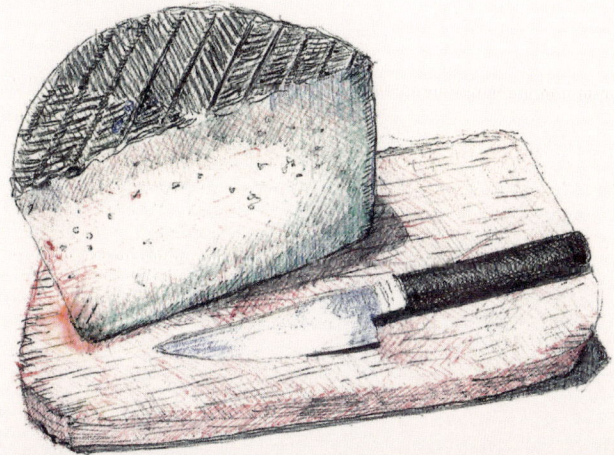

Woven hatching + tick hatching

STEP BY STEP: BIRD BOX

By combining these techniques you can enhance the expressiveness and tonal richness of your artwork. Woven hatching contributes a uniform and dense texture, while tick hatching gives a wide range of tonal values.

1. BASIC PENCIL LINES

Start by outlining the contours with a pencil, doing so subtly to avoid having to erase them at the end of the process.

2. DARKER VALUE

Put in the darkest value with a ballpoint pen, applying a not overly dense and relatively uniform layer using the tick hatching technique.

Apply light pressure with the ballpoint pen at first.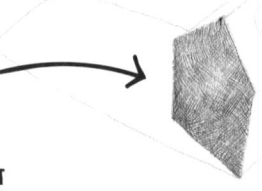

3. SECOND DARKER VALUE

Move on to the next facet of the object; upon completion, assess the tonal relationship between it and the previously shaded area. Adjust the darkest portion of your drawing for clear differentiation.

4. THIRD FACET

Approach the more intricate upper side with care, paying attention to the transition from the darker to the lighter area. Use layers with minimal pressure, overlapping them for the desired tone.

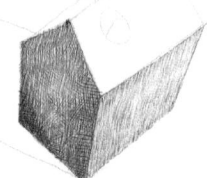

5. VALUES REFINEMENT

Reserve the smaller side for the final touches. After completion, reassess tonal relationships in the reference and refine your drawing by darkening where necessary.

Clean excess ink from the tip of the ballpoint pen occasionally.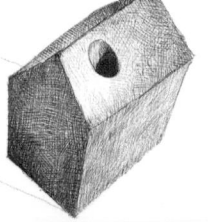

6. WOVEN HATCH

Introduce shadows using the woven hatching technique to swiftly create a uniform tone with an interesting texture.

Change the pressure applied with the ballpoint pen to achieve subtleties in tone.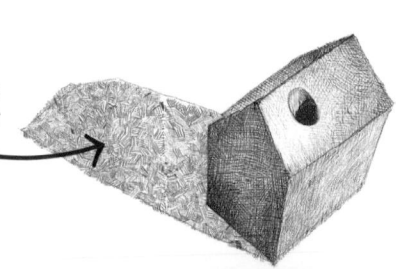

7. FINAL ADJUSTMENTS

Compare your work with the reference and add layers where needed for enhanced contrast. Remember that you can always darken the drawing, but lightening it is more challenging. For this reason, it is recommended not to reach very dark values until the final stages of the process.

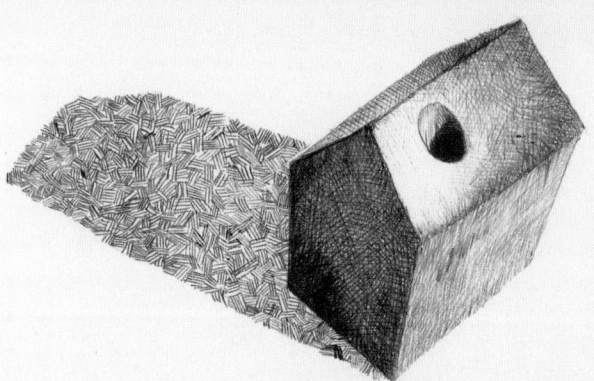

SEE ALSO
Woven hatching, page 52
Tick hatching, page 46

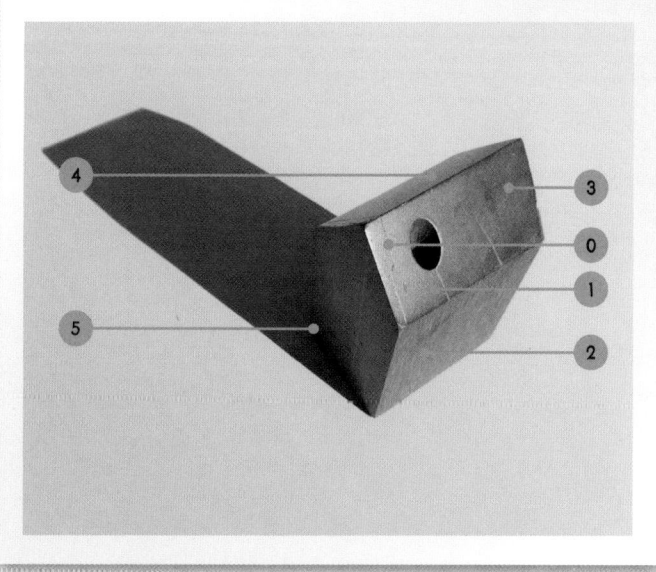

VALUES

0	1	2	3	4	5

GETTING READY FOR ACTION

In this chapter we delve into the steps you need to take to begin your journey into the world of pen-and-ink drawing. We'll explore the crucial importance of choosing projects aligned with your artistic skills and the available time, a vital aspect to avoid unnecessary frustrations, and learn how to employ mindful observation as a bridge between the reality surrounding us and the way it is expressed on paper. Additionally, we will unravel the fundamental principles of perspective and composition, laying the groundwork that will guide you on your path to mastering pen-and-ink drawing.

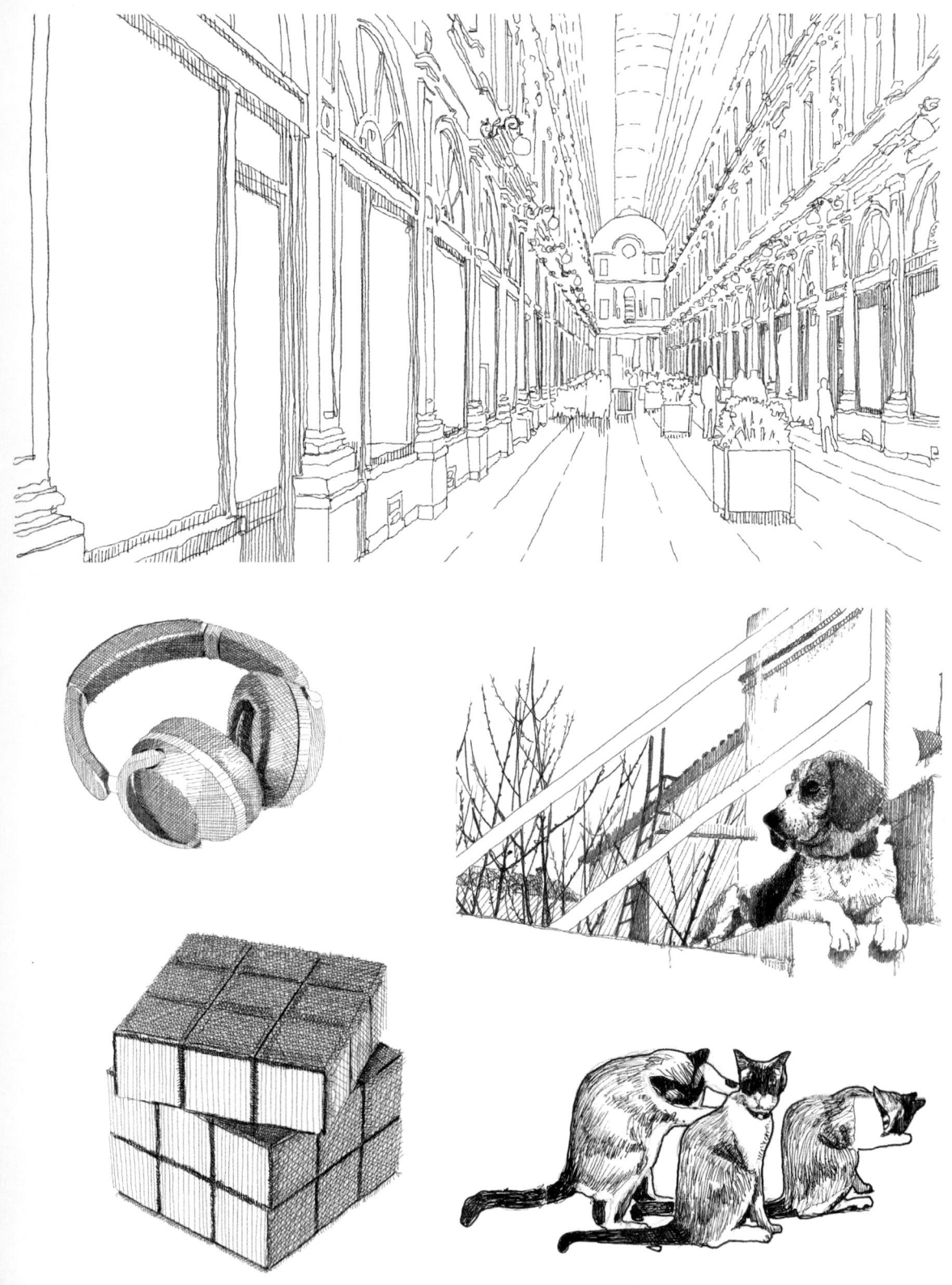

Keep it simple

If you're new to drawing, start with simple, uncomplicated subjects with straight sides, such as books, children's play bricks, cardboard boxes or even suitcases. This allows you to concentrate on the building blocks of art – proportion, perspective and composition – without having to worry too much about complicated curves, overlapping elements or the subtleties of shading, laying a solid groundwork upon which to build your artistic endeavours.

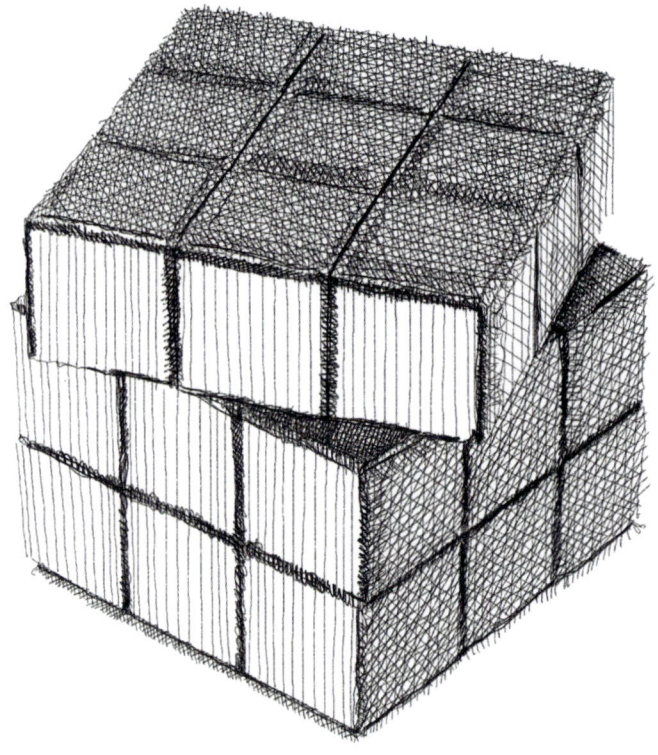

Simple objects can be your allies when practising drawing. At first, your drawings may consist mostly of straight lines; gradually, however, you can add layers of information, such as shadows and details, to make them more appealing.

THE CATALYST

Success with simple drawings is more than just a milestone; it's a catalyst. It will boost your confidence and encourage you to tackle increasingly intricate challenges. You'll find that you'll soon get better at evaluating your work and will be able to approach more complex subjects with a sense of determination and curiosity. This not only boosts your artistic capabilities but also nurtures a sense of accomplishment.

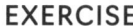

EXERCISE

Copy the books below: This quick exercise, which involves depicting books in various positions, is not only a fun activity – it's also an effective way of refining your observational skills and comprehension. Because the books are straight-edged and have parallel lines, you don't have to worry about drawing complicated shapes and curves.

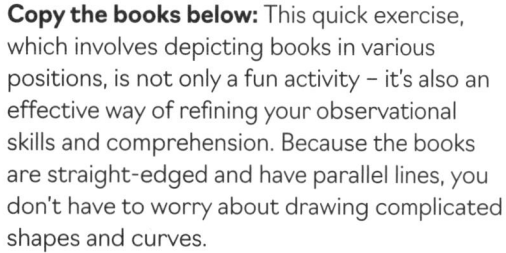

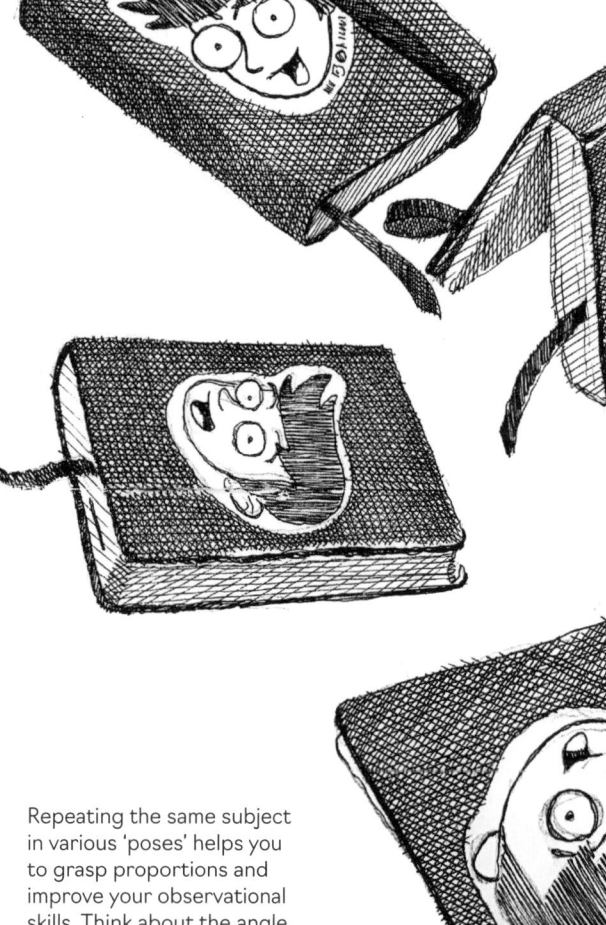

Repeating the same subject in various 'poses' helps you to grasp proportions and improve your observational skills. Think about the angle from which you're viewing the book: how much of each side can you see? It also loosens your hand, enabling you to work more freely.

To prevent frustration when drawing, It is helpful to practise sketching the same object using different approaches. Whether that means starting with a simple outline of a head-on view, and then exploring different perspectives, the practice will help achieve a more realistic result in the long-term.

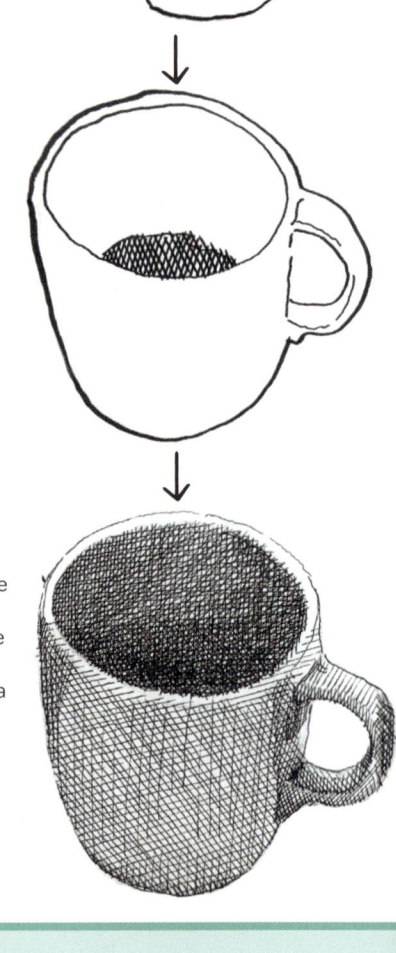

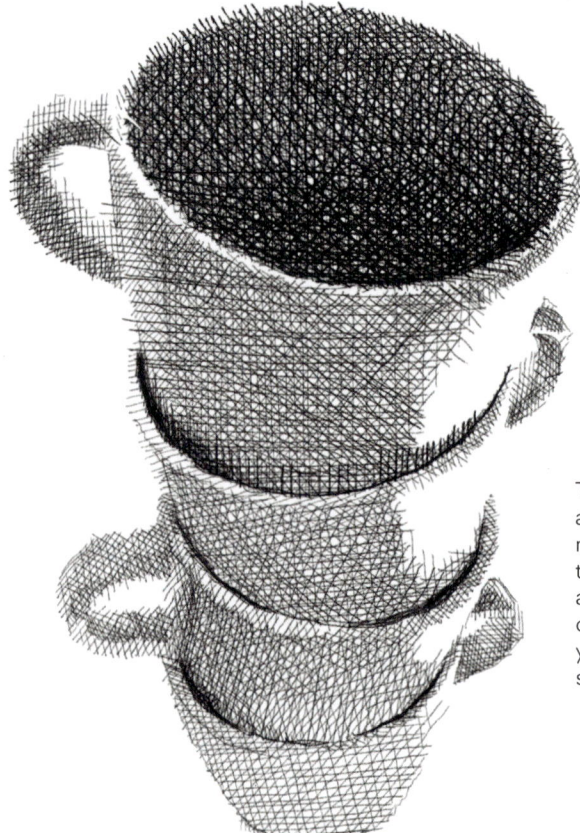

Through exercises such as this you can slowly make your mug look more three-dimensional and add details that would be challenging to capture if you hadn't started from a simple shape.

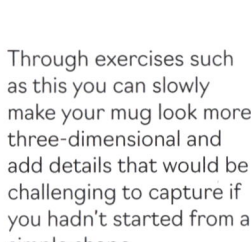

KEEP FRUSTRATION AWAY

Frustration at getting things 'wrong' can lead people to give up drawing altogether – and the cause of that is often that they've tried to do too much too quickly. Choosing a simple object that you can deconstruct to rudimentary shapes will set you on the path towards a more rewarding creative process and provide a solid foundation for building your confidence and skills. It's also important to view your mistakes as steps towards improvement. Embrace drawing as a liberating, enriching experience; the practice itself is the goal, not just a path to artistic excellence.

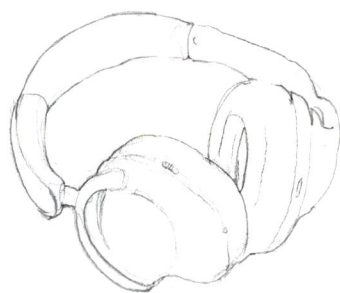

If I have five minutes, I try to quickly take a note, do my best to capture the object's proportions and sketch some basic lines, usually in pencil, to outline the object.

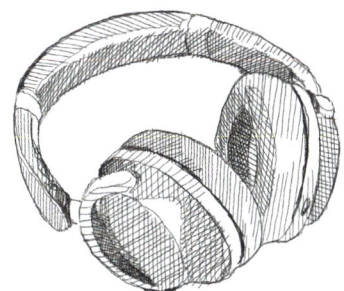

With 15 minutes, I can pay more attention to the proportions. When I'm satisfied with these, I can focus on representing the different tones with quick lines.

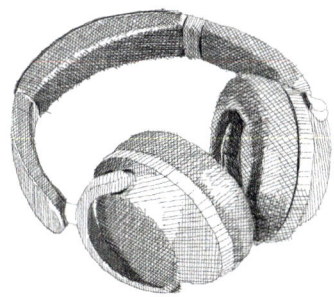

With 30 minutes, the lines can be less hasty, allowing me to pay more attention to textures and produce a more coherent drawing.

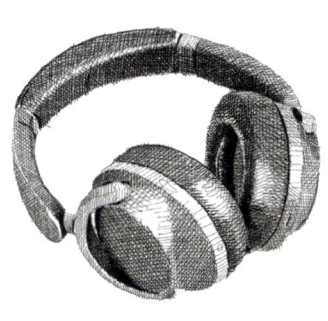

If I have an hour, I can put my effort into adjusting the contrast by adding all the necessary layers.

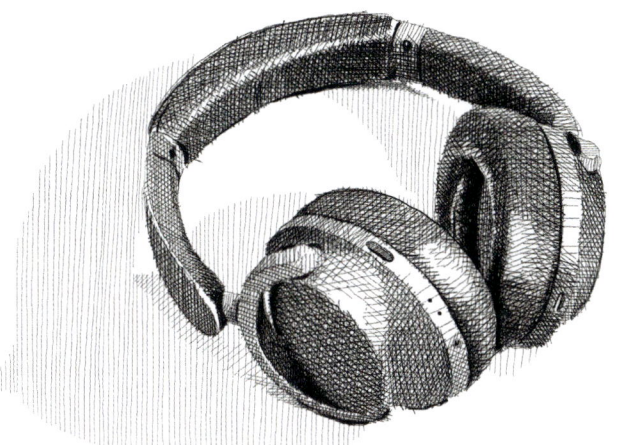

With a little more time, I can focus on small details or include the object's surroundings, the projected shadow or any other elements that add information to the drawing.

BE REALISTIC WITH YOUR TIME

Being realistic about how much time you have available for drawing is essential in establishing achievable objectives. If you only have a few minutes to spare, you won't be able to do much more than establish the basic shape and proportions, so don't expect to produce a really detailed sketch. Start by simplifying the shape(s) and then gradually build up from there – you'll find it far less frustrating than rushing the process and producing something that falls short of your expectations.

Proportions

In this section you'll learn how to use a pencil to transfer measurements and proportions from a real object to paper. The pencil is a practical, portable tool for drawing anywhere, but don't overlook other useful tools. Choose what suits your needs, based on the situation or object.

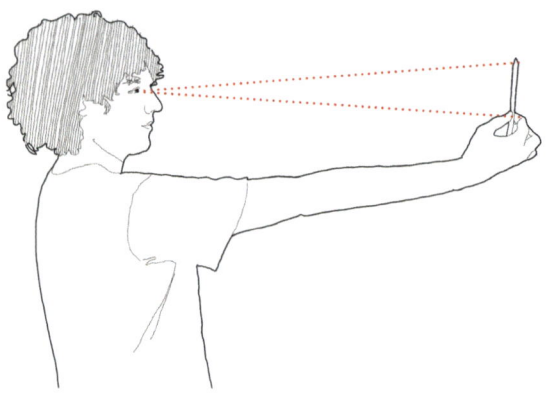

MEASURING THROUGH OBSERVATION

To measure accurately through observation, position yourself at a distance that allows you to observe the object you're about to draw without needing to move your head. Extend your arm and hold a pencil vertically. Close one eye and align the pencil between your eye and the chosen object. This method enables you to establish a direct visual relationship.

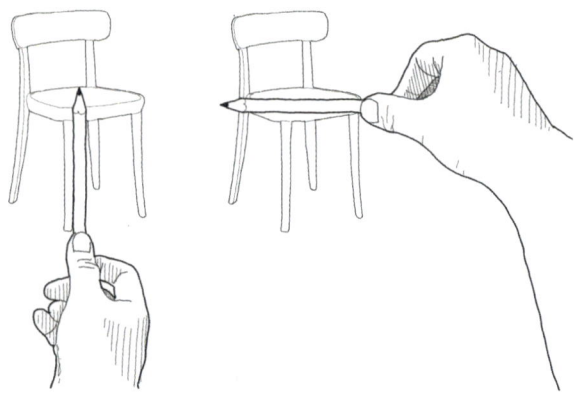

IDENTIFYING PROPORTIONS

Now, focus on identifying proportions within the object. Observe, for instance, that the distance from the bottom of the front leg to the back of the chair seat is similar to the maximum width of the chair. This approach provides a systematic way to compare all parts of the object and understand their relationships and proportions.

CONNECTING WITH YOUR SUBJECT

Dedicating extended periods of time to contemplating an object opens the door to a reality that often goes unnoticed. Investing time in observation while drawing inevitably creates a bond with the object you're depicting. This transforms the act of drawing into more than a mere visual capture; it becomes instead the construction of a lasting memory of the object, the time and the place represented.

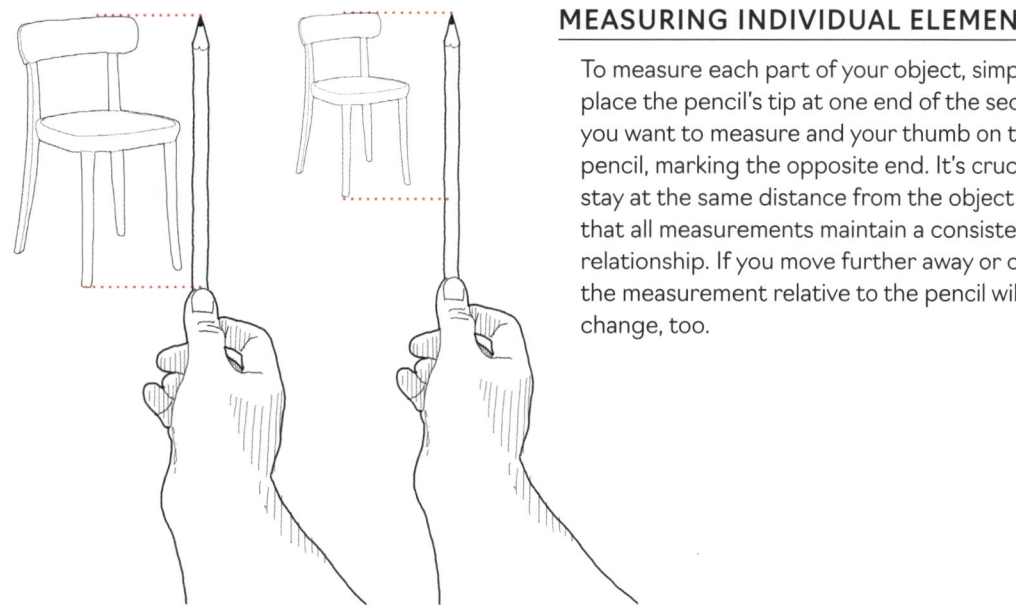

MEASURING INDIVIDUAL ELEMENTS

To measure each part of your object, simply place the pencil's tip at one end of the section you want to measure and your thumb on the pencil, marking the opposite end. It's crucial to stay at the same distance from the object so that all measurements maintain a consistent relationship. If you move further away or closer, the measurement relative to the pencil will change, too.

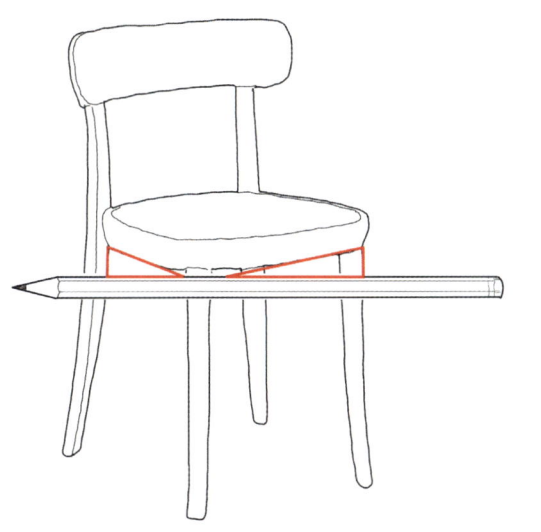

CHECKING ANGLES

You can also use a pencil to help you identify angles. If at any point you have doubts about whether a line is going up or down, simply place your pencil horizontally, and you'll be able to quickly determine the direction of the line. This method also applies to vertical lines.

TRANSFERRING TO PAPER WITH A PENCIL

Let's transfer the measurements to paper using the same approach. Start, whenever possible, with the maximum measurement – in this case, the height of the chair. On your paper, draw a line representing that total height, not necessarily using the exact measurement of the pencil. Remember, the pencil is used to establish relationships, so you can draw the line to whatever size you prefer for your drawing.

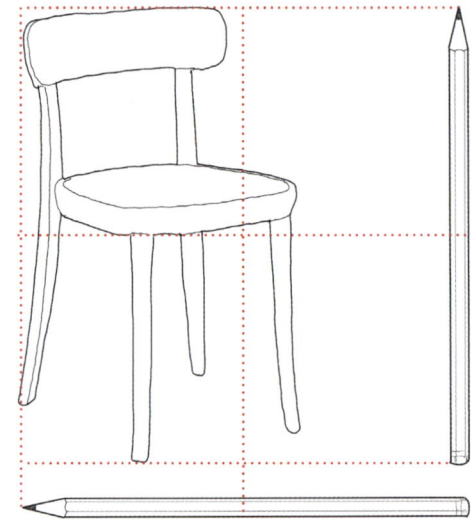

1. FIRST MEASUREMENTS

Using your pencil, note that the front leg is precisely half the total height. Rotate the pencil to compare this measurement with the chair; you'll find the chair's width slightly exceeds the leg's length, and the backrest is slightly shorter. Apply these proportions to your sketch.

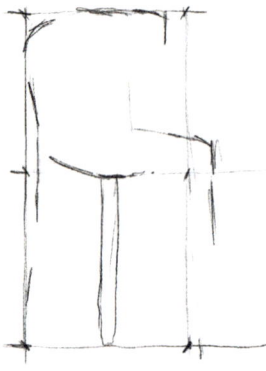

2. RELATIONSHIPS

Holding the pencil horizontally, you can now gauge the length of the other legs in relation to the drawn leg. The same applies to the gap in the backrest.

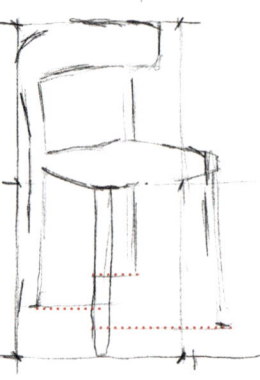

3. ANGLES

You now have all the basic lines to draw the remaining elements of your chair. Use the pencil to identify lines that aren't entirely vertical or horizontal and estimate their approximate angles.

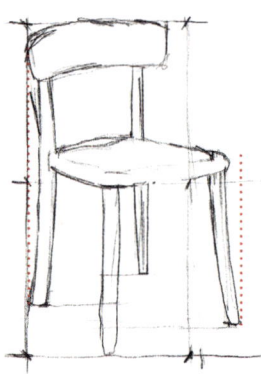

4. OUTLINE

Finally, clean up your drawing by removing unwanted lines and create a firm outline. If you've drawn with a pencil, consider using a pen. This will make the correct lines stand out, enhancing the overall clarity of the drawing.

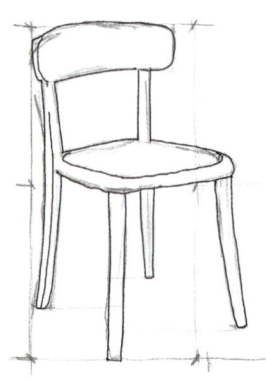

OBSERVATION DEVICES

SIGHTING GRID
The 'sighting grid' is a drawing tool created during the Renaissance, consisting of a visual grid and a sighting tube to fix the point of view. By aligning the object with the grid using a reticle on the paper, you can achieve a more accurate and proportional representation of the object under observation.

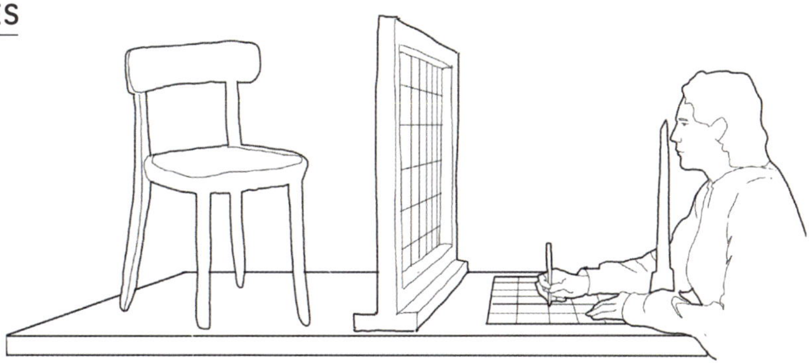

CAMERA OBSCURA
Also very popular during the Renaissance, a camera obscura consists of a dark chamber where the image of an object or scene is projected through the passage of light. This projection serves as a reference to draw an accurate and proportional representation on paper.

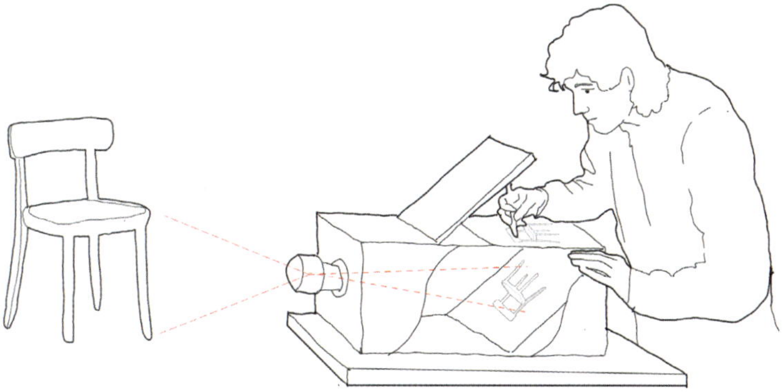

CAMERA LUCIDA
The camera lucida is an optical system that, through a prism or mirror, creates the illusion that the observed object is projected onto the paper. Using this device you can see both the reflected image and your hand on the paper, so you can precisely trace the contours and details of the object directly onto the paper

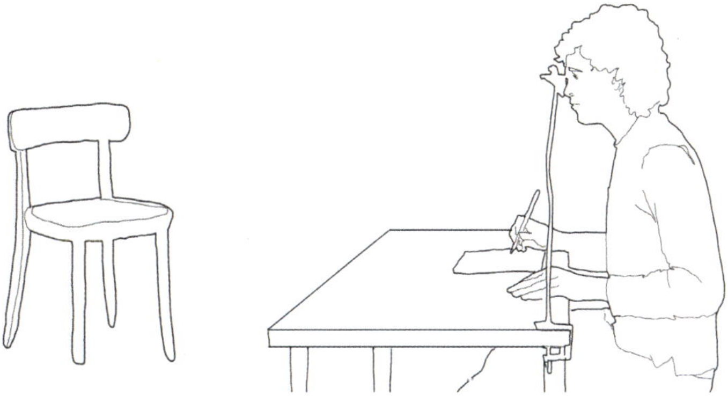

MODERN EQUIVALENTS

Over time, artists and engineers have devised various contraptions to transfer reality to a two-dimensional surface: mirrors, grids and cameras are tools that can aid in this transfer. Nowadays, a large function of these devices can be replaced with applications on mobile phones. Taking photos and using them as references resembles the function of the camera obscura, while applying grids to these photos can be equivalent to using the sighting grid. Regardless of the historical period, technology can play an important role in the realm of observation.

Composition

The term 'composition' refers to the way the visual elements within a drawing are arranged. This is rarely done casually: instead, guidelines are applied to make the work pleasing, striking or capable of capturing the observer's interest. Composition involves making decisions about the way elements are distributed. These decisions aim to achieve visual balance and a coherent aesthetic narrative. Understanding the importance of composition is crucial for creating works that are not only visually appealing but also convey emotions, tell stories or communicate specific messages.

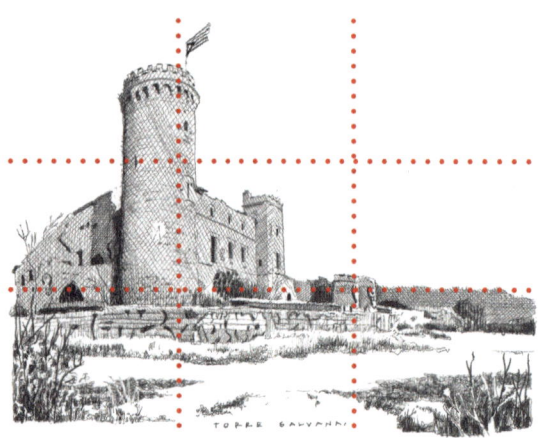

THE RULE OF THIRDS

The rule of thirds divides the composition into nine equal parts through two horizontal and two vertical lines, creating a set of smaller squares or rectangles. The fundamental idea is that points of interest or key elements of the composition should be positioned near the intersections of these lines.

EXPERIMENT WITH DIFFERENT COMPOSITIONS

Regardless of the simplicity of your drawing, always consider where you place the elements you want to depict. The time you dedicate to this decision is never in vain and will make a significant difference when finishing your drawing.

In this section, I describe some compositional guidelines; however, it is worth noting that there are more guidelines and variations of them than are shown here. Feel free to use those you find suitable and experiment to discover which ones best fit your preferences. Try out different compositions for the same subject and analyse the various moods and emotions they create. Exploring and being flexible in how you apply these guidelines will allow you to develop a personal style in your drawings.

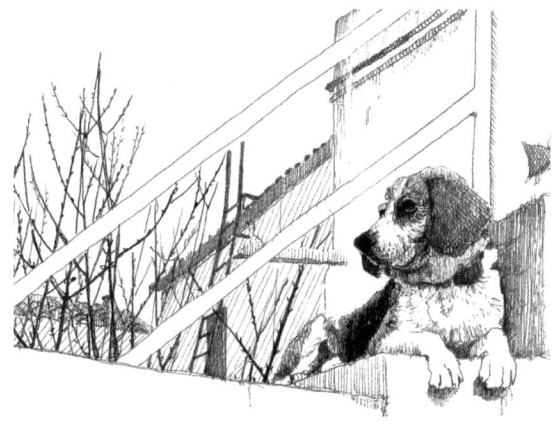

THE LAW OF GAZE

The law of gaze states that elements should have more free space in front of them than behind them. This way, additional space is provided in the direction towards which the eyes or attention of the subject are oriented.

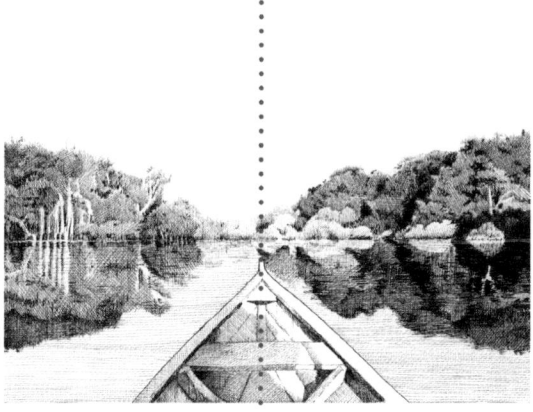

THE LAW OF SYMMETRY OR AXIALITY

The law of symmetry or axiality is based on creating visual balance through the symmetrical arrangement of elements. In simple terms, it involves dividing the image into two halves, symmetrically reflecting the elements on both sides of a central axis, whether that is horizontally or vertically (as in this image). This type of composition typically conveys a sense of calm and balance.

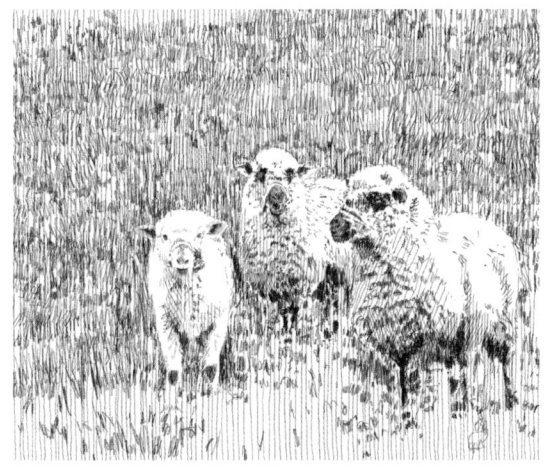

THE RULE OF ODD NUMBERS

An odd number of elements in a composition tends to be more appealing than an even number. This rule aims to avoid perfect symmetry and adds visual interest and a sense of asymmetry and dynamism to your drawings.

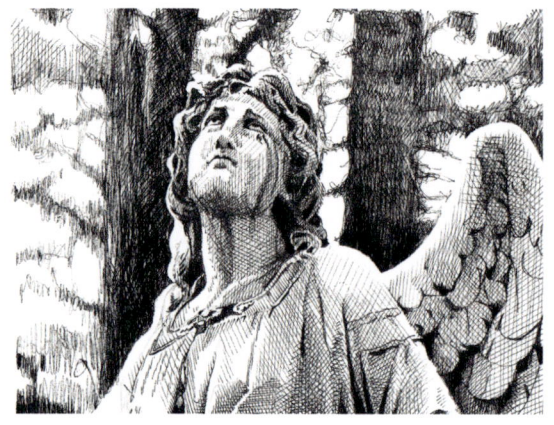

NARROW FOCUS

This rule aims to guide the viewer's gaze towards a particular element within the composition, enhancing its importance and enriching the visual narrative.

While drawing, we can use various tools to achieve focus. Contrast, variations in the typology of our strokes or the amount of details applied to certain elements are key features. These tools work together to centre the viewer's attention on the focal point, providing a more impactful and meaningful visual experience.

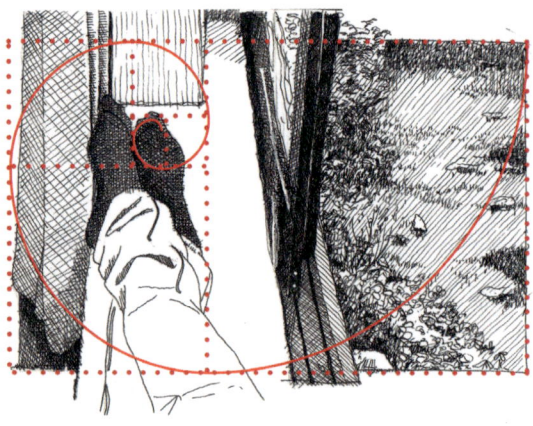

THE GOLDEN RATIO

The Golden Ratio is a mathematical principle based on a special relationship between two segments, where the ratio of the whole to the larger part is equal to the ratio of the larger part to the smaller part. With an approximate value of 1.618, this ratio is considered aesthetically pleasing. The Golden Ratio is also associated with the Fibonacci spiral (seen here in red), a naturally occurring spiral shape found in nature and art, further highlighting its significance in composition and design.

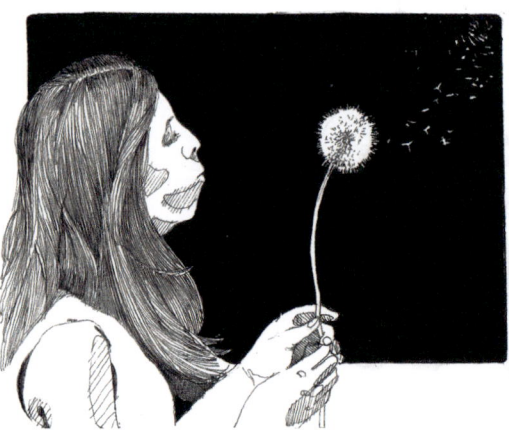

FRAMING

Framing refers to the practice of using elements such as borders, arches or other objects to highlight the main subject. This technique aims to direct the viewer's attention towards the focal point of the composition.

Framing can be natural, utilizing elements already present in the scene, such as tree branches, doors or windows, or it can be deliberately created in the drawing process.

MASS COMPENSATION

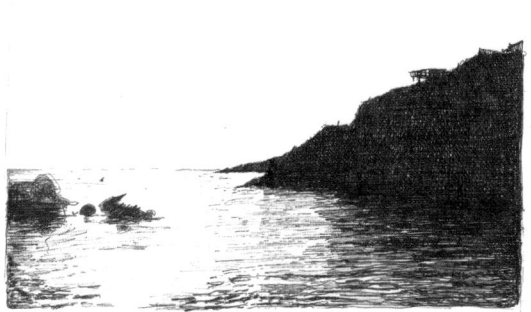

Mass compensation is a key element in the pursuit of a visual composition. This concept shifts the main subject away from the centre of the frame and compensates for this change by including smaller, secondary focal points. By strategically balancing masses in the artwork, an attractive visual distribution is achieved, infusing dynamism into the composition.

NEGATIVE SPACE

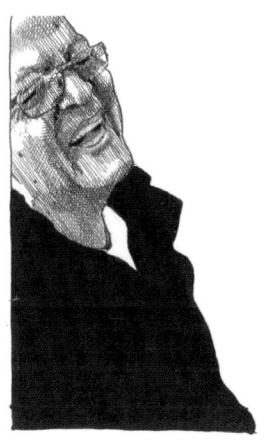

Negative space composition involves the consideration and manipulation of the space surrounding elements in a drawing. The key lies in strategically utilizing negative space to highlight and define the main subject, contributing to clarity and balance in the composition. When employing this technique, the goal is to achieve harmony between what is present and what is not, with negative space playing an active role in the visual narrative.

FILLING THE FRAME

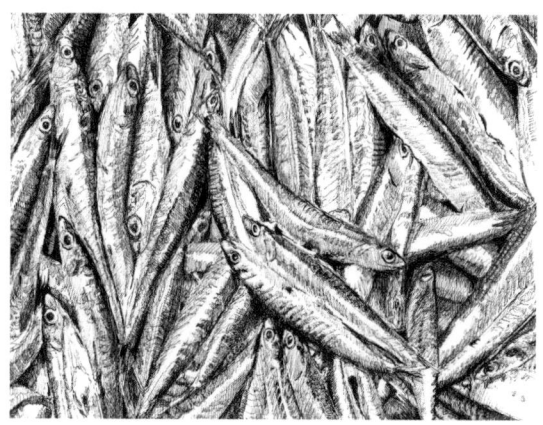

Filling the frame refers to the practice of occupying every visual space in our drawing with relevant elements, avoiding any empty areas. This concept aims to optimize the use of available space in the composition, ensuring that each region contributes effectively to the visual narrative of the artwork.

Perspective

Perspective is like a magic wand that creates the illusion of a three-dimensional space on a two-dimensional sheet of paper. Essentially, there's one basic rule: things that are closer appear larger and more detailed, while things that are further away are smaller and simpler. There are different types of perspective, but here we'll focus on linear perspective. This is based on the idea that parallel lines receding away from you will appear to converge at a single point on the horizon.

GENERAL PRINCIPLES

There are three things to bear in mind when dealing with perspective – namely, the vanishing point, the horizon line and lines of convergence. The simplified drawing on this page shows how to work out how much smaller objects need to be when they are further away from you. The same basic principles apply to one-, two- and three-point perspective, which you will find examples of on the pages that follow.

EXERCISE

Imagine you're creating a scene with a straight path and a group of trees lining it.

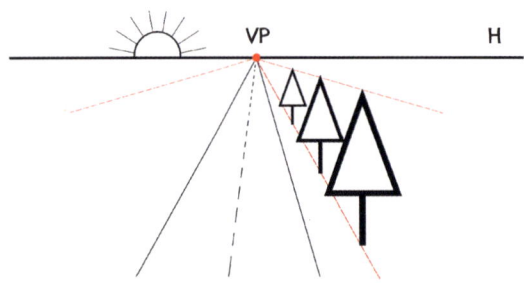

1. VANISHING POINT (VP) (THE RED DOT IN THIS IMAGE): The trees in this diagram are all the same height, but as they recede away from the viewer the lines of their tops and bases seem to converge at the vanishing point – so the further away the trees are, the smaller they seem. (Note that all vertical lines – the tree trunks in this diagram – remain vertical.) This creates an impression of depth and distance. The vanishing point coincides with your eye level (also known as the horizon line).

2. HORIZON (H): The horizon is the line marking the meeting point between the sky and the earth. It is usually positioned at the viewer's eye level, and its placement is critical since altering it significantly changes the perception of the scene.

3. LINES OF CONVERGENCE (RED LINES IN THIS IMAGE): These imaginary lines act as visual guides pointing towards the vanishing point on the horizon. They function as arrows indicating the direction in which elements recede or converge. These lines are essential in creating the illusion of depth.

FINDING THE VANISHING POINT

To find the vanishing point in a scene like the one on this page with a road and trees, we must follow the parallel lines of the road's edge and the lines formed by the bases and top of the trees. Imagine how these lines extend towards the horizon. The point where these extended lines intersect is the vanishing point – the point at which they disappear from view. This point is on the horizon line, which is always at eye level, and it's where all parallel lines meet as they recede into the distance.

ONE-POINT PERSPECTIVE

One-point perspective occurs when one of the faces of an object or scene is parallel to the picture plane (see the below panel for a description). Parallel lines receding away from the observer will appear to converge at a single vanishing point on the horizon. Parallel lines that are above the viewer's eye level (the tops of the trees in this diagram) will appear to slope down towards the vanishing point, while those that are below it (the bases of the trees in this diagram) will appear to slope upwards.

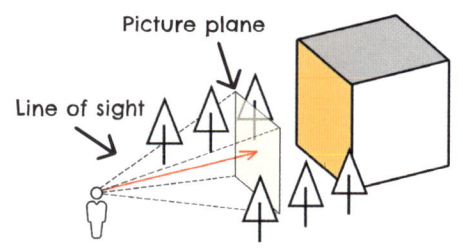

Picture plane

Line of sight

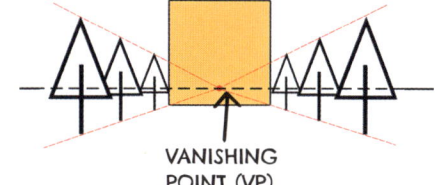

VANISHING POINT (VP)

This image illustrates the view point of the observer.

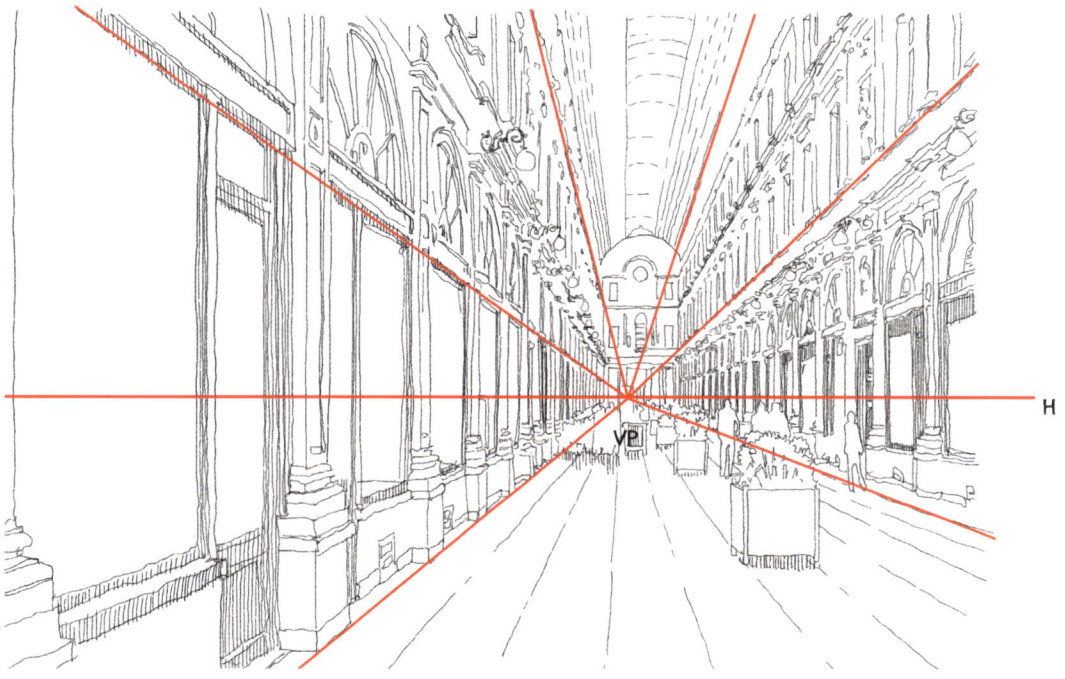

Les Galeries Royales Saint-Hubert in Brussels, Belgium (2023).

PICTURE PLANE

The picture plane is an imaginary two-dimensional surface onto which the three-dimensional view of a scene is projected. It's like a transparent window through which the three-dimensional world is observed and drawn onto a flat surface.

TWO-POINT PERSPECTIVE

Two-point perspective occurs when two sides of an object can be seen – for example, two sides of a box or building. In this case, the parallel lines receding from each side converge towards their own vanishing point, providing greater depth. As with one-point perspective, vertical lines remain vertical. Two-point perspective is especially useful for compositions emphasizing corners and edges.

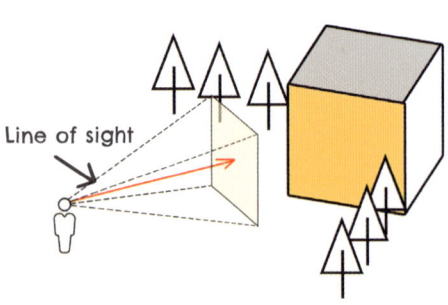

The observer can see two sides of the cube as they are stood at the corner.

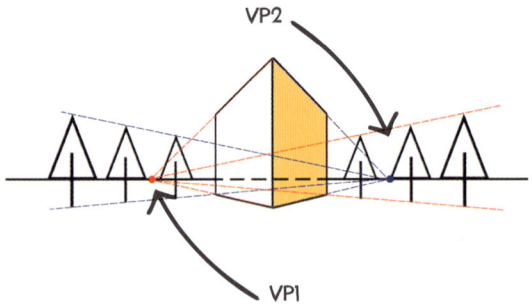

This image illustrates the view point of the observer.

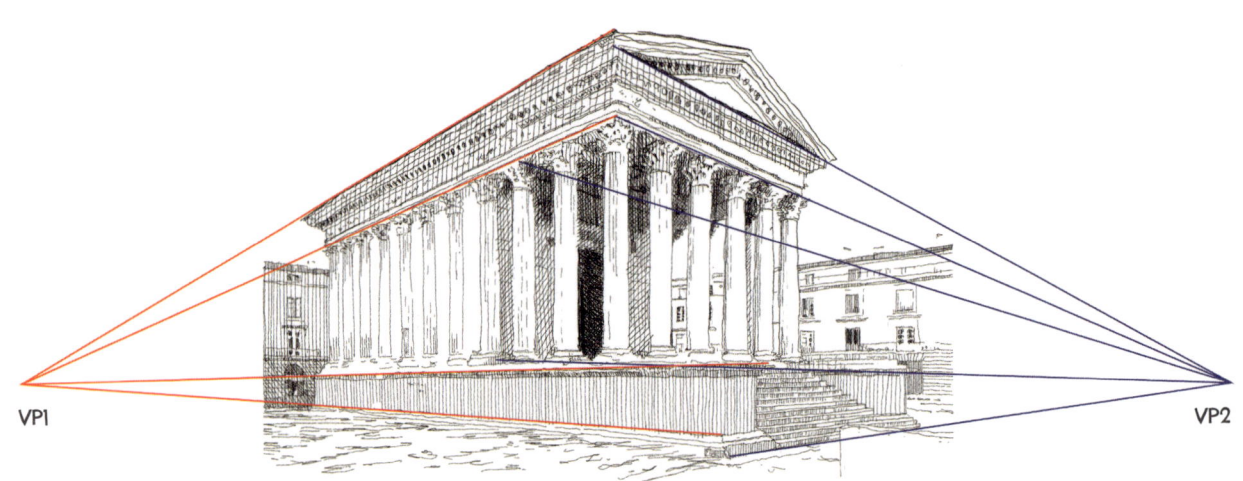

A Roman temple (the Maison Carrée) in Nimes, France (2024).

THREE-POINT PERSPECTIVE

Three-point perspective comes in to play when positioning ourselves in front of an object, facing an edge, *and* looking either up or down. In this approach, parallel lines from planes converge towards three vanishing points: two on the horizon and one vertically. If you're drawing a very large scene, such as the city street below, you may find that some of the vanishing points lie outside the picture area, but that's fine: just try to plot the angles of the converging lines accurately and you'll create a realistic-looking drawing.

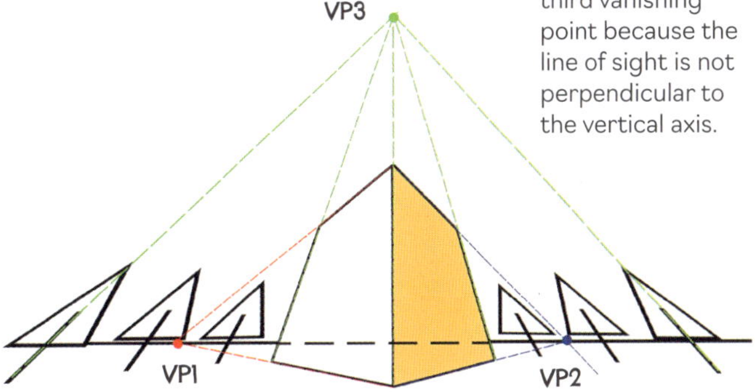

Vertical lines converge at a third vanishing point because the line of sight is not perpendicular to the vertical axis.

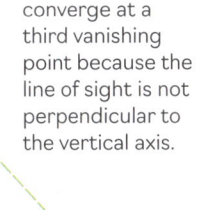

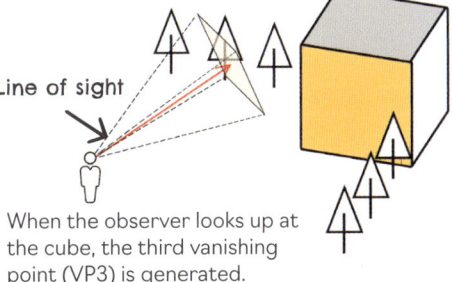

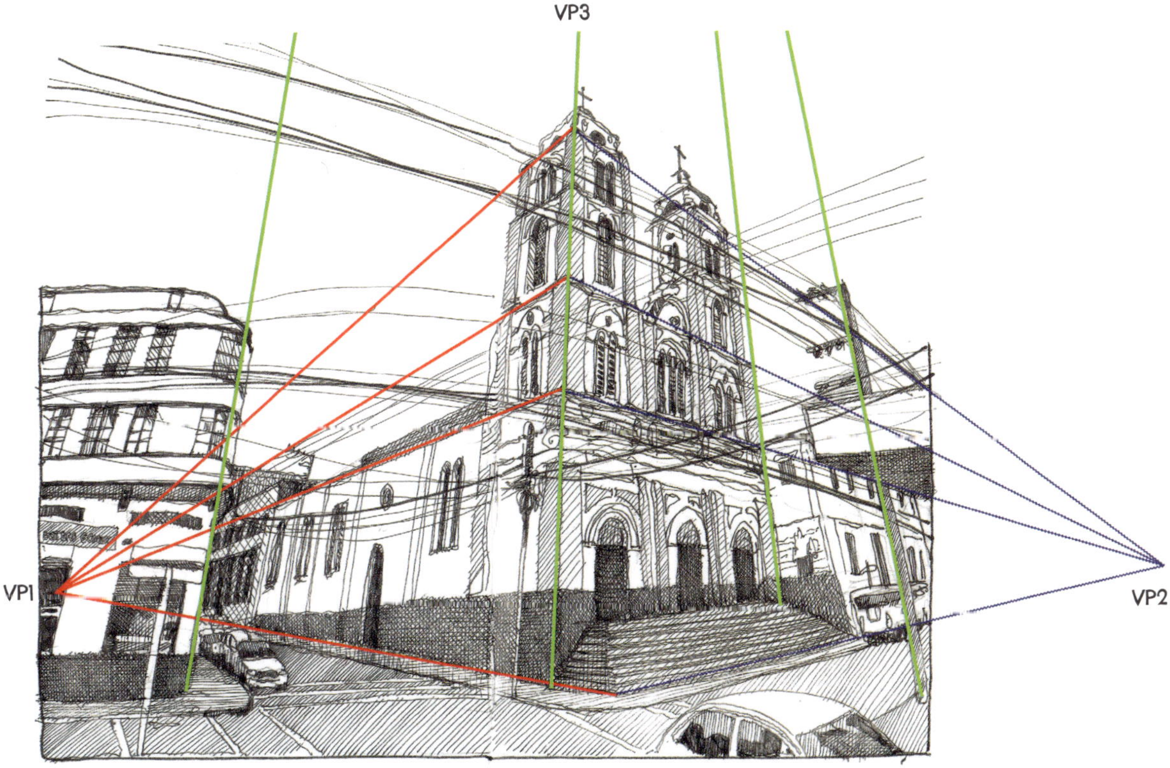

Line of sight

When the observer looks up at the cube, the third vanishing point (VP3) is generated.

San Roque church in Ibagué, Colombia (2019).

The world around us

We don't need to search far and wide to find reasons to draw; they are right in front of us, in our daily routine. This makes it easier to incorporate drawing into our everyday lives, as elements that can inspire us are always within arm's reach.

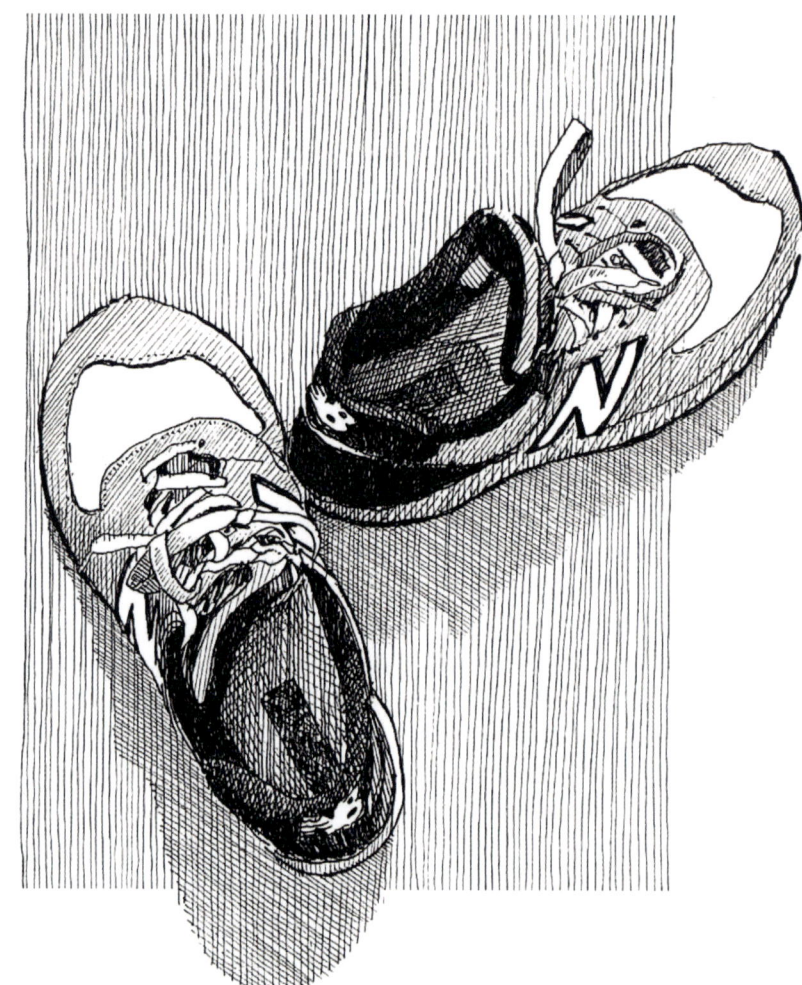

Just by looking around, you'll realize that your surroundings are filled with drawable objects.

USING A SKETCHBOOK

By drawing the world around us, we are not only visually documenting our lives but also giving these elements a place in our personal narrative. Doing this chronologically in a sketchbook turns your drawings into a visual record of the things or places that make your existence unique. Each drawing is an act of documentation, immortalizing places, fleeting moments and common objects that, together, weave the fabric of your story.

Thus, the sketchbook becomes more than a drawing notebook. It's a tool to explore the

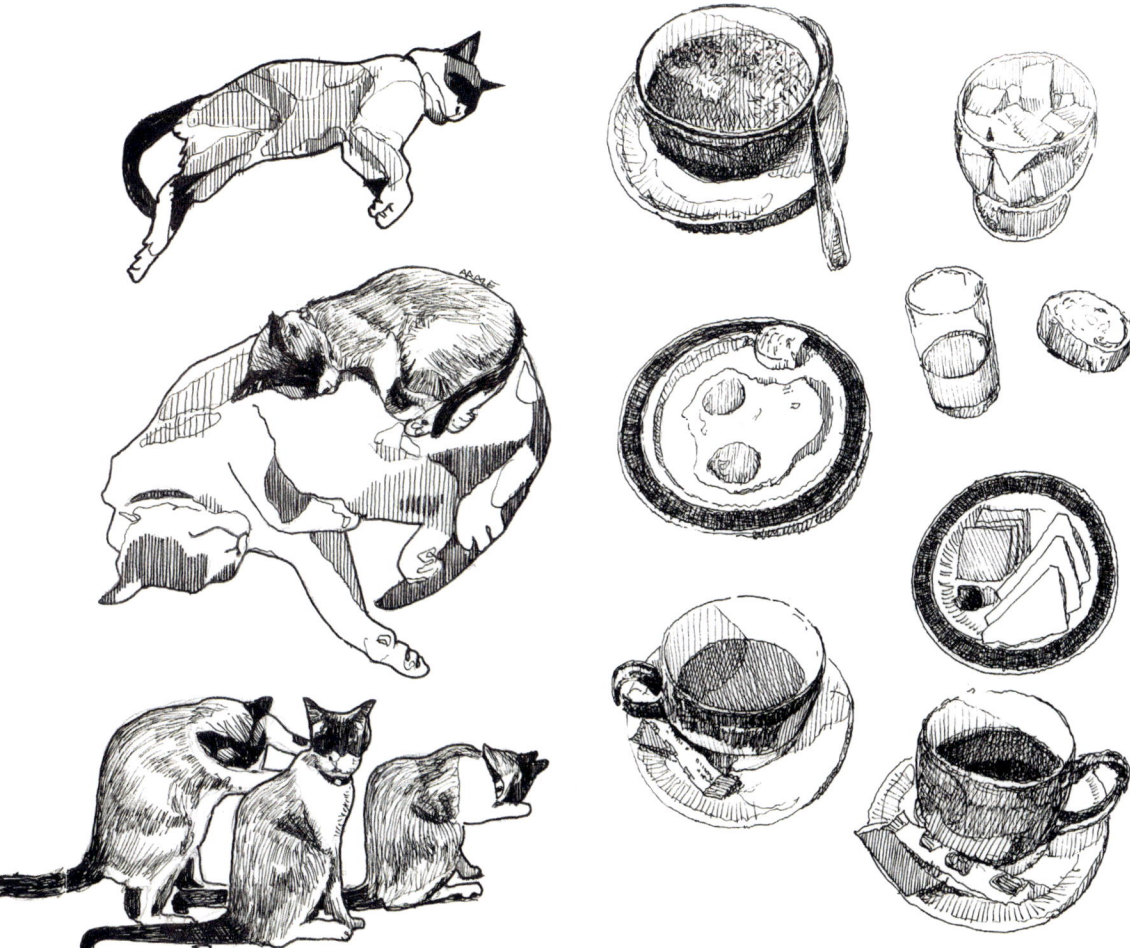

Our pets, family and the places we frequent are endless sources of inspiration. Moreover, repeating these elements is very simple since they are always within our reach.

Even a simple hotel breakfast can become a perfect subject for documentation through drawing.

beauty in everyday simplicity and a means to maintain a continuous connection with artistic practice. Drawing close, familiar elements creates a unique graphic novel, where each page tells the visual story of our lives, capturing our essence. Personally, I categorize drawing themes into three sections: everyday objects (including food), people and animals (usually family, friends and my cat), and places (architecture and interiors). These groups cover almost everything in my daily life.

EVERYDAY OBJECTS

Inanimate objects surrounding us offer the easiest way to practise daily drawing. These drawings can be as simple or as complex as you desire, ranging from a cereal box to the intricacies of your car, including chairs, fruits, plants or any inanimate object within your reach. Due to their size and weight, some of these objects can be moved, allowing you to position them optimally for a good composition.

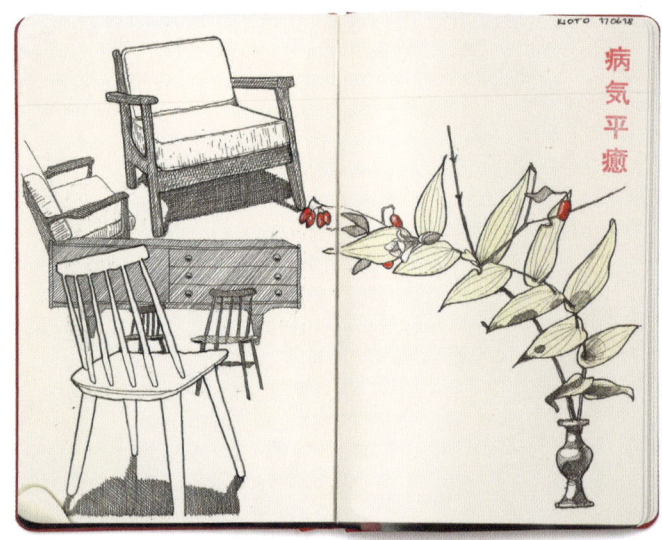

SURROUNDING PLACES

Drawing places requires a bit more attention and time to capture them in your sketches. They are a recurring source of inspiration, especially for documenting the places we visit or that are part of our lives. Unlike objects, when drawing places, it's up to you to find the ideal spot to position yourself. It's important to consider details such as the movement of the sun, whether you want to draw from the shade or otherwise, and to find a comfortable place to sit in case the drawing session is relatively long, among other things. The key to making it an enjoyable experience, is to be comfortably situated.

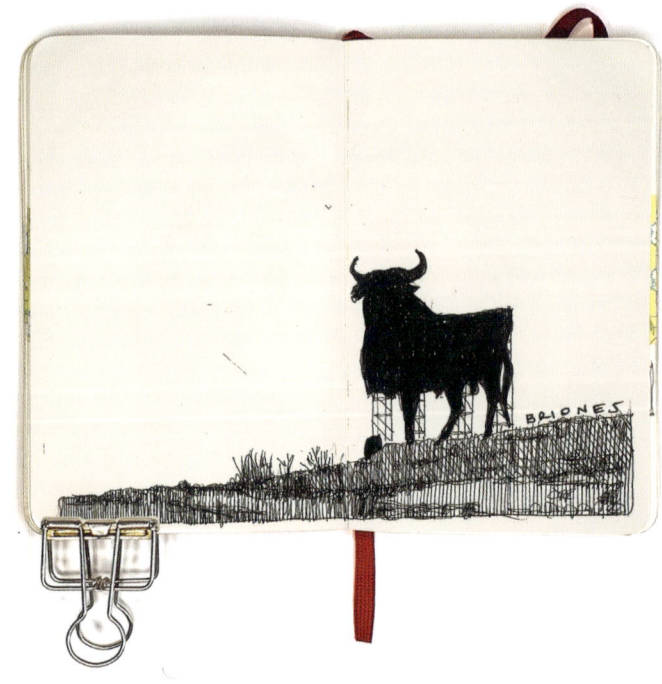

FAMILY, FRIENDS AND PETS

From my experience, this section represents the greatest complexity, as I have had far fewer hours of practice drawing people than buildings. Drawing family members and friends, despite the challenges it presents, is highly rewarding. It allows us to observe them as never before, providing a fantastic experience even when based on a reference photo. This section includes, of course, self-portraits that can be created by positioning yourself in front of a mirror, perhaps focusing on your hands or any other part of your body. I assure you – you won't find a more patient model than yourself!

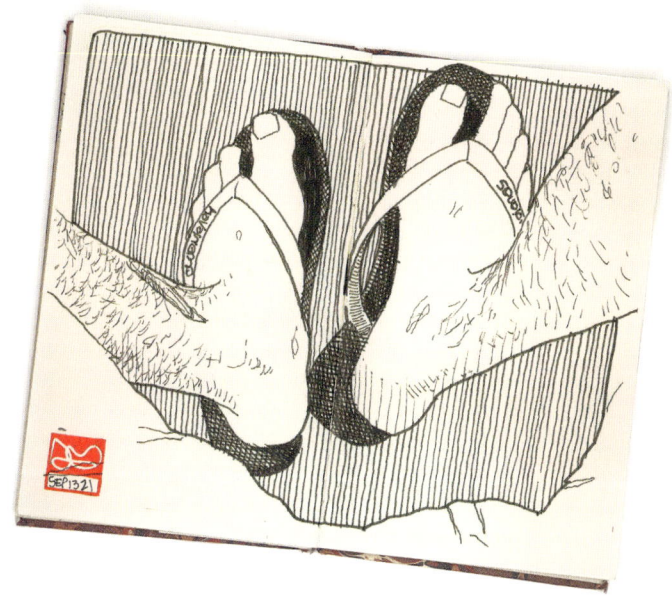

CONTEXT CUES

Finally, it is crucial not to overlook the inclusion of any additional information that helps you recall the context of the moment when you created the drawing. Details such as the date, associated names, particular anecdotes or even small tangible mementos, such as the receipt from the coffee you were savouring at that moment, become key pieces. These elements not only enrich the experience of revisiting your sketchbook in the future, but also immerse you once again in the unique atmosphere of that moment. Each additional piece of information becomes a thread connected to memory, woven into the tapestry of your visual story, ready to be unravelled and relived each time you gaze upon your drawing.

LET'S DRAW

So far, we've delved into the materials and techniques essential for ink drawing, alongside acquiring skills in composition and observation. Now, it's time to put those skills into practice!

In this chapter I've provided ideas for subjects that you can easily draw in your home or close by, with suggested durations: 15, 30, 60 and 120 minutes. To help you get started, I've included step-by-step demonstrations for some of those topics so that you can see the stages I generally go through. Towards the end of the chapter you'll find templates to assist you in the initial drawing process so that you can focus on your pen-and-ink work.

Inspiration for drawing can come from all kinds of sources and it's a good idea to challenge yourself by trying out subjects and approaches that are new to you. The chapter ends with some prompts for you to interpret in any way you choose.

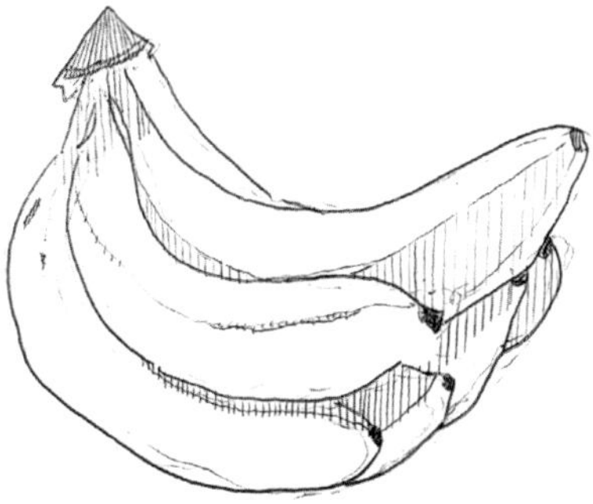

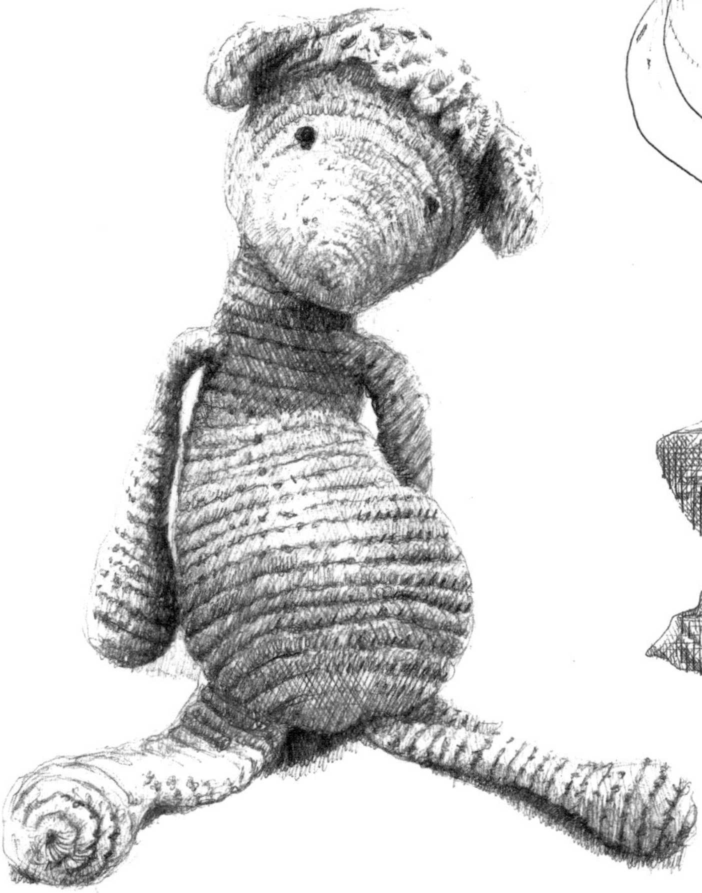

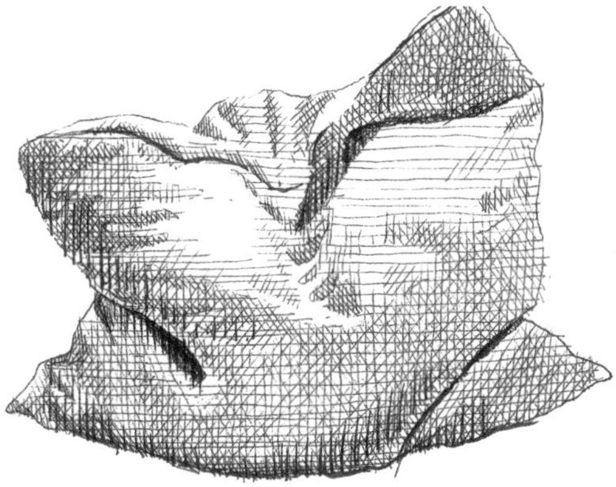

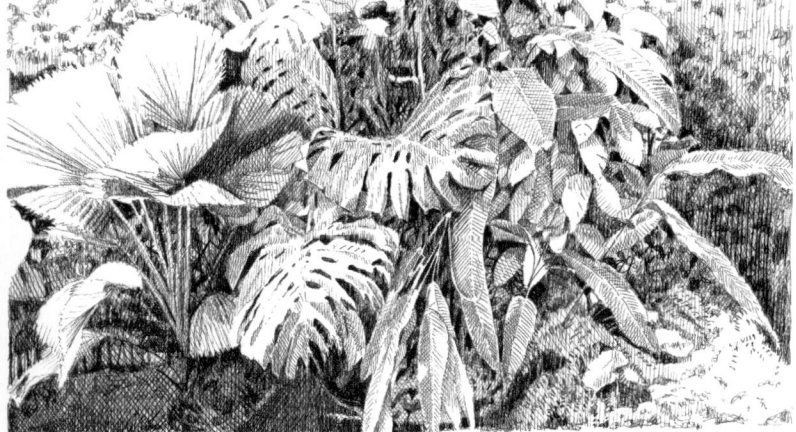
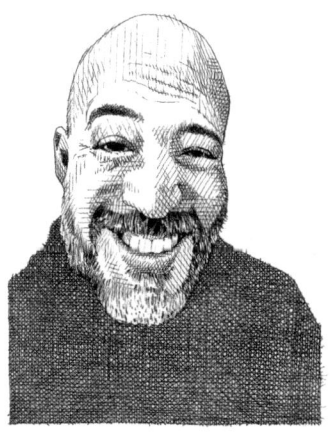

Timed exercises

Let's dive in and explore creativity across various time frames! From quick, 15-minute sketches to immersive two-hour sessions for detailed work, by following these exercises you'll discover the full range of creative possibilities offered by different time spans.

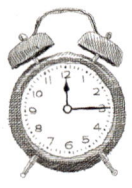

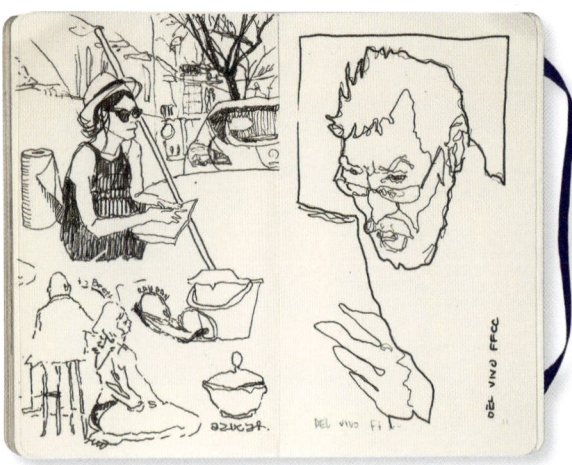

15-minute drawings are essential for strengthening your ability to capture the essence of your subject quickly and precisely. The time constraint forces you to hone in on what truly matters, avoiding distractions and leaving aside superfluous details. Before you start to draw, take a moment to study the subject. When you've finished, reflect on any errors of proportion or areas where you could improve.

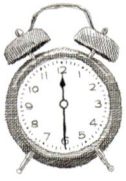

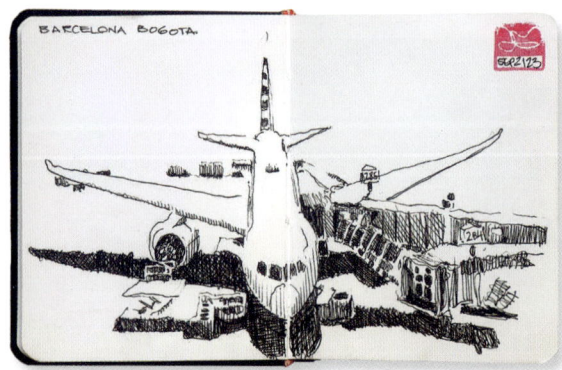

30-minute drawings offer a valuable balance between detail and speed. This amount of time allows you to focus on form and structure with greater precision. It also enables you to explore different techniques and styles, while adding textures and values for depth and realism. Despite the extra minutes, maintaining focus on capturing the essence of the subject is key. These drawings foster artistic growth by combining detail and efficiency.

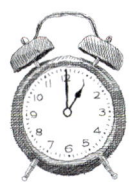

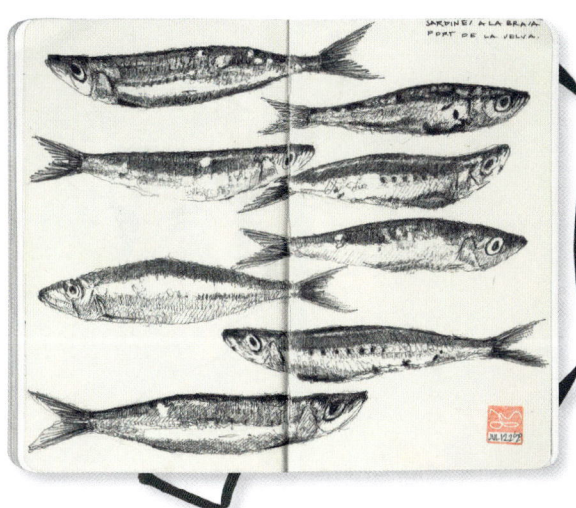

60-minute drawings allow you to examine objects and scenes thoroughly, delving into their details and complexities. You have time to develop a strategic approach to your composition, enhancing visual depth and cohesion. This practice fosters patience and endurance, which are invaluable for your artistic development. Despite the generous time, capturing the essence of your subject remains paramount. With a 60-minute drawing you can immerse yourself in your subject, studying it in detail; this significantly enriches the drawing experience.

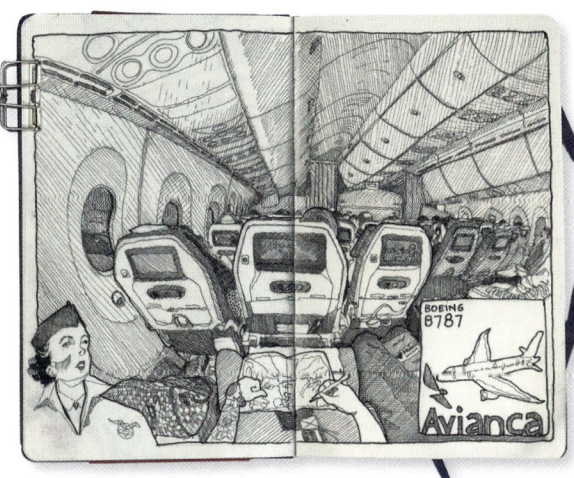

120-minute drawings provide ample time for you to delve deeply into spatial and compositional relationships. They require continuous dedication and concentration. Though time is generous, the fundamental principle remains the same: to focus on the essence of the subject. Each stroke contributes to a meaningful representation. In conclusion, 120-minute drawings offer an immersive and enriching experience, fostering patience, concentration and a deep exploration of art.

Exercises

Here are some ideas for drawing exercises that you can easily do close to home. I've given some ideas for the amount of time you might take for each one, from 15 minutes to two hours. To help you get started, the exercises that are detailed on the following pages are listed in bold.

FOOD	🕐	👁	📷
The napkin holder at a restaurant	15	●	
A bunch of bananas	15, 30	●	
The dishes from your family meal	15, 30	●	●
A glass of water	15, 30 60	●	●
Your favourite dish	30, 60	●	●
A plate of noodles	30, 60	●	●
The packaging from your favourite snack	60, 120	●	●
Different kinds of mushrooms	60, 120	●	●
Your favourite fast-food dish	60, 120		●
The ingredients for your favourite recipe	120	●	●

FIGURES	🕐	👁	📷
A co-worker during a meeting	15	●	
People in a public place before they move	15	●	
A family member while they take a nap or read	15	●	
Your non-dominant hand	15, 30	●	
Your feet	15, 30	●	
Your facial expression while looking in the mirror	15, 30, 60	●	
Your pet	60, 120		●
A family member's face	30, 60, 120		●
A group of people	30, 60, 120		●
The face of your favourite person in the world	30, 60, 120		●

Suggested time in minutes: This is my personal recommendation for the list of subjects below but is entirely dependant on your time constraints.

Observation: More challenging as it requires the subject and the artist to remain in the same place.

Photo reference: You may need more time for your drawing – capture the moment with a photo.

NATURE AND URBAN	🕐	👁	📷
A plant you have at home	15	●	
An urban rubbish bin	15	●	
A bench in a park	15	●	●
A manhole cover	15, 30	●	●
The house or building where you live	30, 60	●	●
The texture of a tree trunk near your home	30, 60	●	●
The most iconic building in your town	60	●	●
A glass-walled building	60	●	●
What you see from your window	60	●	●
The market in your town	120		●
A forest scene that evokes a special feeling for you	120	●	●

OBJECTS	🕐	👁	📷
The tool or device you use the most at home	15, 30	●	
The interior of the car while you wait inside it	15, 30	●	
A clock you have at home	15, 30	●	
Your bag on the table	15, 30	●	
A pillow or a wrinkled cushion	30	●	●
A bicycle	30, 60	●	
Your bed before making it	15, 30, 60	●	
Your favourite shoes	30, 60	●	●
A reflective metallic balloon	60, 120	●	●

15-minute exercises

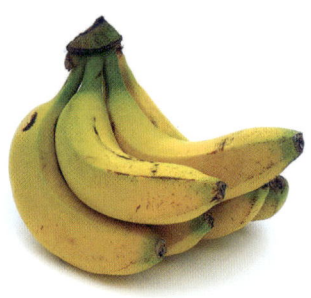

DRAW A BUNCH OF BANANAS

Take a moment to observe the proportions and spatial relationships between the elements before you start the drawing. Using a ballpoint pen is a good choice, as it allows you to make strokes with different intensities.

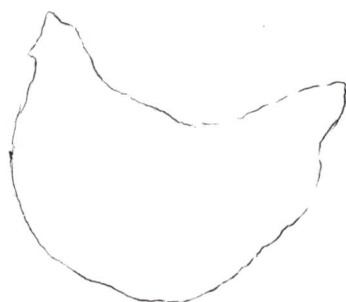

1. DRAW THE CONTOUR

Begin by subtly drawing the outline of the object. This will help establish the overall framework of the drawing.

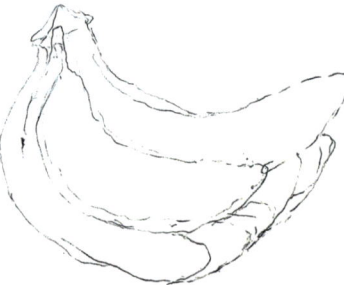

2. ADD THE INTERIOR LINES

After outlining, focus on the interior lines to define the structure and shape of the object. Adjust the outline if necessary to match the interior lines.

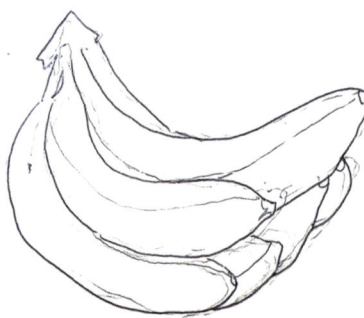

3. ADD THE FINAL LINES

Once you are satisfied with the proportions and structure, you can apply more pressure to the pen to create sharper and more defined lines.

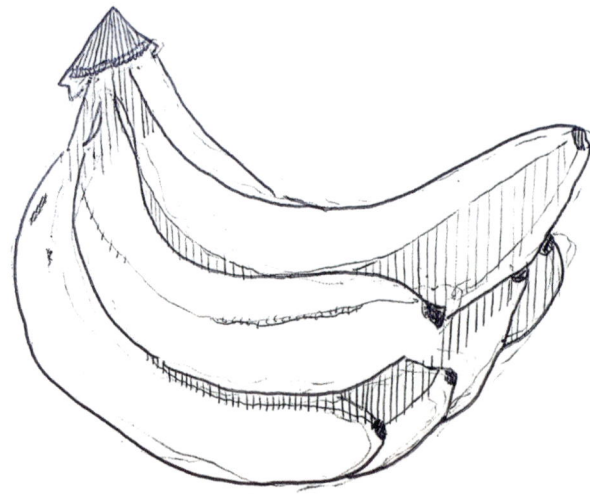

4. ADD DETAILS AND FINISHING TOUCHES

If time permits, add details such as shadows or subtle lines to enhance the appearance of the drawing.

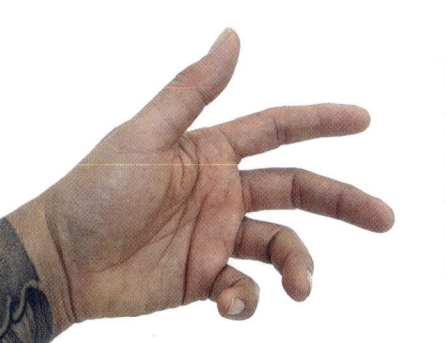

DRAW YOUR NON-DOMINANT HAND

Drawing your own body, especially the hands, doesn't require any special preparation. You always have your hand available for practice. You can use a pencil to create the initial strokes or, as shown in the example, a ballpoint pen, as it easily allows for strokes with different intensities.

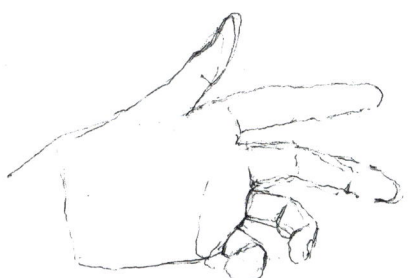

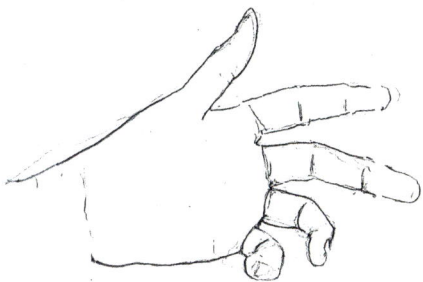

1. DRAW THE OUTLINE

Begin by delicately tracing the outline of your hand. Observe how the fingers form different angles with each other and how the lines relate to each other.

2. ADD THE INTERIOR LINES

Mark the divisions of the fingers – the phalanges. This will help you verify the proportions and relationships between them. If you notice any discrepancies with your actual hand, correct the lines with gentle strokes.

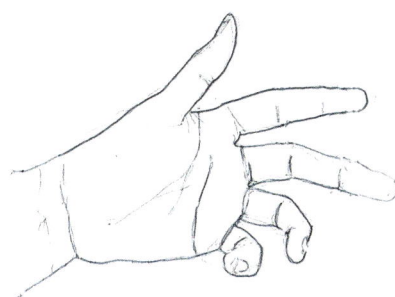

3. REINFORCE THE CORRECT LINES

Go over the correct lines with more pressure to emphasize them over the rest.

4. FILL IN THE BACKGROUND

Filling in the background serves two purposes: it allows you to practice textures and it highlights the negative space around the hand, which helps confirm that the relationships between the fingers are correct.

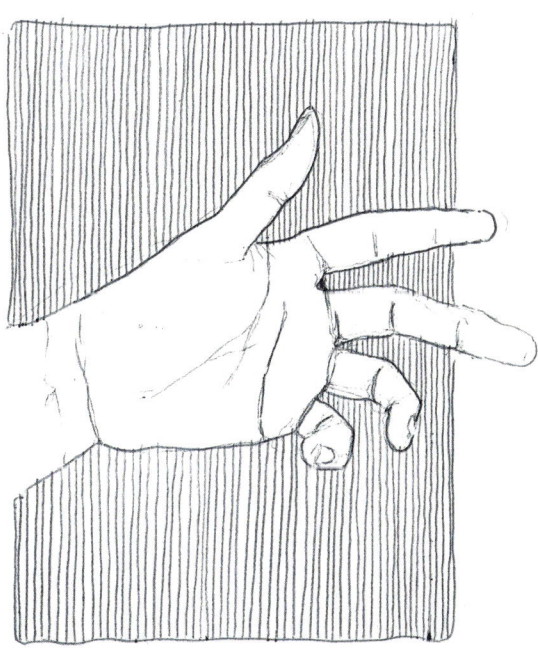

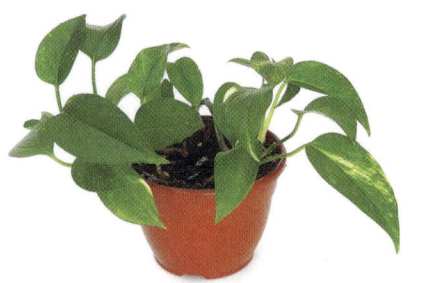

DRAW A PLANT YOU HAVE AT HOME

Drawing plants, especially those with few leaves and large, recognizable features such as this one, can be very useful. It allows you to practise relationships between elements – and even if you make mistakes, it will still resemble a plant.

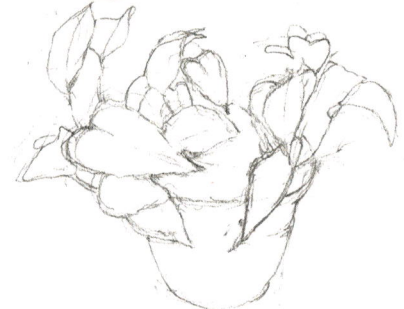

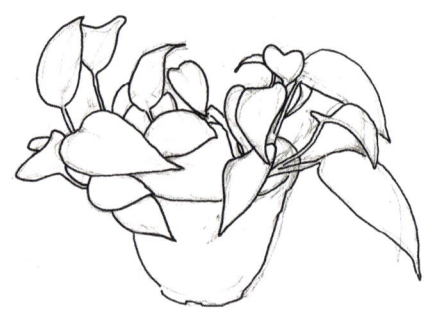

1. DRAW THE CONTOUR

In this exercise, use a pencil to begin. Start from the general form and work towards the specific details. Pay attention to the overall proportions: mark it and begin placing the leaves while observing how they relate to each other.

2. OUTLINE WITH A FINELINER

When you're satisfied with the general lines, switch to a 0.5 fineliner or similar to draw the outlines. Pay special attention to the empty spaces created between the leaves; they will help you understand if you're on the right track.

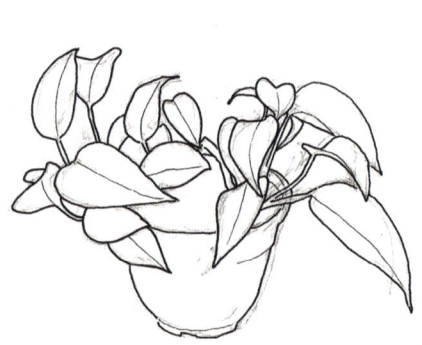

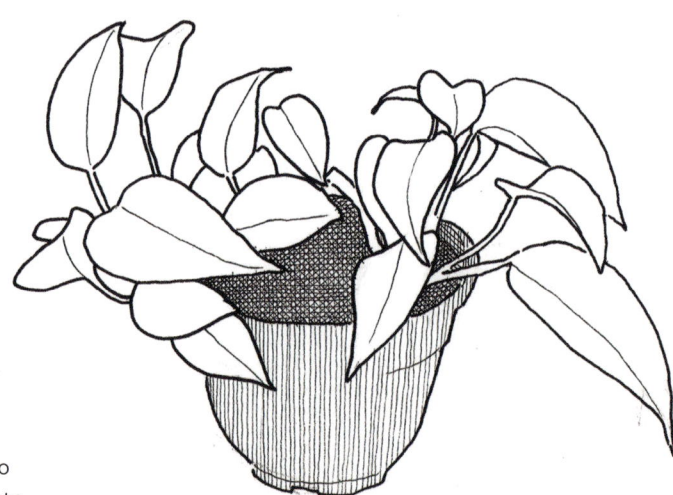

3. ADD THE INTERNAL LINES

Now draw the internal lines of the leaves. As you do this, recheck the proportions. Dividing elements into smaller parts can help you check whether the overall proportions are correct.

4. PRACTISE TEXTURES AND ADD DEPTH

If you still have some time, practise textures and add depth to your drawing. You can also rotate the pot and start a completely new drawing.

DRAW THE TOOL OR DEVICE YOU USE THE MOST AT HOME

Drawing small objects is the first step towards tackling larger projects. Pay attention to the direction of the object's lines, which ones are parallel to others, and what angles they form. Take your time to observe the different pieces that compose the object.

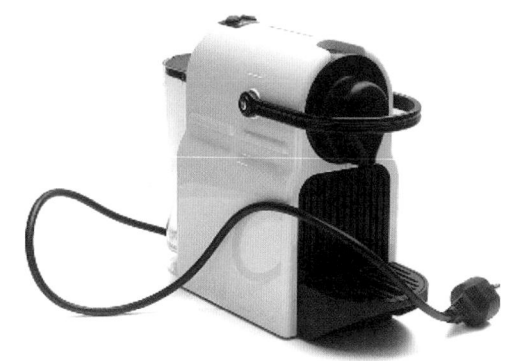

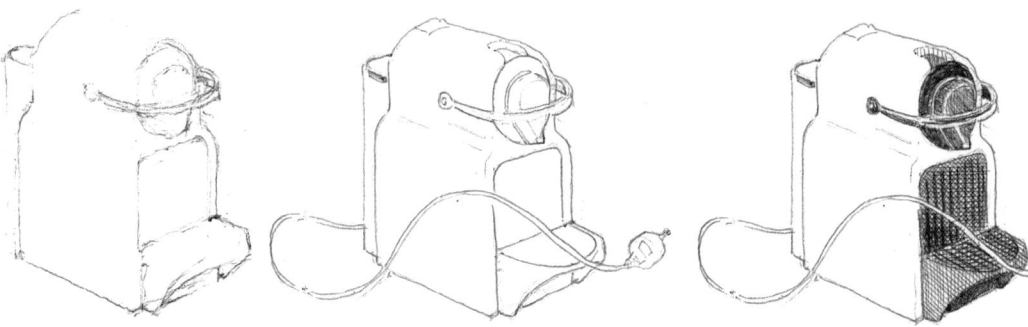

1. DRAW THE CONTOUR

Begin with the outline lines; don't focus on the details initially. There's a white part and a black part; try to subtly draw the relationship between them.

2. EMPHASIZE DEFINITIVE LINES

Once you have it, go over the final lines with a bit more pressure to highlight them from the rest.

3. DETAIL THE BLACK PART

Now focus on detailing the black part. Pay attention to the highlights that give volume to this area. By applying more or less pressure with a ballpoint pen, you can create tones, just as you would with a pencil.

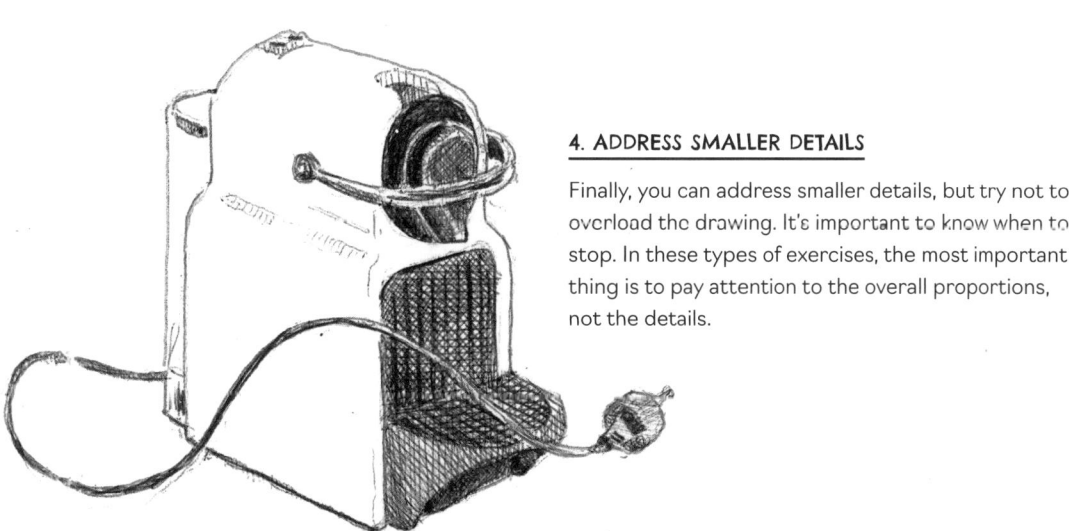

4. ADDRESS SMALLER DETAILS

Finally, you can address smaller details, but try not to overload the drawing. It's important to know when to stop. In these types of exercises, the most important thing is to pay attention to the overall proportions, not the details.

30-minute exercises

DRAW A PILLOW OR A WRINKLED CUSHION

As with the 15-minute sketches, take a moment to observe how the cushion is illuminated. Imagine a line bordering the highlights and another bordering the shadows. Got it? Let's draw them. This exercise will use cross hatching in all four directions.

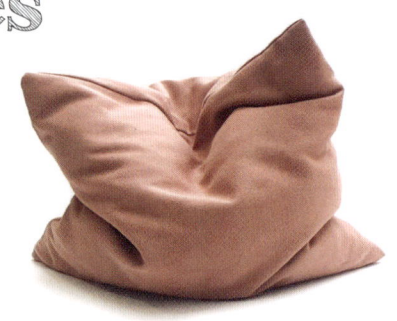

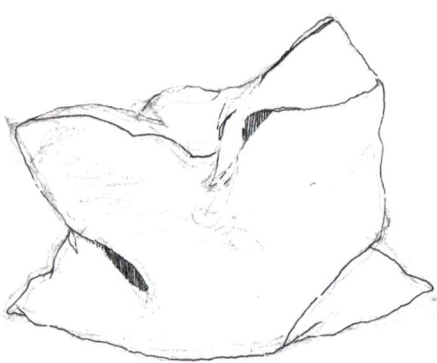

1. START WITH PENCIL OUTLINES

Begin with a pencil by drawing the contour until you are satisfied with the proportions. Then, draw those imaginary lines separating the light and shadows. It's important that these lines are very subtle and drawn with minimal pressure to maintain delicacy and avoid harsh lines.

2. DEFINE CONTOURS WITH A FINELINER

Using a 0.05 or 0.1 fineliner, draw the cushion's outline and densely shade the darkest areas where the folds are almost black. This will be the darkest part of the drawing. These dark areas serve as reference points for locating the rest of the shadows.

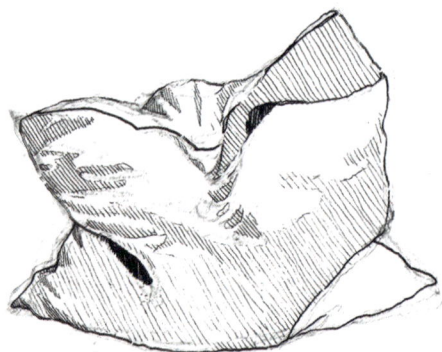

3. APPLY THE FIRST DIAGONAL HATCH MARKS

Now make the first diagonal hatch marks on the area that receives less light on the cushion. You don't need to reach the final tone; this is just the first layer of hatching. You can draw the hatching lines in any direction you choose.

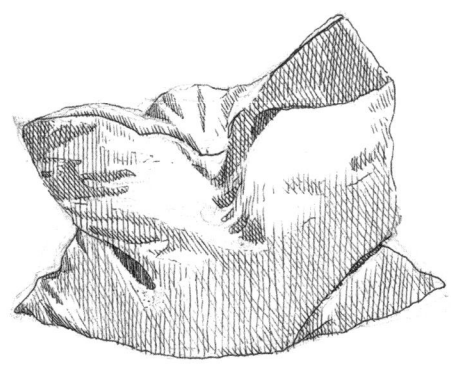

4. ADD A SECOND LAYER OF HATCHING

Repeat the process with a second set of hatching over the dark areas, in the opposite direction to the first. This hatching can slightly overlap the initial imaginary lines, which helps achieve a smooth transition between tones.

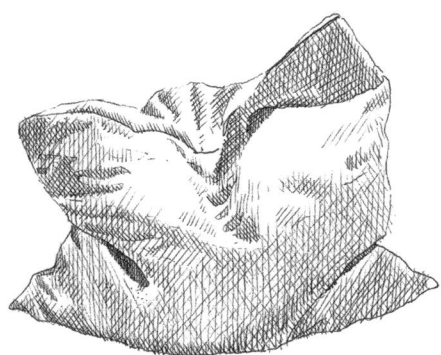

5. PUT IN DARKER FOLDS

Note that within the shaded areas there are some folds that are slightly darker. You can highlight them with a third set of hatching in a different direction.

6. ADD THE LAST LAYERS AND DETAILING

We only have one direction of hatch available, as we have already used the other three. With this direction you can cover the entire cushion, leaving only the brightest areas blank.

If you want to darken any part because you're not satisfied with the contrast, use a thicker fineliner and apply strokes where you want to deepen the shadows.

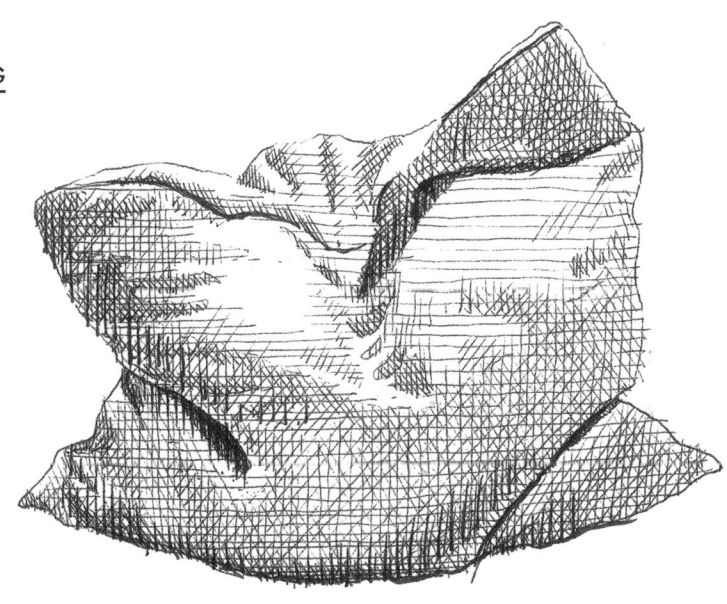

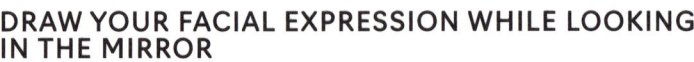

DRAW YOUR FACIAL EXPRESSION WHILE LOOKING IN THE MIRROR

You can do this exercise either by looking at yourself in a mirror or, if you prefer, use a reference photo. Whichever way you choose, ensure there's side lighting to create illumination on one side of your face and shadows on the other. This will generate better contrast and understanding of volumes.

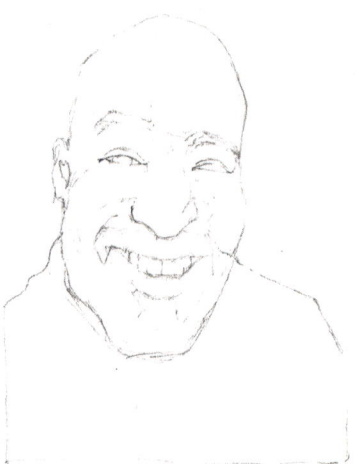

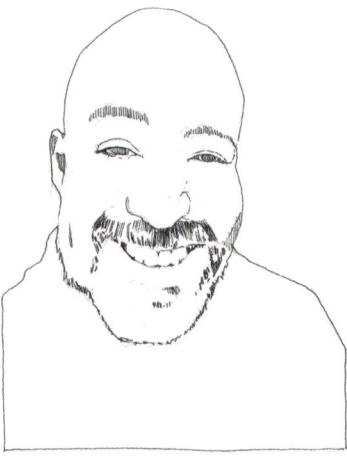

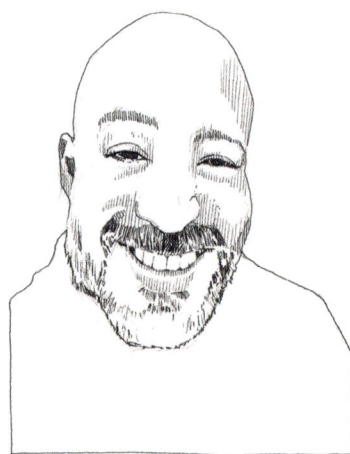

1. DRAW THE CONTOURS

Begin by outlining the face with a pencil, starting with the eyes and moving to the nose, mouth and general shape. Focus on observing rather than perfect resemblance.

2. HATCH THE DARKER AREAS

Create the first hatching layer on the darker areas. You can also ink the outer and inner contours such as the edge of the nose and the teeth. These dark areas serve as reference points for locating the rest of the shadows.

3. PUT IN THE SHADOWS

Now draw the first skin hatching layer over the areas that are in shadow. Remember, you don't have to achieve the final value at this stage – this is only the first layer.

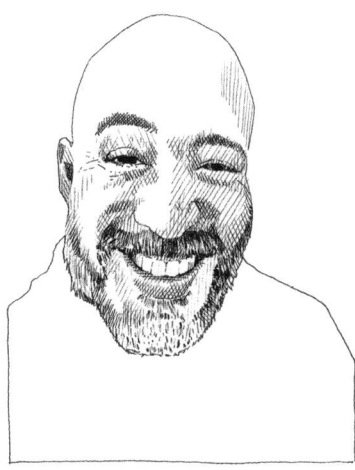 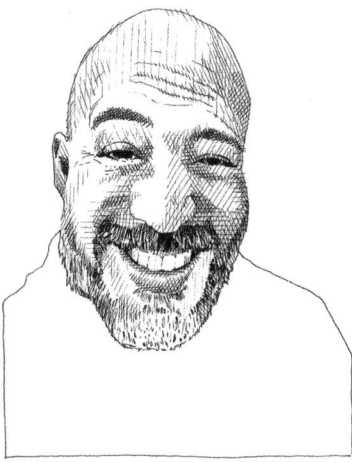 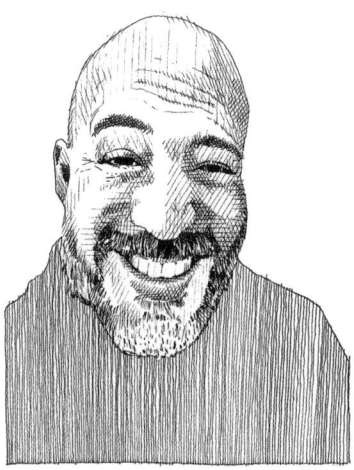

4. CREATE MORE SHADOWS

Create another layer of hatching in a different direction to the first to cover the previous set and extend over the next darkest area, gradually increasing the darkness.

5. ADD NECESSARY DETAILS

Add any missing details but be careful not to make the lines too prominent. The goal is to gradually build up layers. It's easy to clutter the drawing with strong lines.

6. PRACTISE LONGER STROKES

You can utilize clothing areas to practice uniform hatching, which helps improve your stroke control. Ensure the hatch marks are made as close together as possible without the lines overlapping.

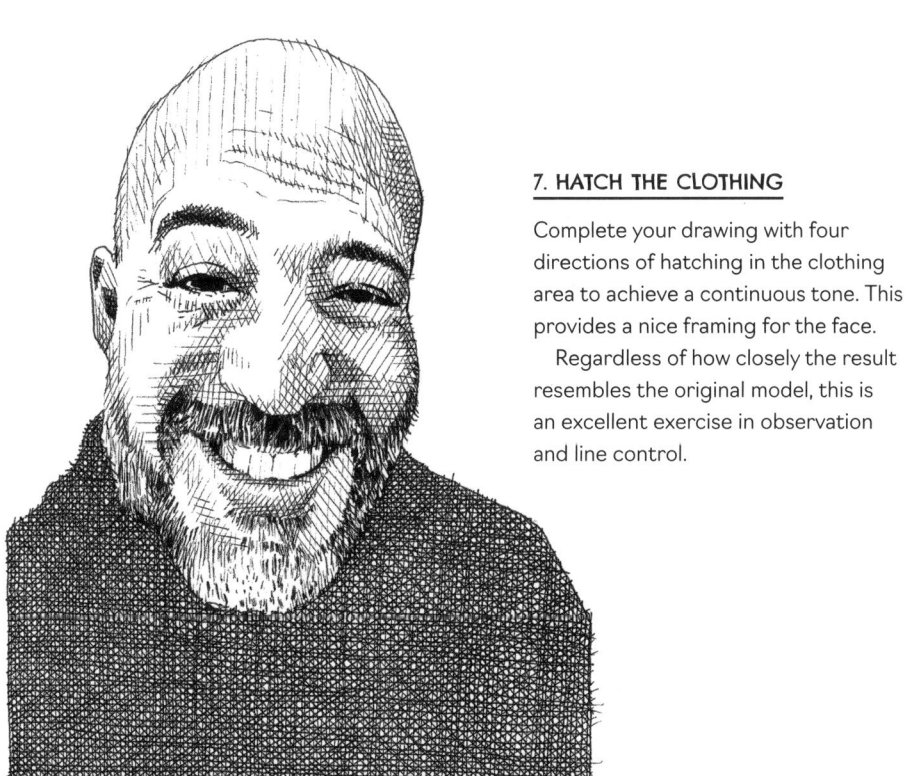

7. HATCH THE CLOTHING

Complete your drawing with four directions of hatching in the clothing area to achieve a continuous tone. This provides a nice framing for the face.

Regardless of how closely the result resembles the original model, this is an excellent exercise in observation and line control.

60-minute exercise

DRAW THE HOUSE OR BUILDING WHERE YOU LIVE

In this exercise we'll use this house as a model. There are several reasons why it's a good subject for ink drawing. Firstly, it's a single-point perspective, making it relatively easy to draw. Additionally, it has a wide range of values, with distinct shadows, dark areas and very light areas, creating an interesting contrast. As in other exercises, take a moment to understand the relationships between the different elements in the image.

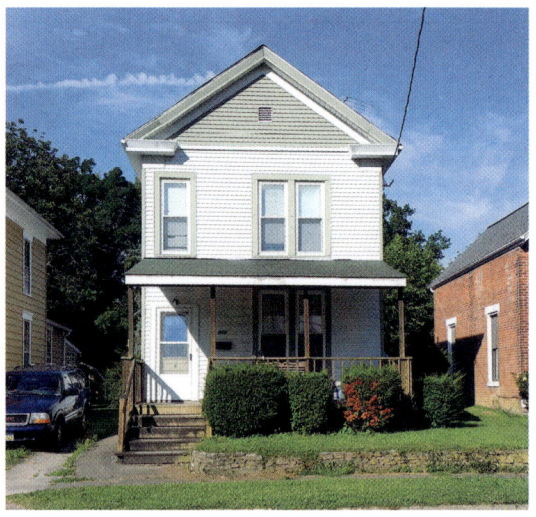

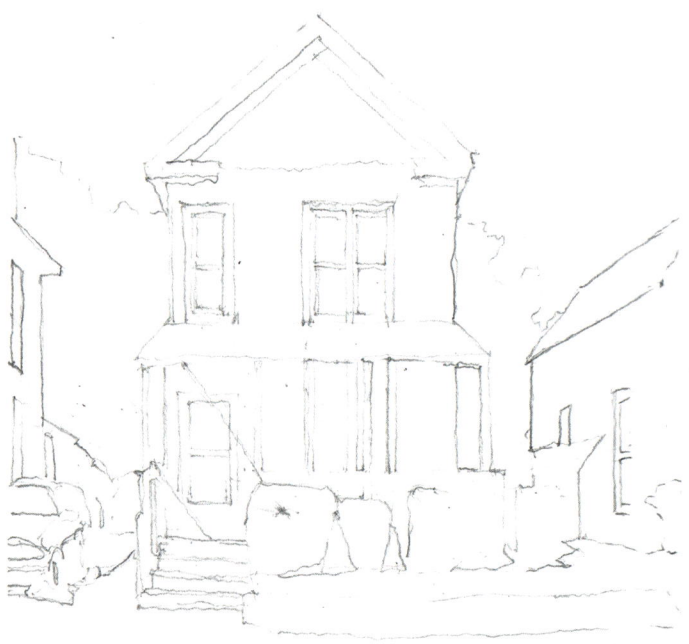

1. ESTABLISH THE BASIC LINES

Start by creating basic lines with a pencil, locating the most prominent elements of the image without going into too much detail. Locate the vanishing point by extending the imaginary lines of perspective (the sloping lines of the roofs on the adjacent buildings) until they intersect. Note that the vanishing point is at the centre, near the steps.

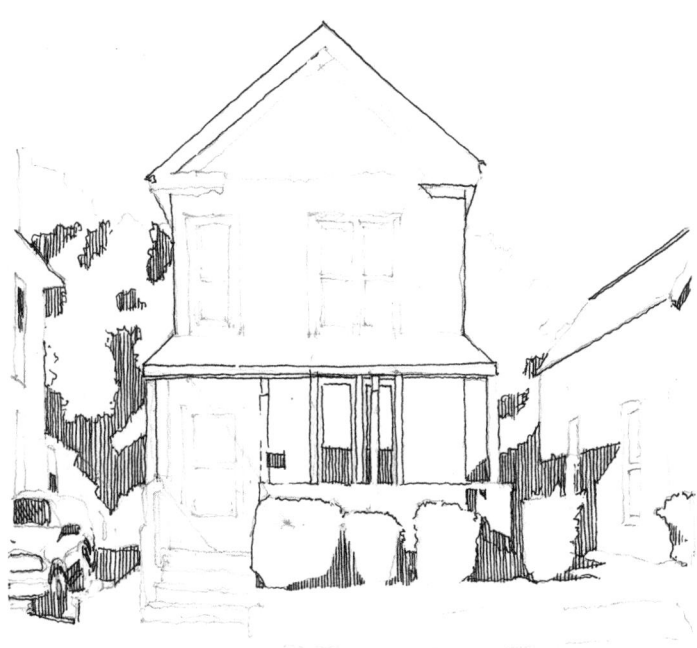

2. ADD **THE DARKER CONTOURS**

Use a 0.05 fineliner to draw the darker contours and apply hatching to the darker areas. Despite these being the darkest areas of the drawing, you don't need to darken them to the final value at this stage. This will be achieved gradually throughout the process. It's important to have patience and not rush the darkening process.

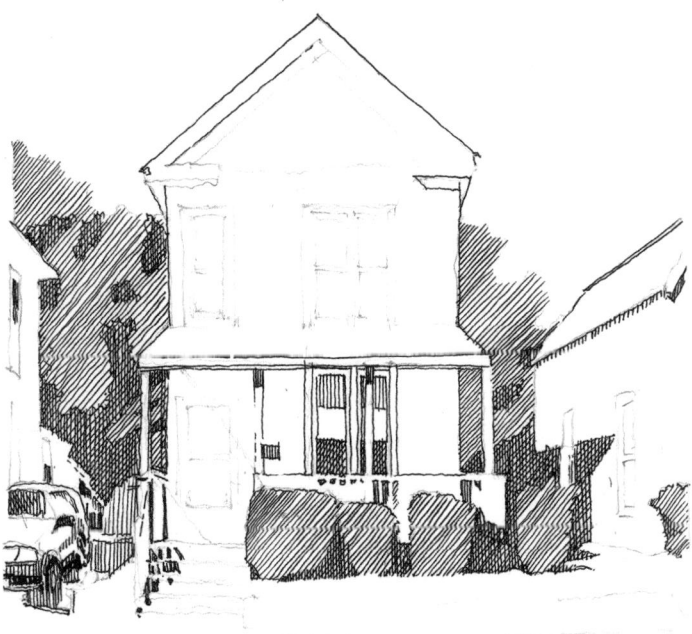

3. HATCH **THE VEGETATION**

Cover the vegetation, the darkest element of the image, with hatching in the opposite direction. Note that trees don't require a linear outline; you can define their shape with hatching. Additionally, there are other elements such as the windows of the porch that have tonal values similar to the vegetation. Now is a good time to apply hatching to these elements as well.

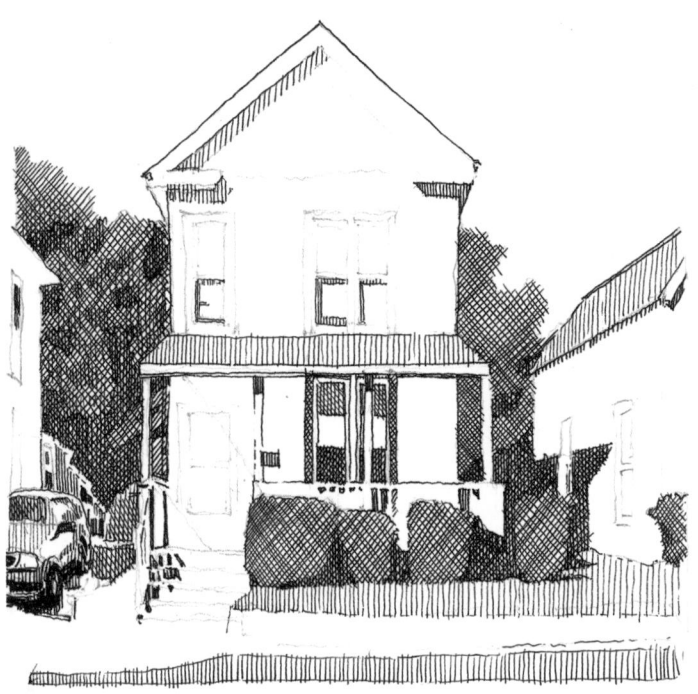

4. HATCH OTHER DARK ELEMENTS

After covering the darker areas, apply hatching in a single direction to the second darkest areas. These areas include the front garden lawn, the shadows of the cornice, the roofs and some areas of the car. It's worth noting that detailing the car isn't essential; instead, observe it as a succession of shapes without delving into too much detail, since it's not the main focus of the drawing.

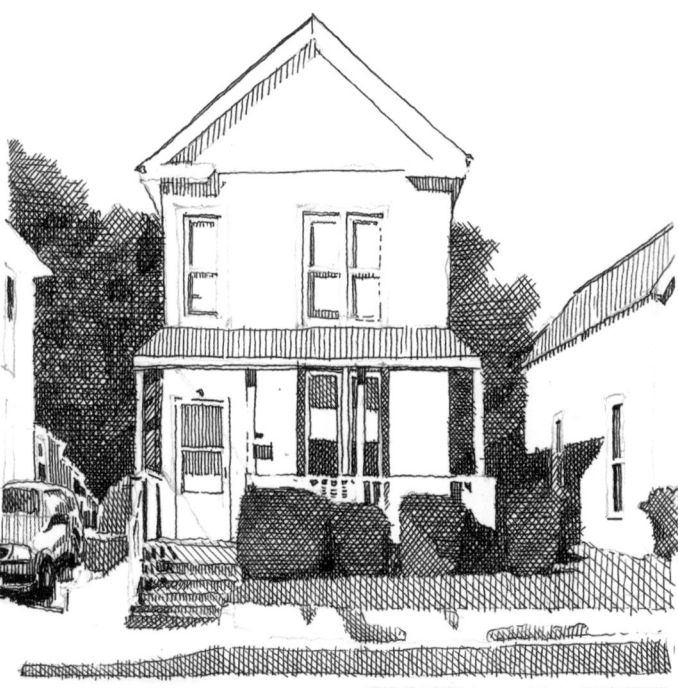

5. DEEPEN THE SHADOWS

You might feel the need to darken the vegetation further. Remember, we've only used hatching in two directions so far – there's still a way to make it darker. Apply a third direction of hatching marks and observe again. By doing this you are creating more contrast in the image and enhancing the depth of the shadows.

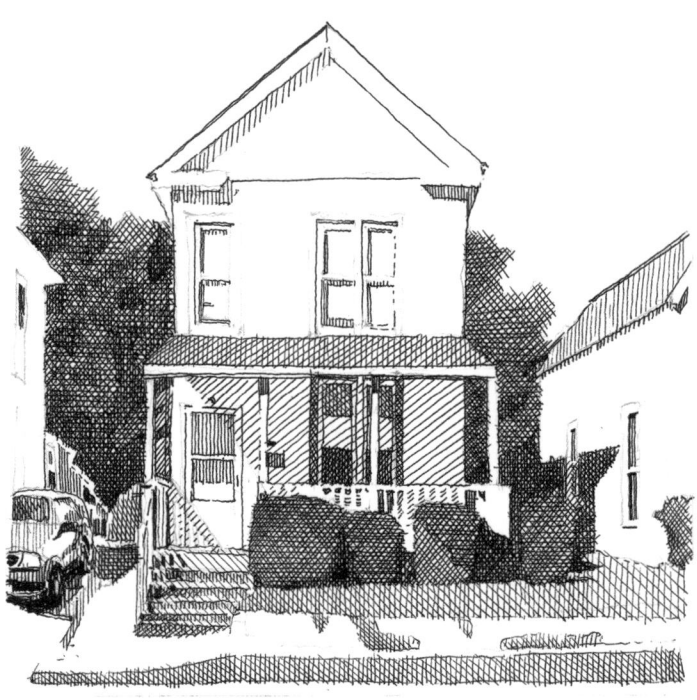

6. GRADUALLY FILL AND DARKEN

Within the areas without hatching, choose the darkest one, such as the shadow under the porch, and apply the first layer of hatching. As you gradually fill in the blank spaces, it's beneficial to pay attention to how the shadow is applied behind the porch railing, without outlining it. This approach prevents the ink outline from dominating small areas, resulting in excessive darkness.

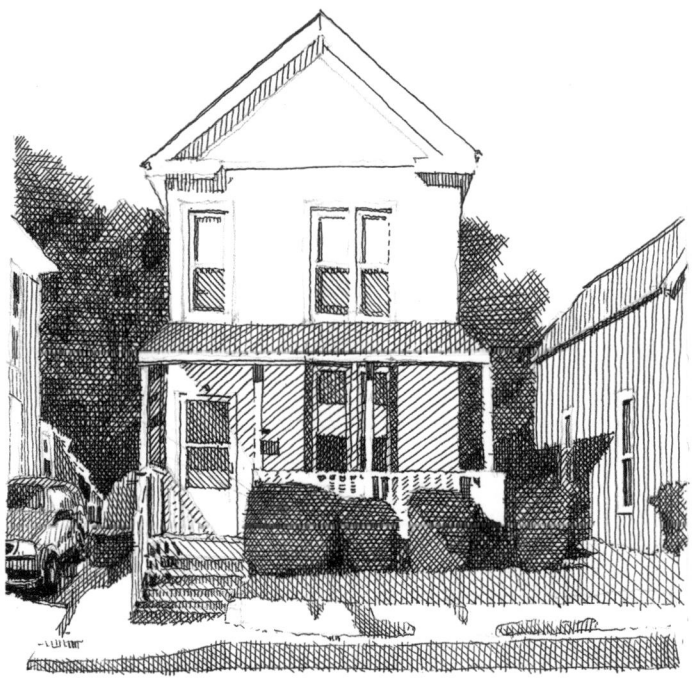

7. IDENTIFY THE LIGHTEST AREA

As you add layers and darken the drawing, become aware of which area will remain the lightest. This could be the facade above the porch. Make sure that as you darken the drawing you also progressively add layers to those previously drawn to maintain overall tonal coherence.

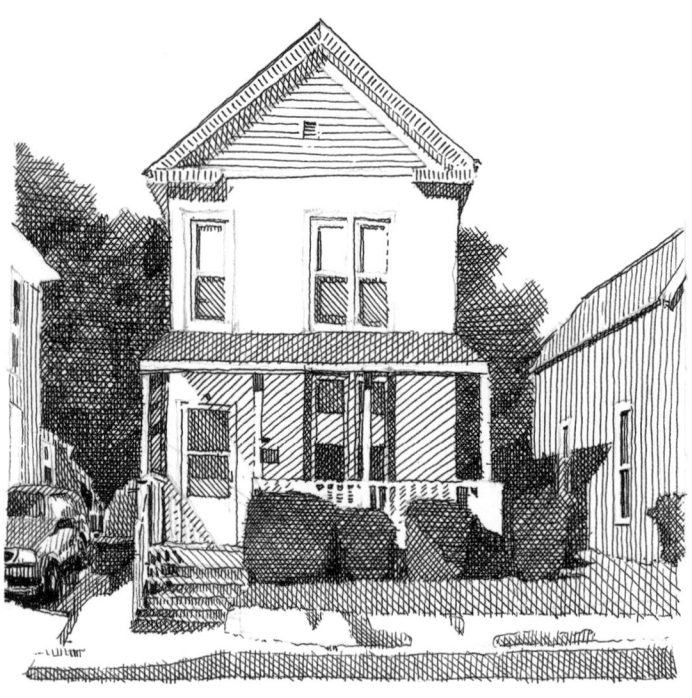

8. EMPHASIZE LIGHTER AREAS

As you near the end of the drawing, highlight the lighter areas by applying hatching on the grey cornice, creating contrast with the lower part.

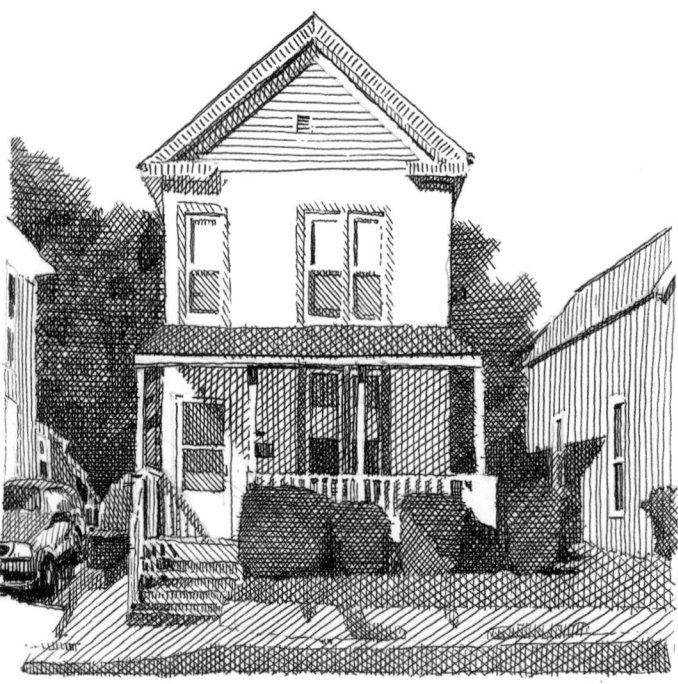

9. ADJUST CONTRAST WITH HATCHING

With the lighter areas delineated with hatching, add more hatching where you want to adjust the contrast – in this case, the shadow under the porch and the garden in front of the house.

Pay attention to small tonal variations such as the window frames in the lighter area. When incorporating these variations, use subtle lines and try to avoid inking the contours to prevent overloading the drawing.

10. FINAL TOUCHES

Finally, use a thicker fineliner to add hatching in some darker areas to increase the sense of depth. Additionally, pay attention to small details at this stage and darken them to highlight them. Remember: you can always darken areas but you can't lighten them, so it's crucial to practise patience and build tonal coherence layer by layer.

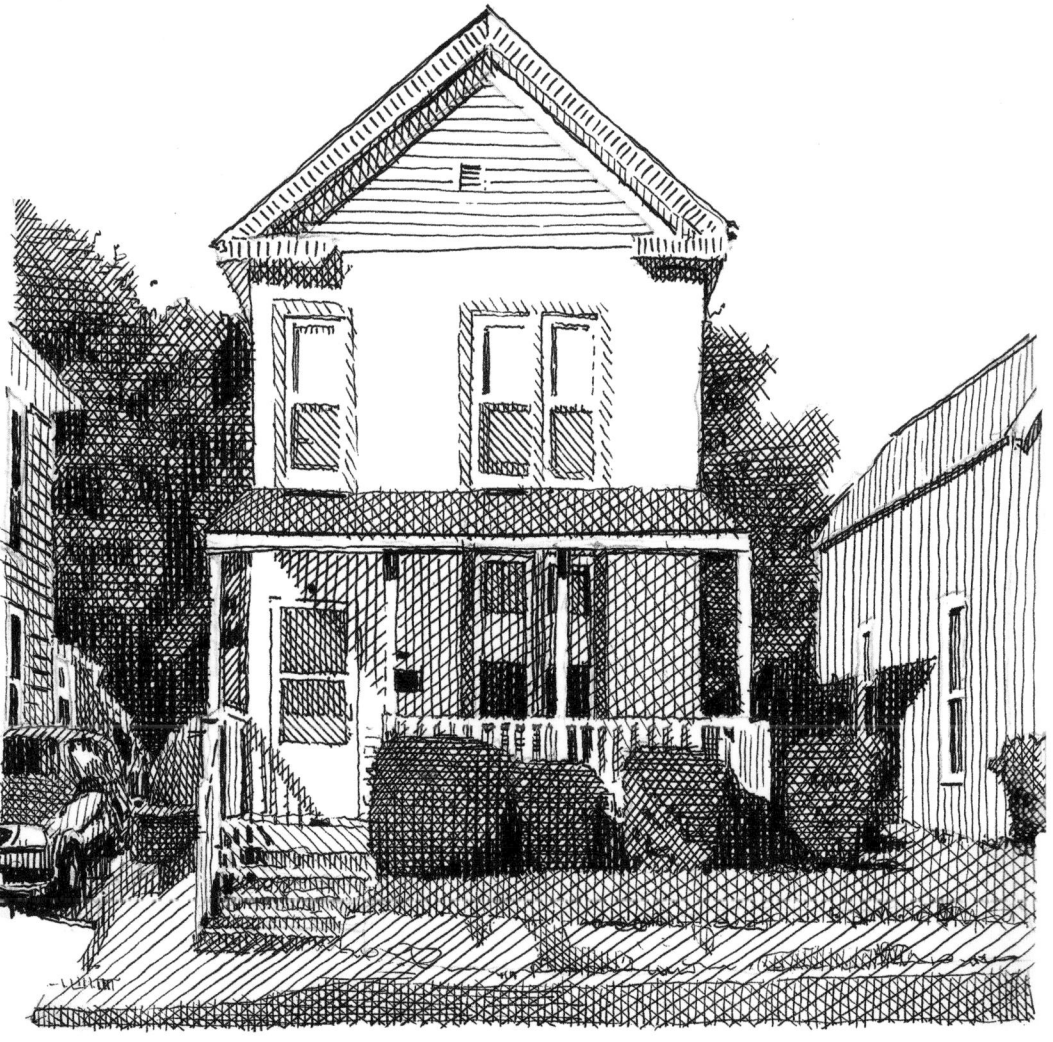

120-minute exercise

DRAW A FOREST SCENE THAT EVOKES A SPECIAL FEELING FOR YOU

Don't let the complexity of this image overwhelm you. To simplify your understanding of the range of values, convert the image to black and white to avoid dealing with colour, since this is information you won't represent.

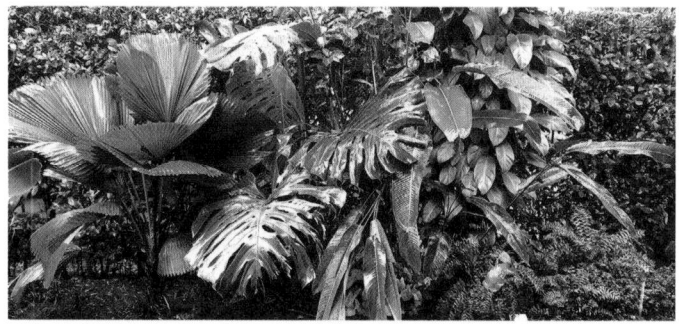

1. PUT IN THE BASIC LINES

Identify the largest and most representative volumes of the image. Lightly draw them with a soft pencil, such as a 2B. Pay attention to proportions and the relationship between the elements you're delineating. Avoid too many details; draw them as simple shapes.

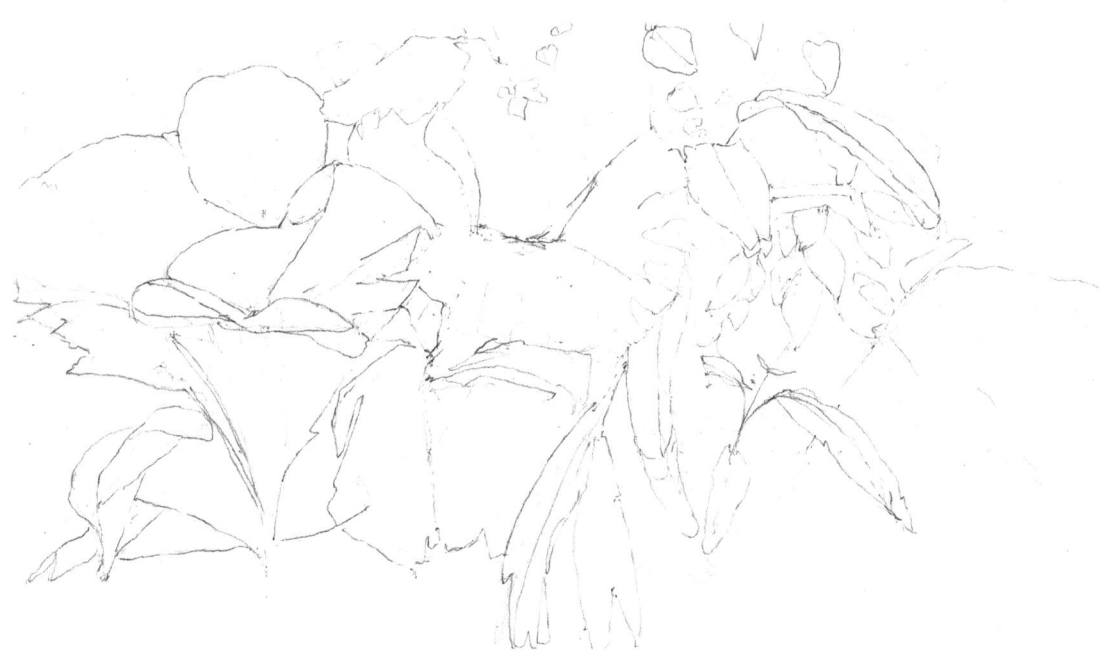

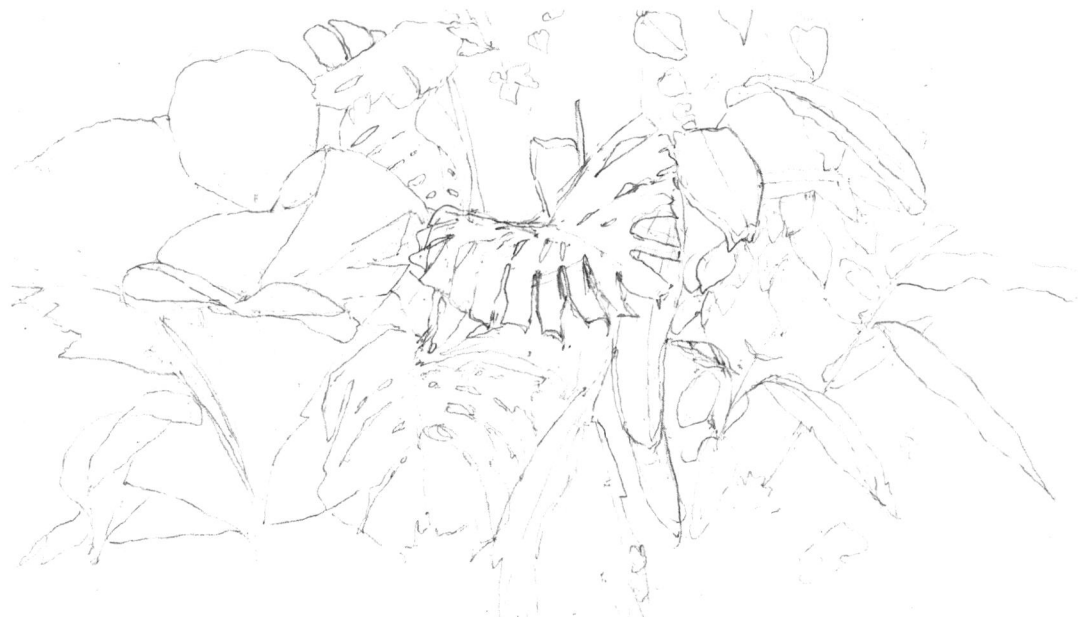

2. REFINE ELEMENT DETAILS

Once located, detail the elements better, especially those that are more difficult to read, such as the Monstera leaves in the centre of the image, which are also the most prominent element of the composition.

3. INITIAL INK STEP

Locate and hatch the darkest areas of the image. This will serve as a reference to help you navigate your way through the drawing.

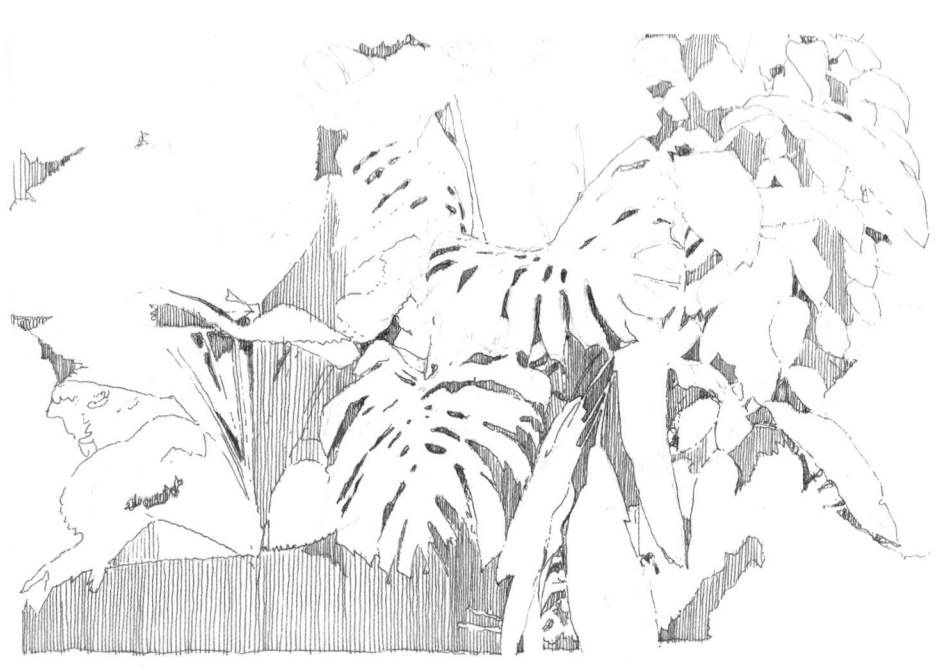

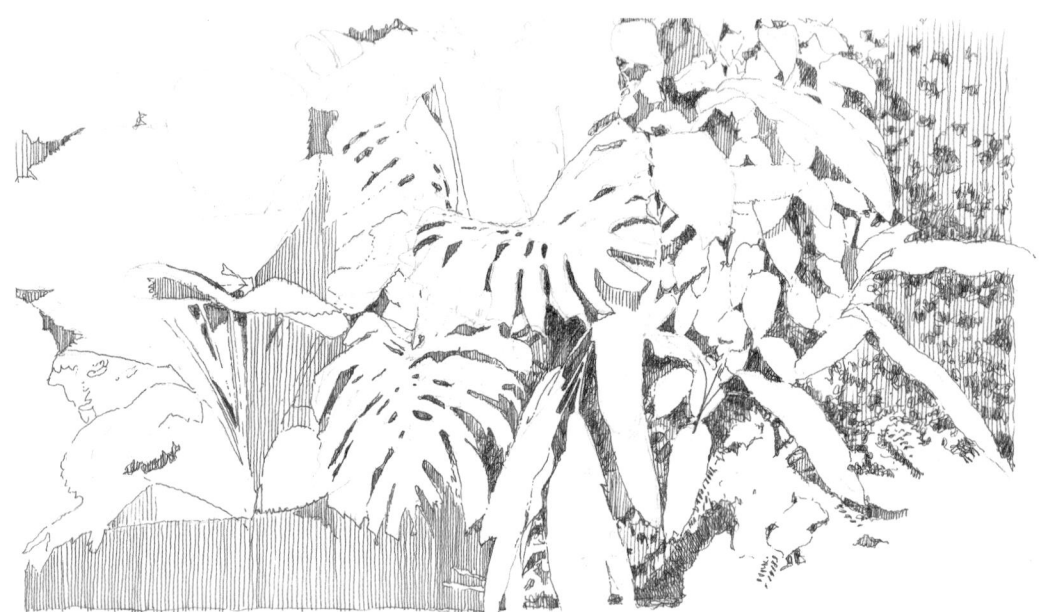

4. ADD STROKES

Continue adding strokes and working solely on these dark areas. Foliage areas are easier to represent by experimenting with textures; in this case, a bit of scribbling seems to work well.

5. EXPAND DETAIL

As you add details to these areas, you can expand the range of action without moving away from the darker areas. Remember to always start by drawing the darkest elements, but without necessarily reaching the final value.

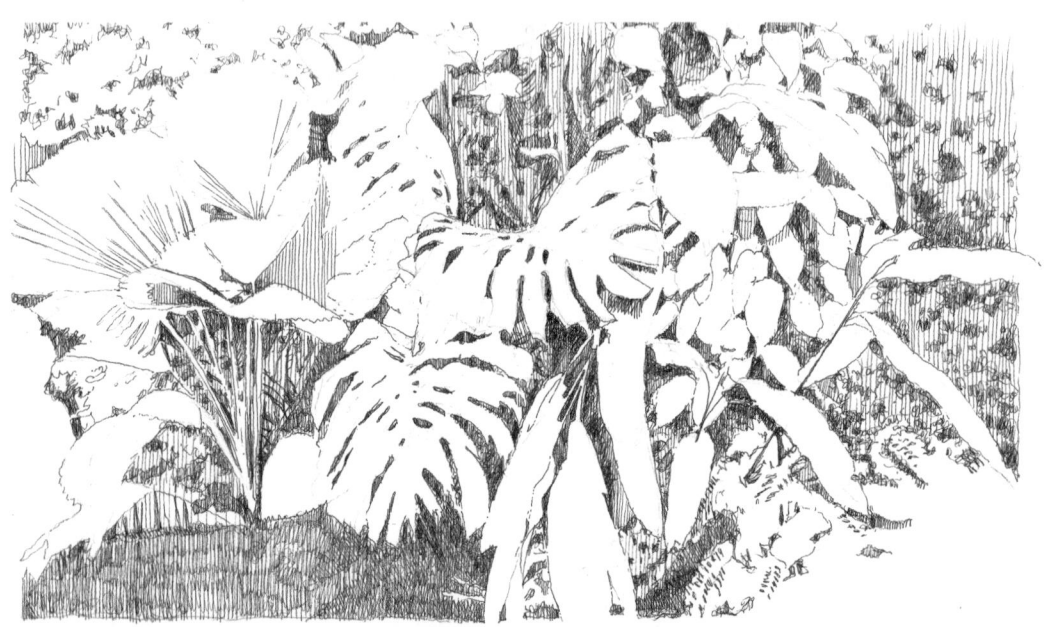

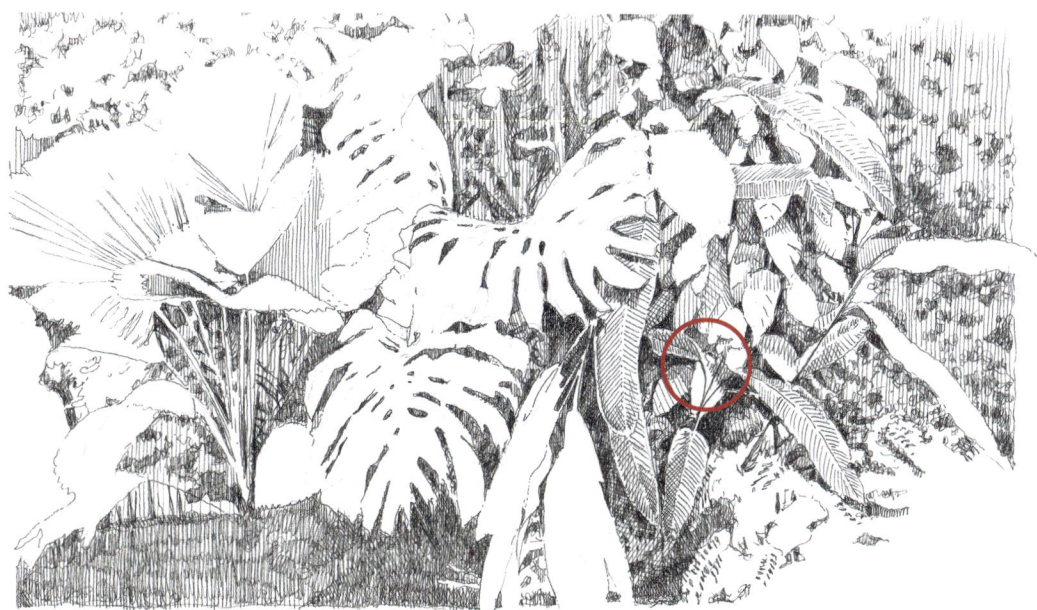

6. INK LEAVES IN GROUPS

When the dark areas are well defined with several
layers of hatching, start inking the leaves in groups.
In this case, begin with the group on the right.
Remember to start with the darkest areas within each
group and gradually work towards the lighter areas.

7. ADJUST VALUES

Add another layer of hatching to this group of leaves
to adjust the values and create greater depth.

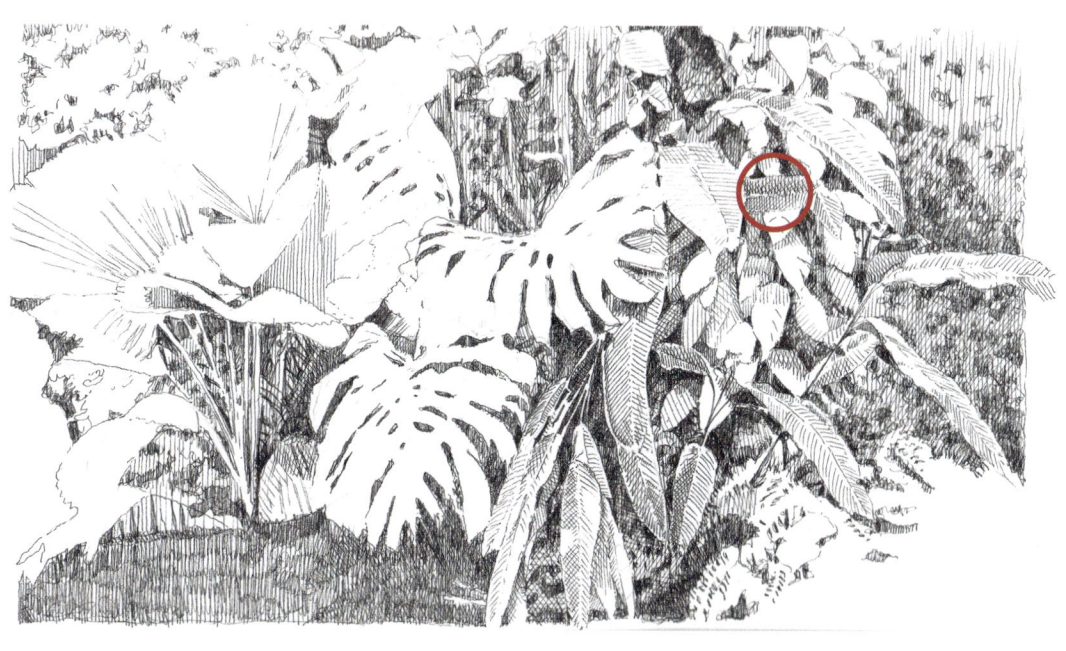

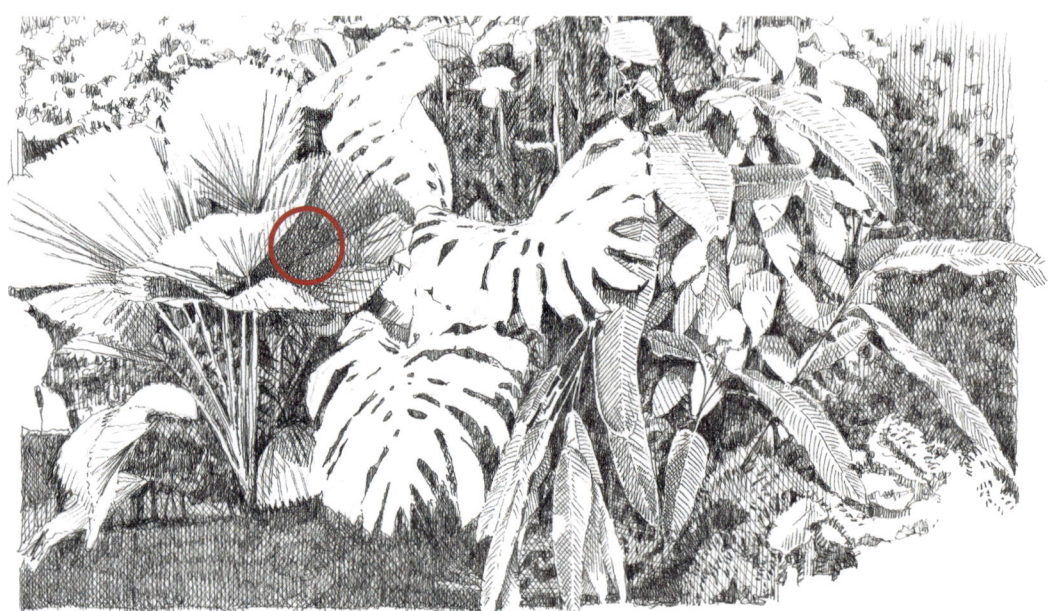

8. CONTINUE WITH OTHER GROUPS OF LEAVES

Move on to another group of leaves, repeating the process by adding layers from the darkest to the lightest areas.

9. WORK ON THE CENTRAL LEAVES

It's time to begin with the central leaves, always with a layer of hatch over the darkest area. Note that it's the hatchings that delineate the tonal variation, not lines on the contours of the elements.

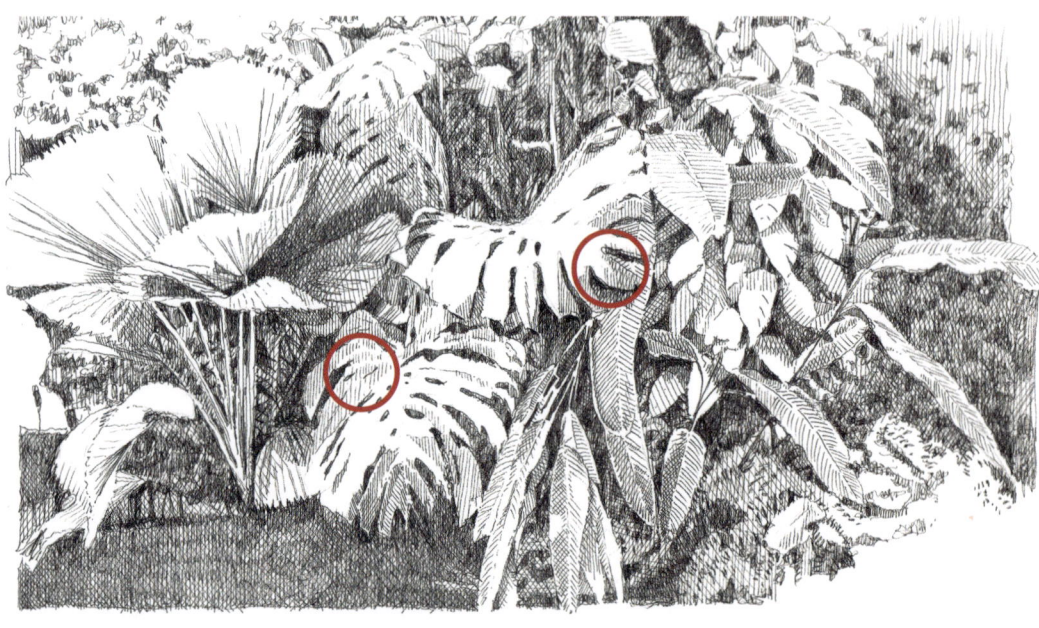

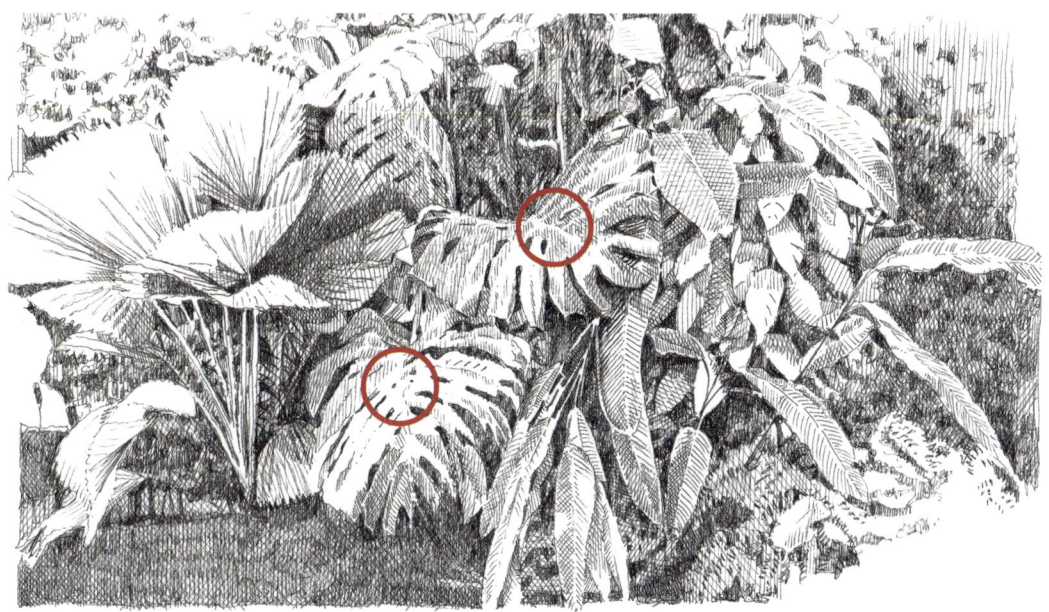

10. ADD LAYERS TO THE CENTRAL LEAVES

Add more layers to these leaves, paying particular attention to the light areas. These are just as important, if not more so, than the hatched areas, as they are essential for creating the sensation of depth and contrast.

11. REFINE THE DARK AREAS

Now that you have hatching on all elements, revisit the darker areas, adding details to create depth. If you've exhausted the directions of hatching, remember you can use scribbling or a thicker fineliner to achieve darker hatches.

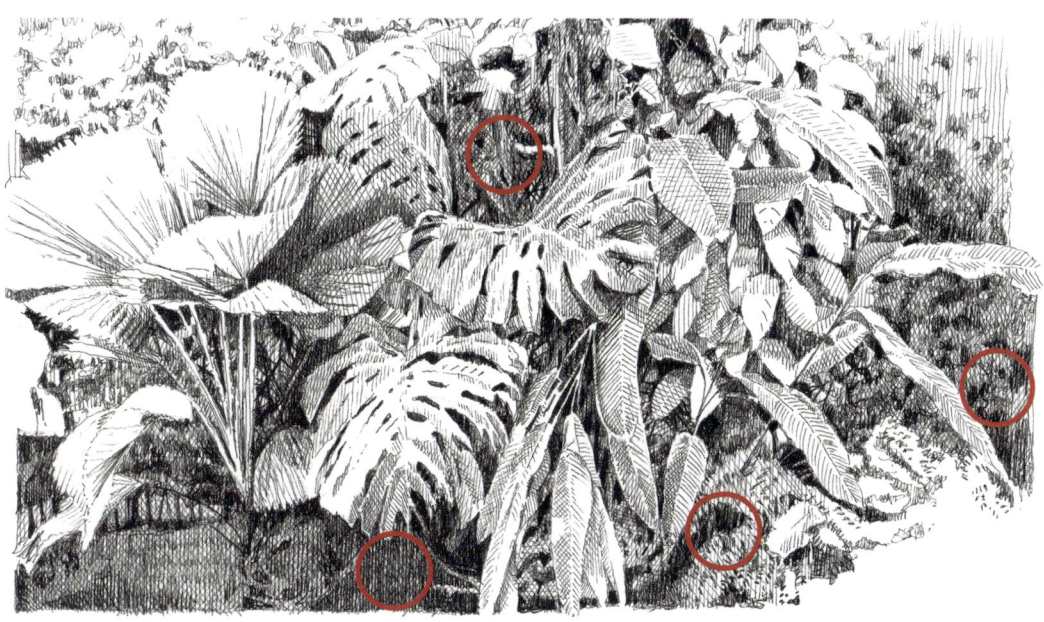

12. FINAL TOUCHES AND TIME CONSIDERATION

Always keep in mind that you can add more details, but each line darkens the image. You must respect the value relationship to maintain coherence. When adding details to lighter areas, work delicately; otherwise, you'll need to darken other areas, reaching a point where you can't do more. This is the point where you

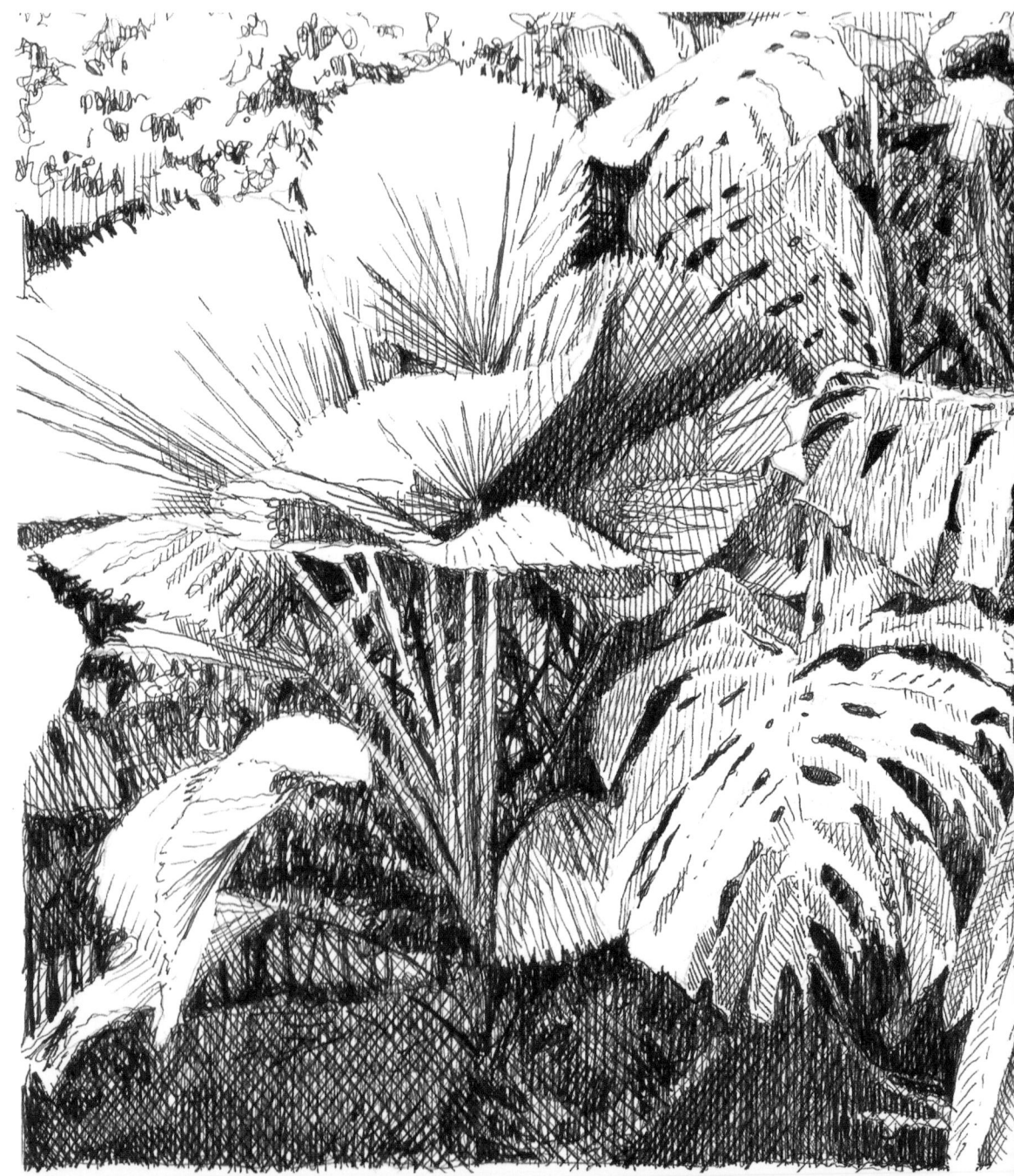

should stop, since further overworking will damage the visual coherence. Remember, the time for these exercises is only indicative, especially in longer times and more complex projects. As you can see, the process is similar in all cases, regardless of the complexity of the subject being drawn.

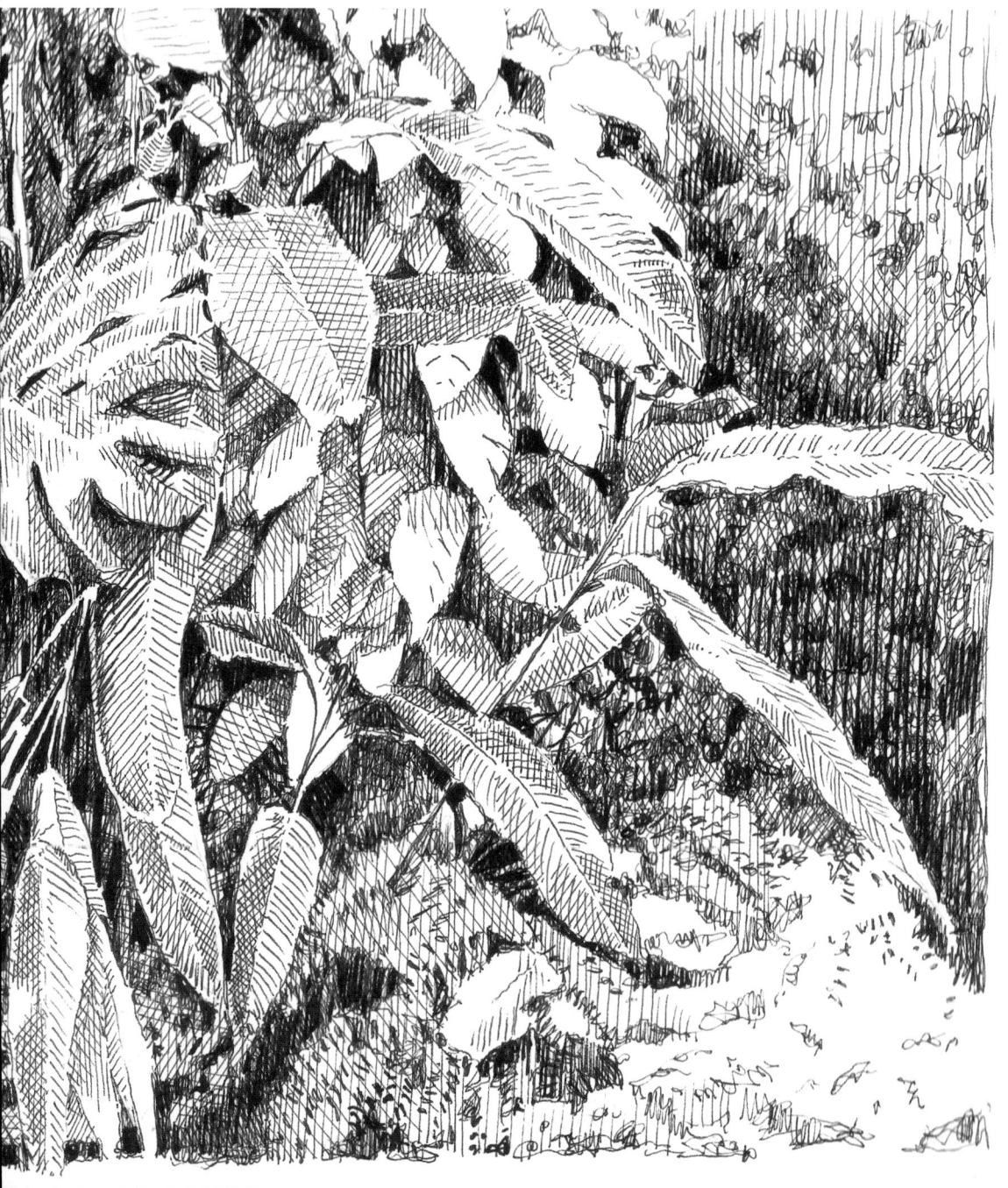

Templates

Nervous about drawing? Use the grid on each template to help draw the object proportionally on a piece of paper. Use the suggested pen-and-ink techniques to achieve a similar result, or choose another from this book.

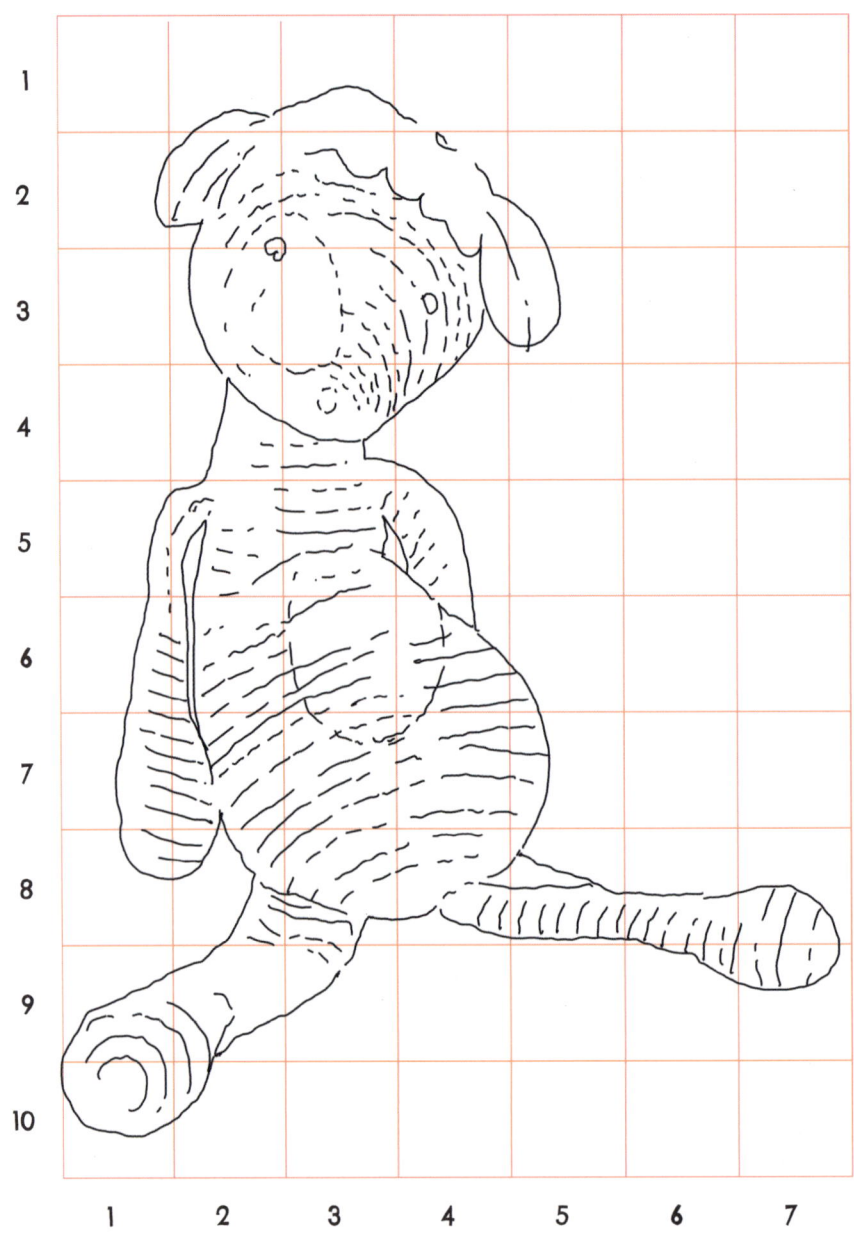

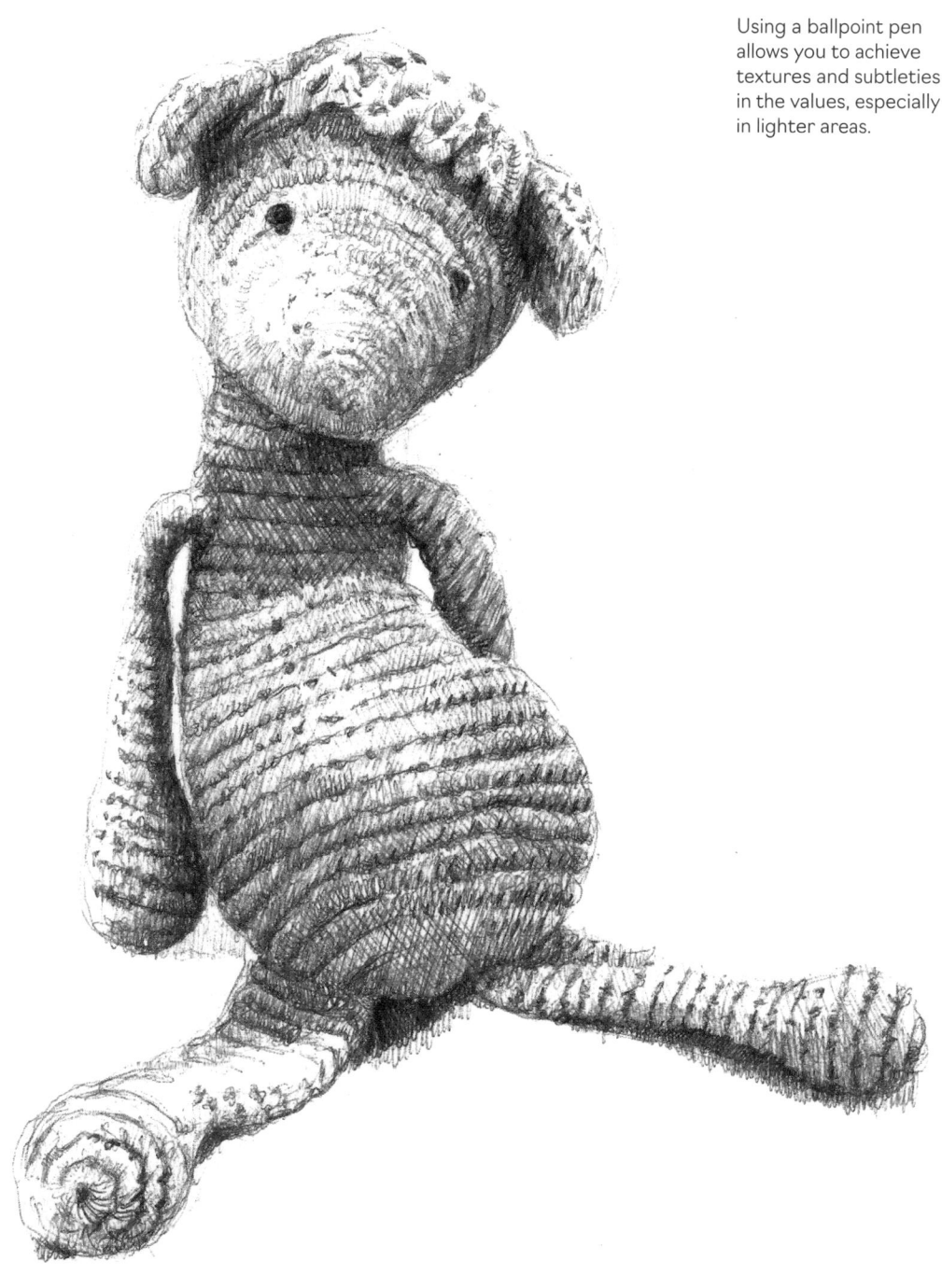

Using a ballpoint pen allows you to achieve textures and subtleties in the values, especially in lighter areas.

Techniques used: Cross hatching and scribbling
Supplies: Ballpoint pen

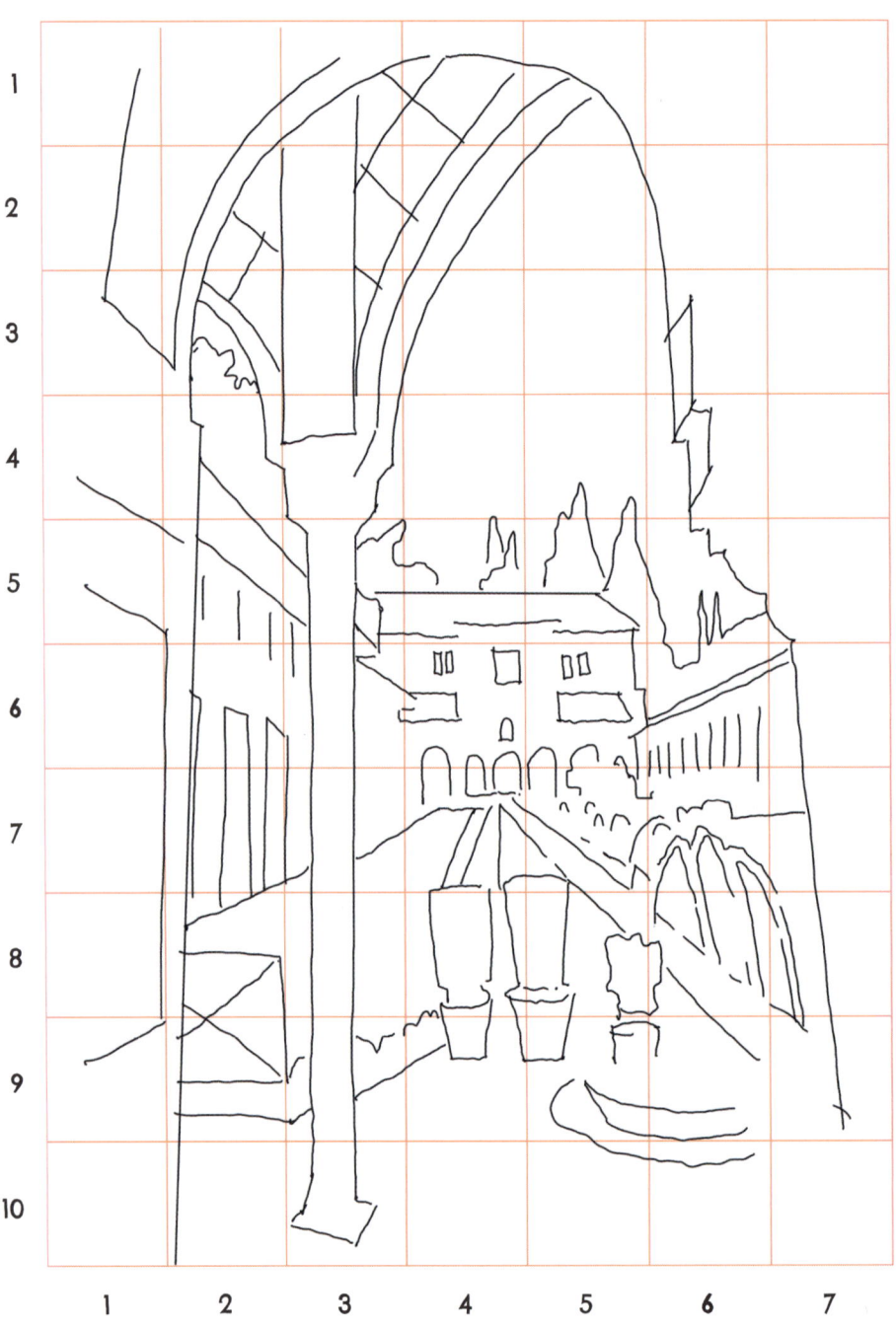

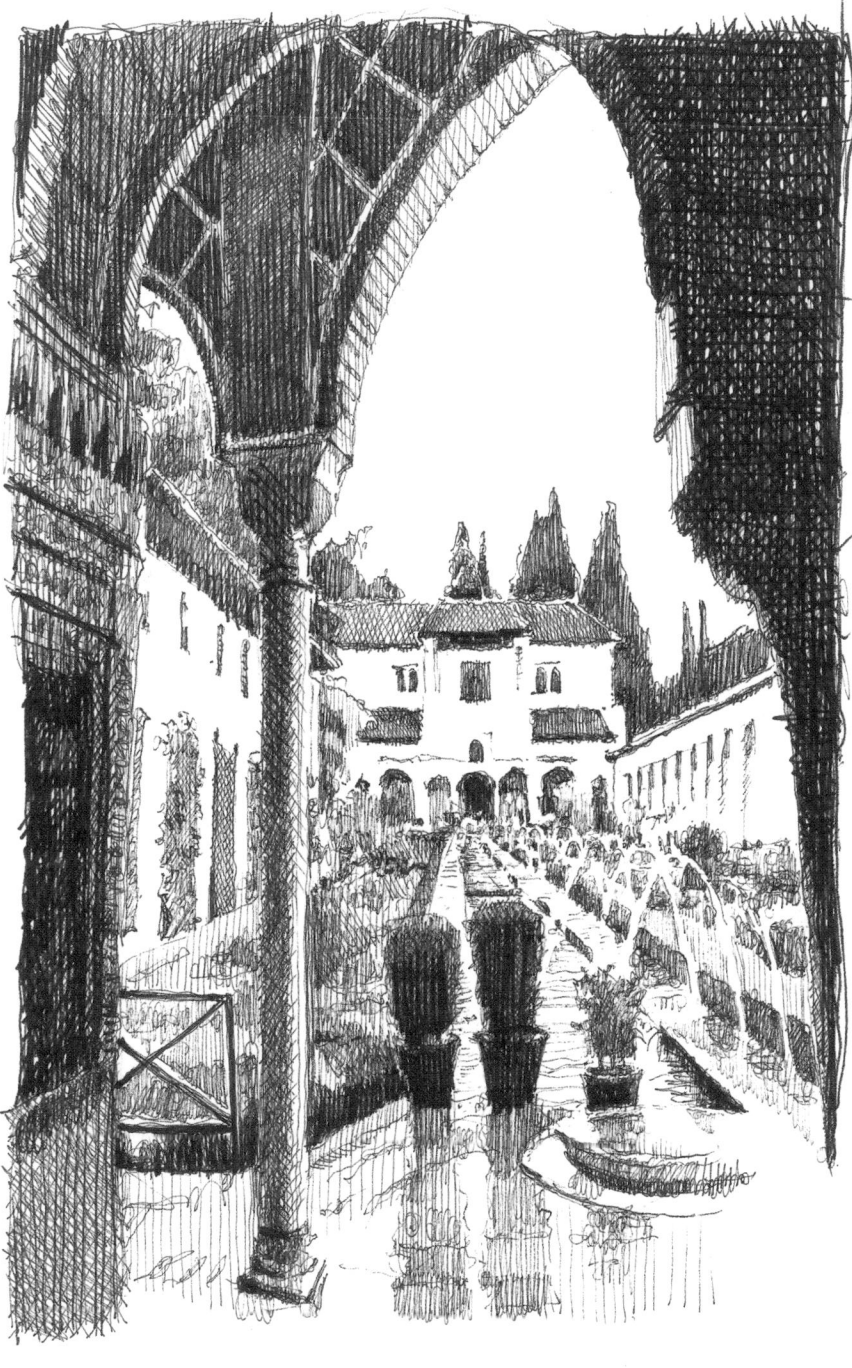

Use fineliners of different thicknesses to create contrast in your drawing quickly and effectively.

Techniques used: Cross hatching and scribbling
Supplies: Fineliners of different thicknesses

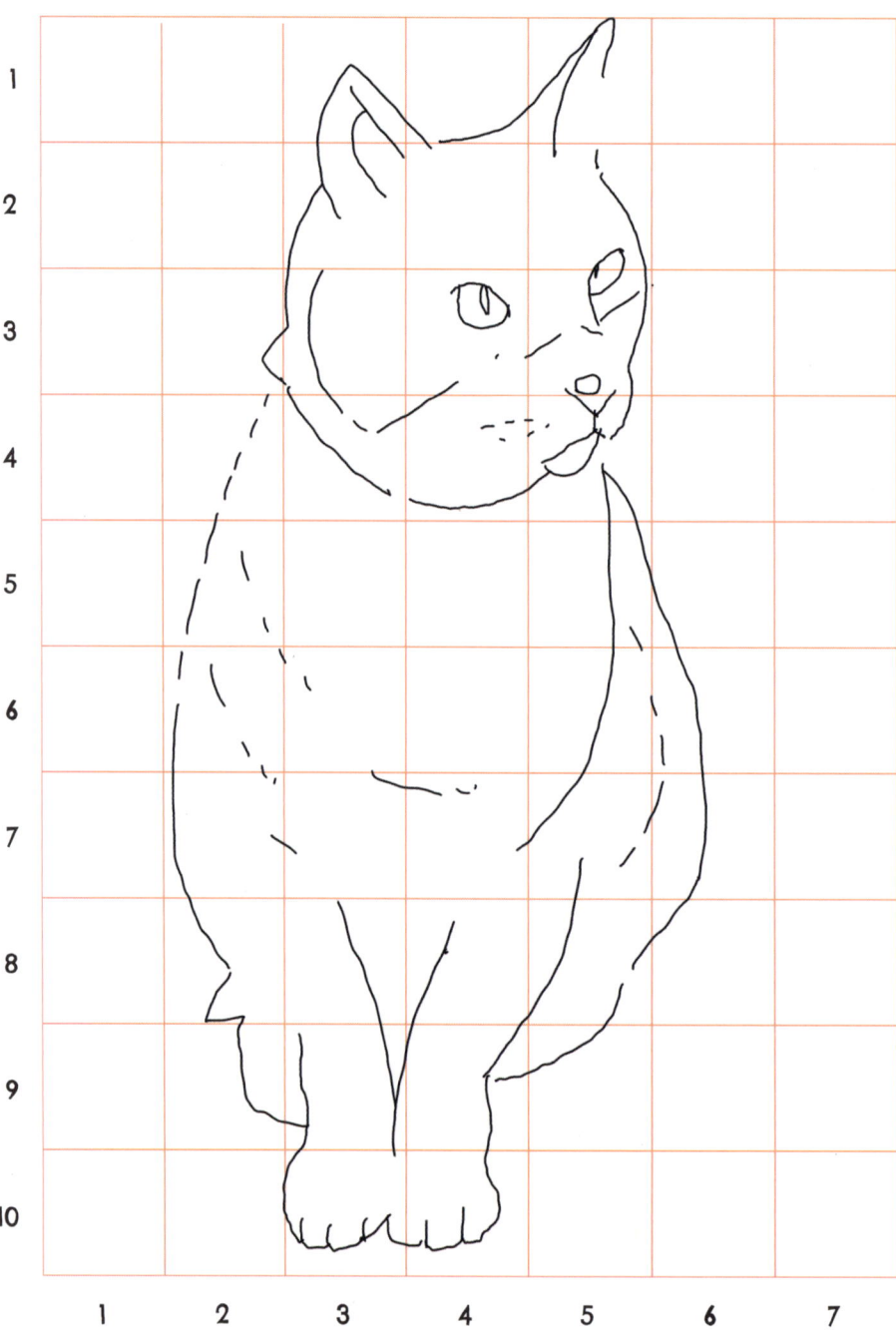

The areas left blank, without inking, are almost more important than the inked areas; pay attention and avoid overloading the drawing.

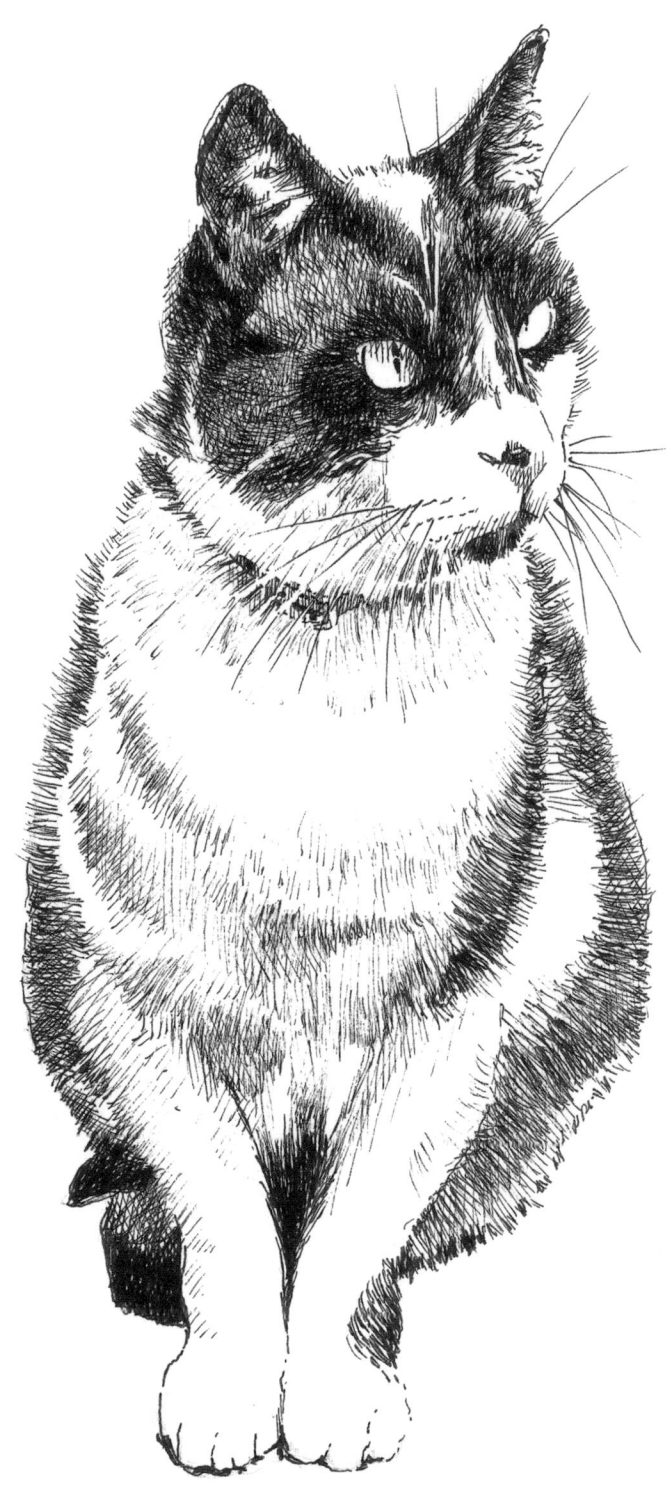

Technique used: Cross hatching
Supplies: 0.05 fineliner

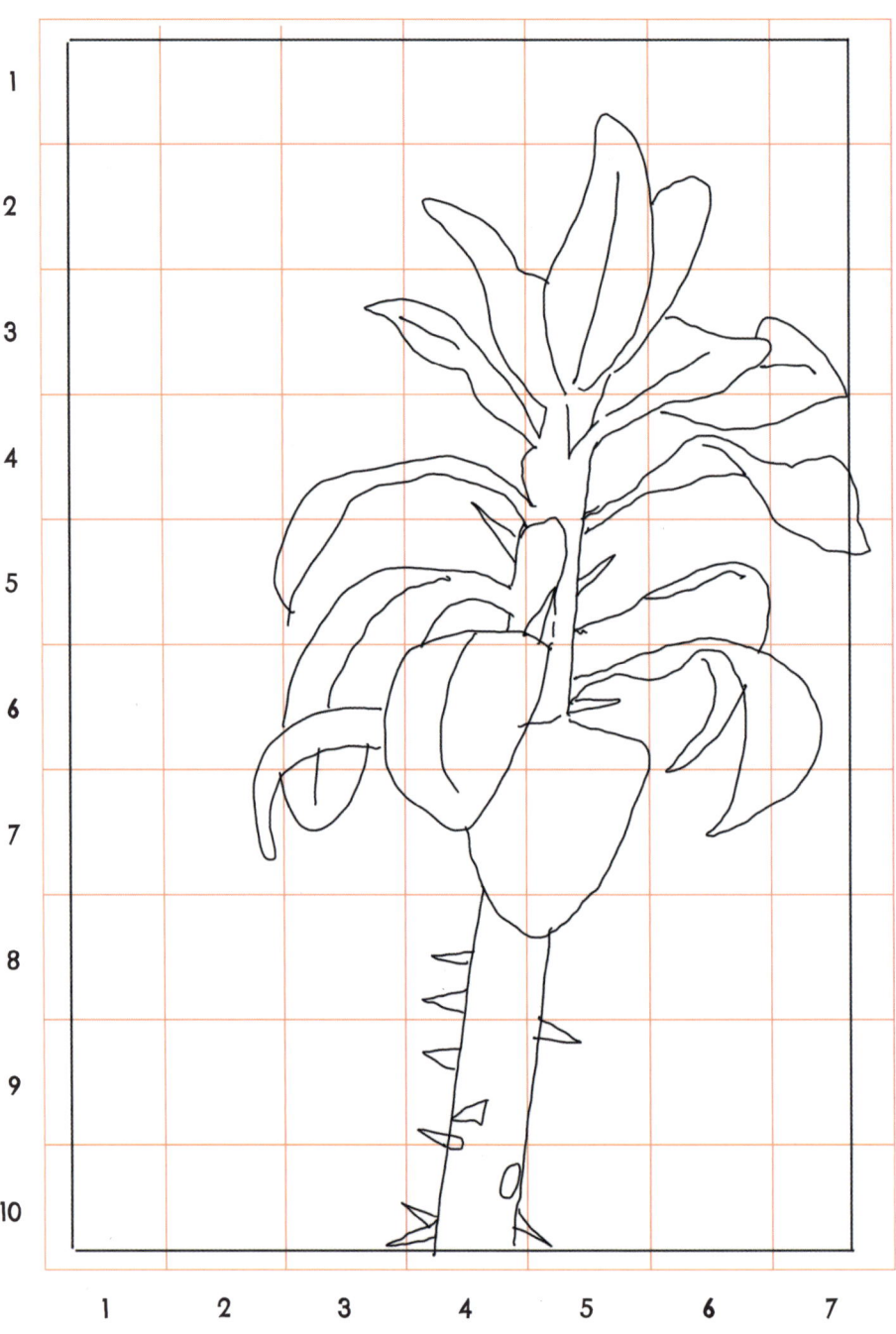

Outlining the contour or framing the object with thick lines can create an attractive effect.

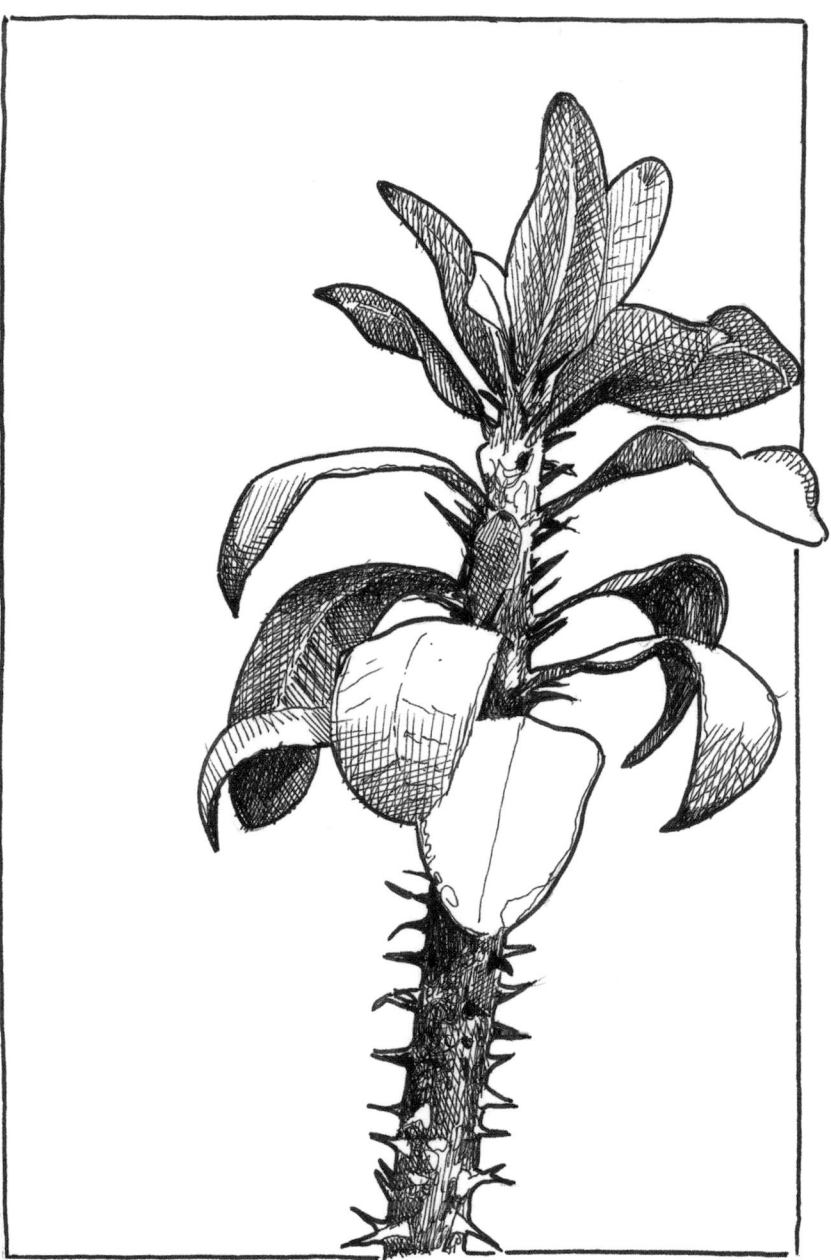

Technique used: Cross hatching
Supplies: Fineliners of different thicknesses

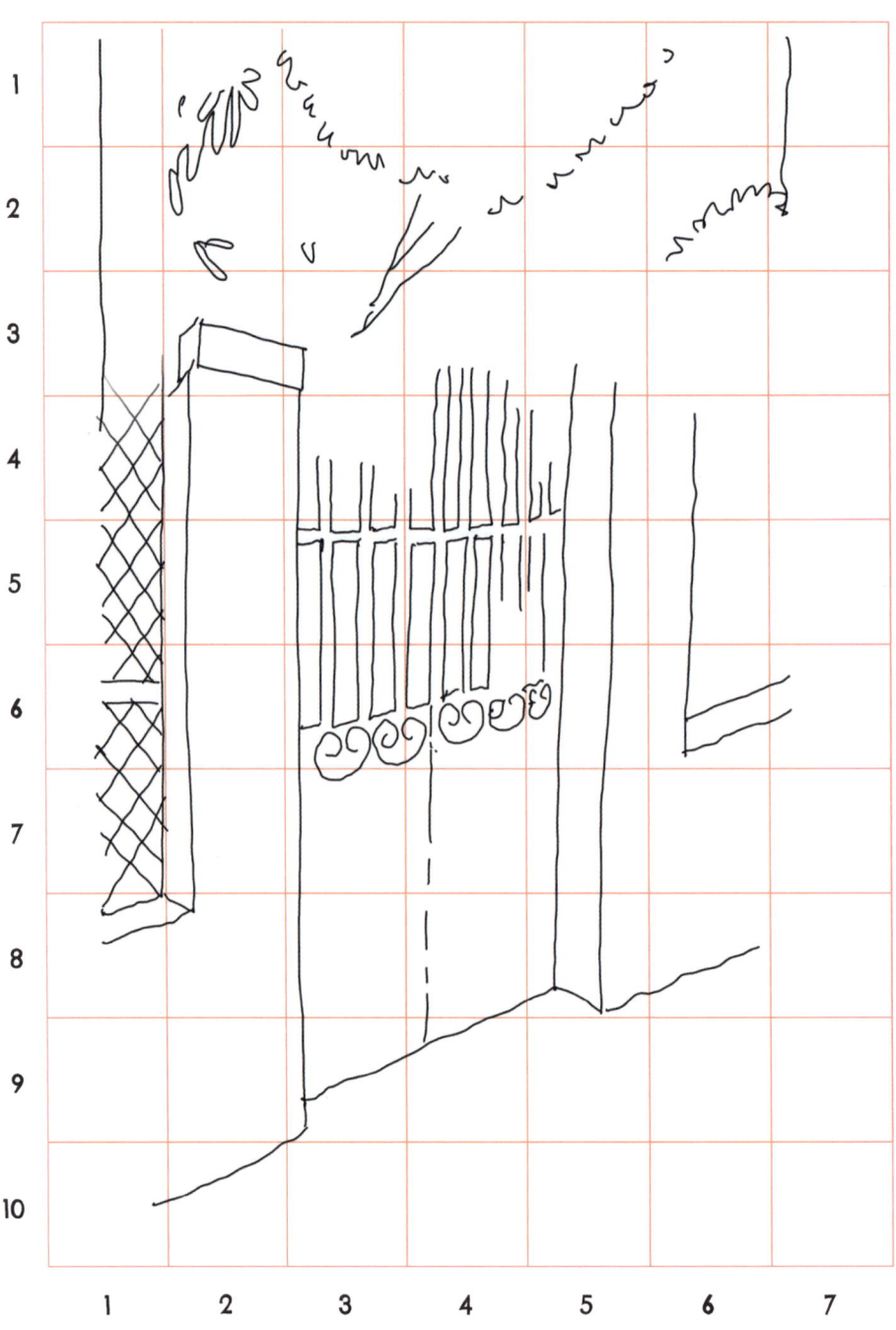

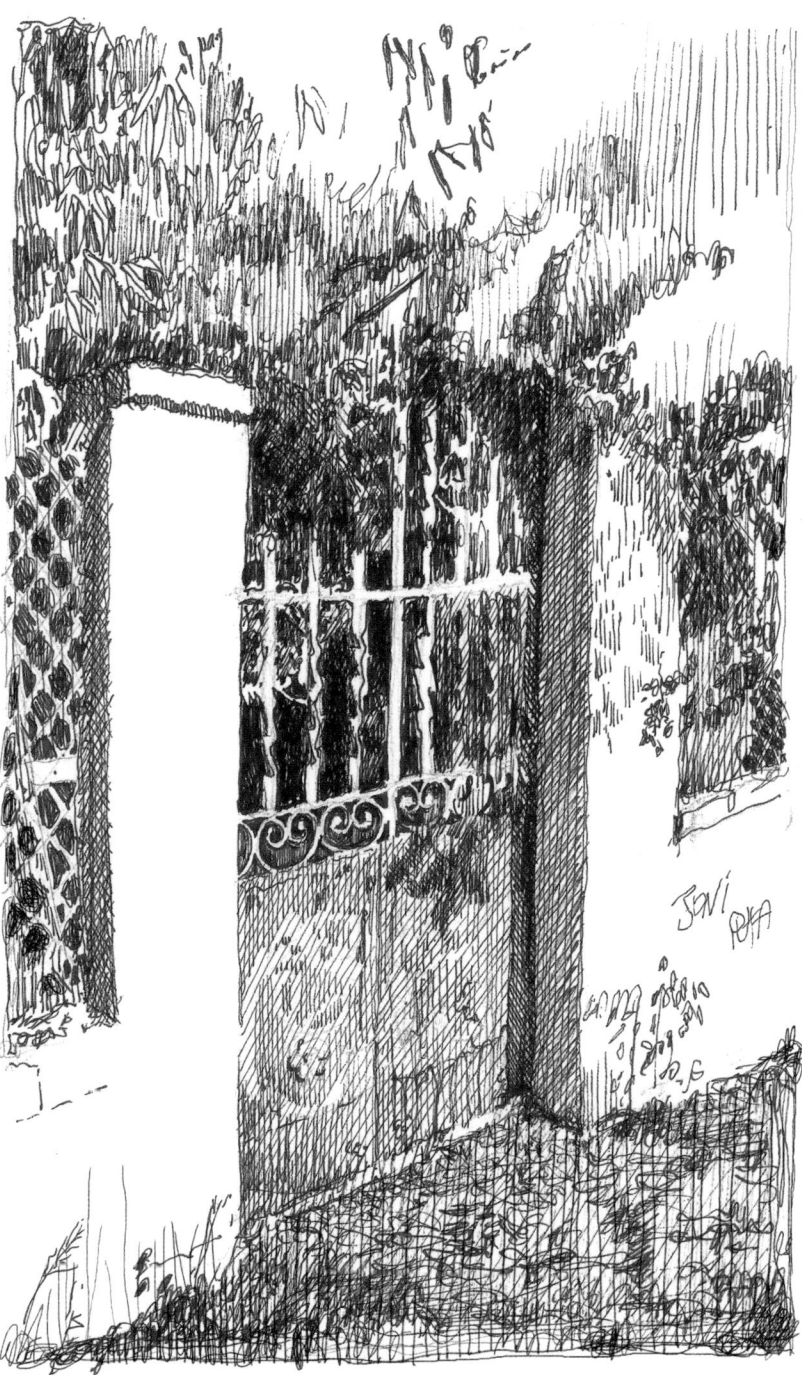

The texture of vegetation can be achieved through a blend of scribbling and controlled strokes without the need for detailed work.

Techniques used: Cross hatching and scribbling
Supplies: 0.05 fineliner

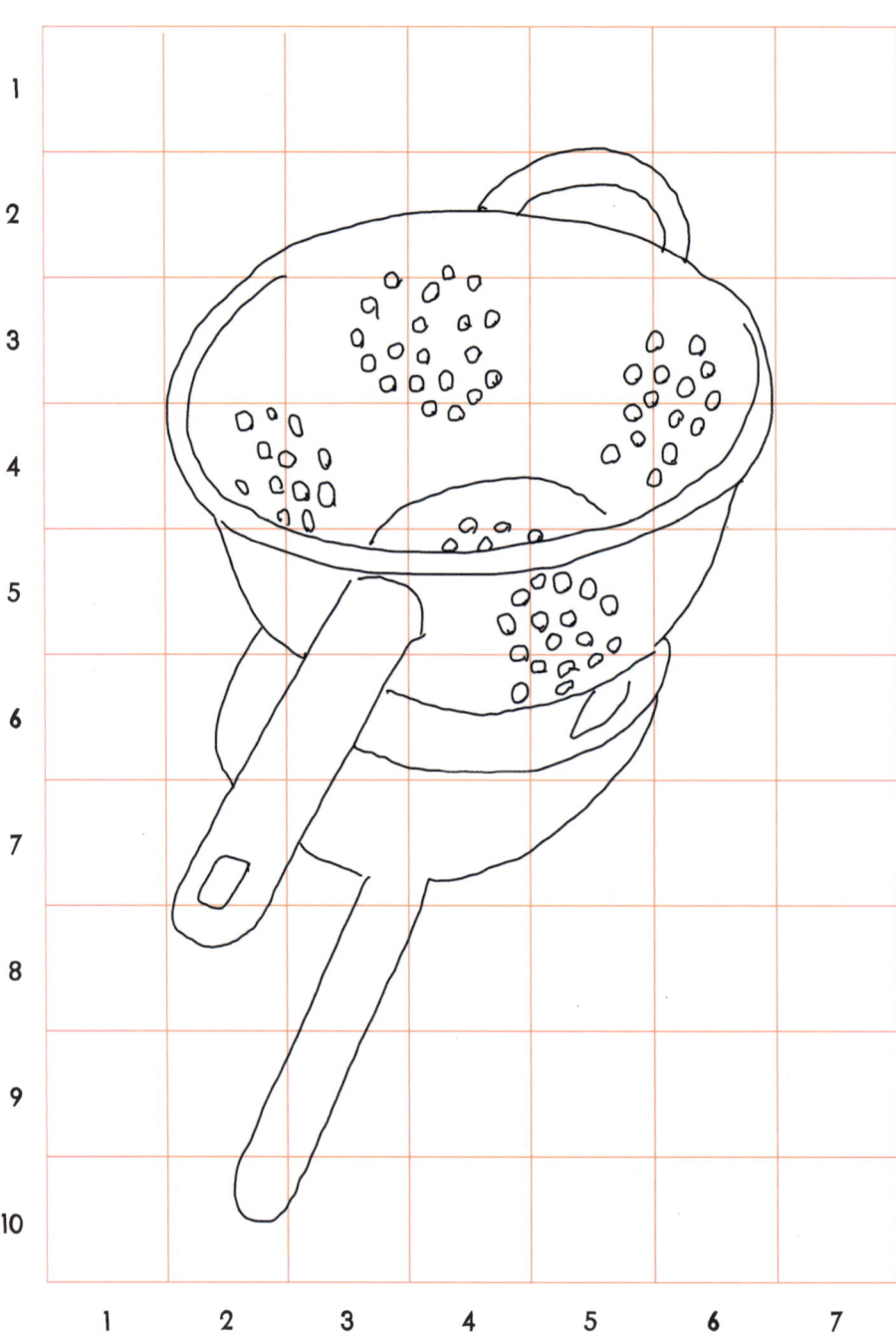

1
2
3
4
5
6
7
8
9
10

1   2   3   4   5   6   7

Do not underestimate the power of values; in this case, they are indispensable for creating the highlights and shadows necessary for us to understand the volume of the colander.

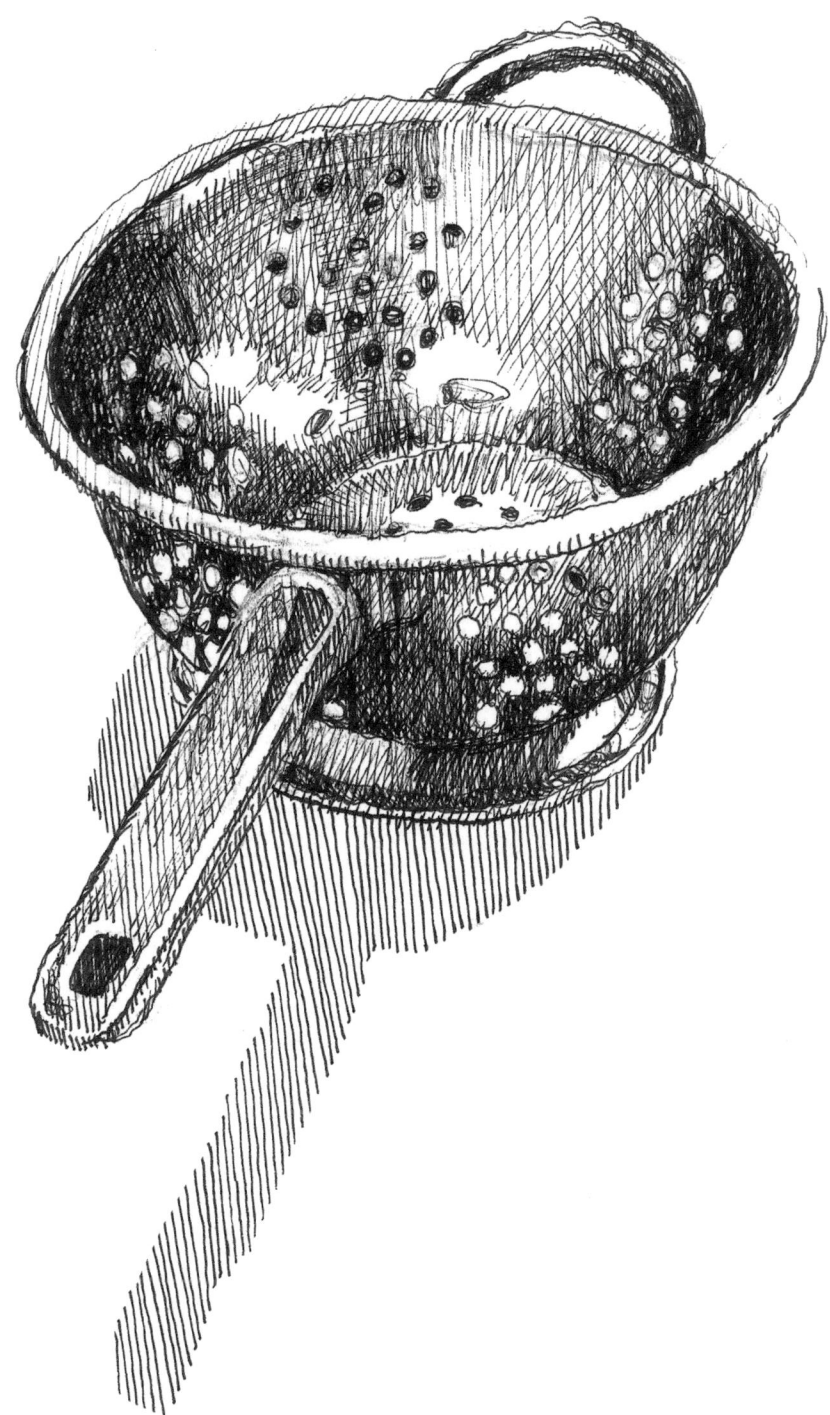

Technique used: Cross hatching
Supplies: 0.05 fineliner

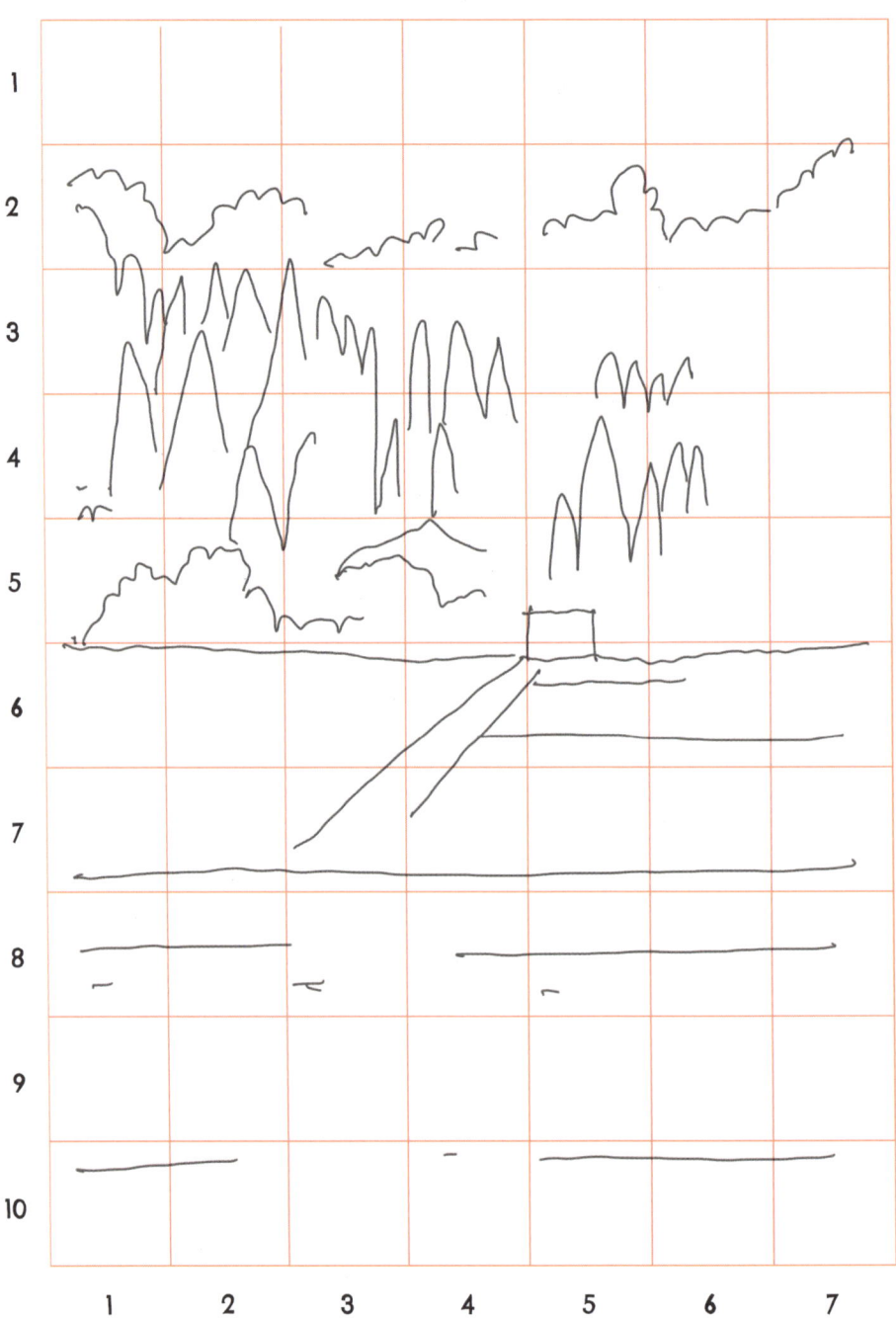

Outlines are not always necessary; a variety in values is sufficient to understand the image.

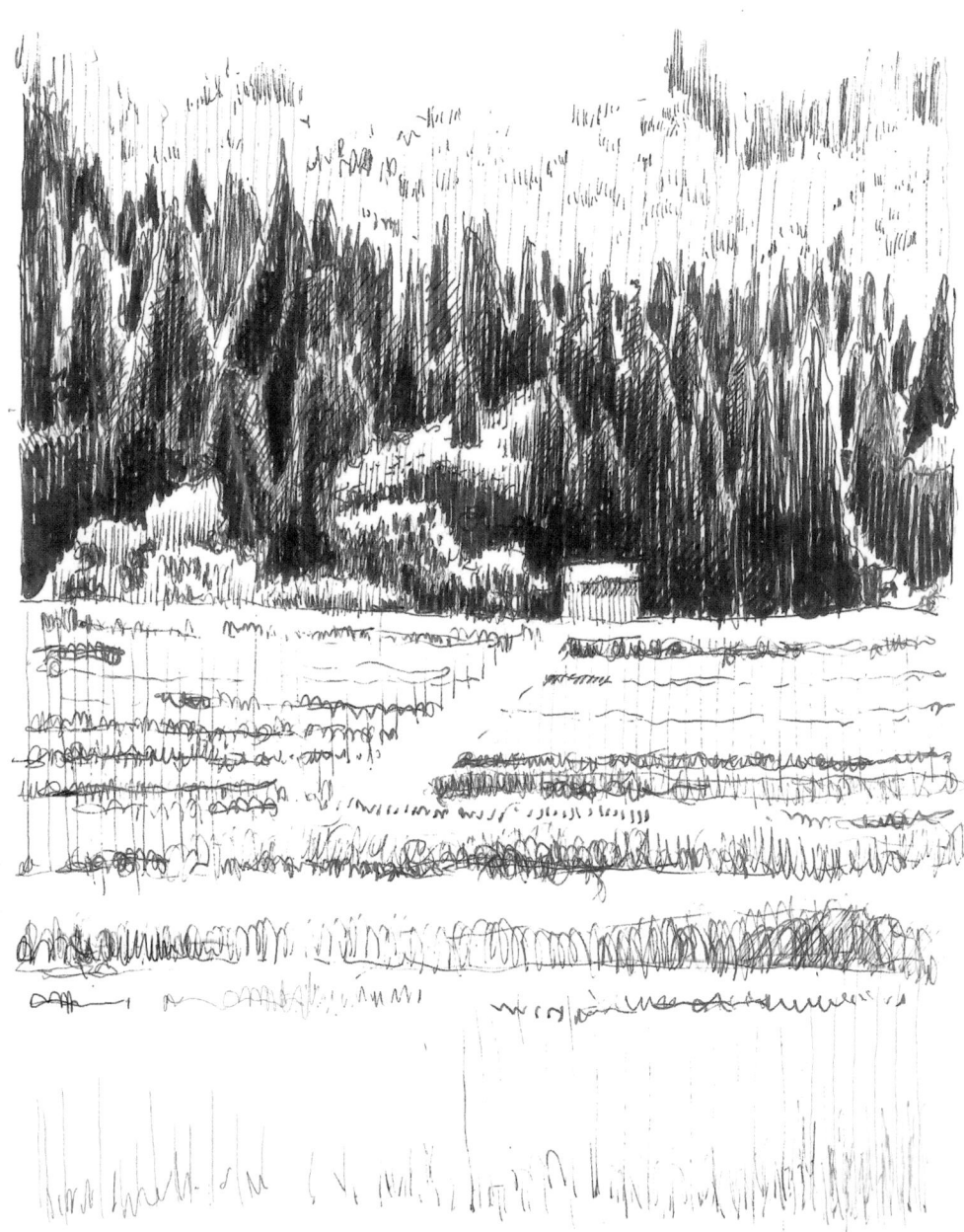

Techniques used: Cross hatching and scribbling
Supplies: Fineliners of different thicknesses

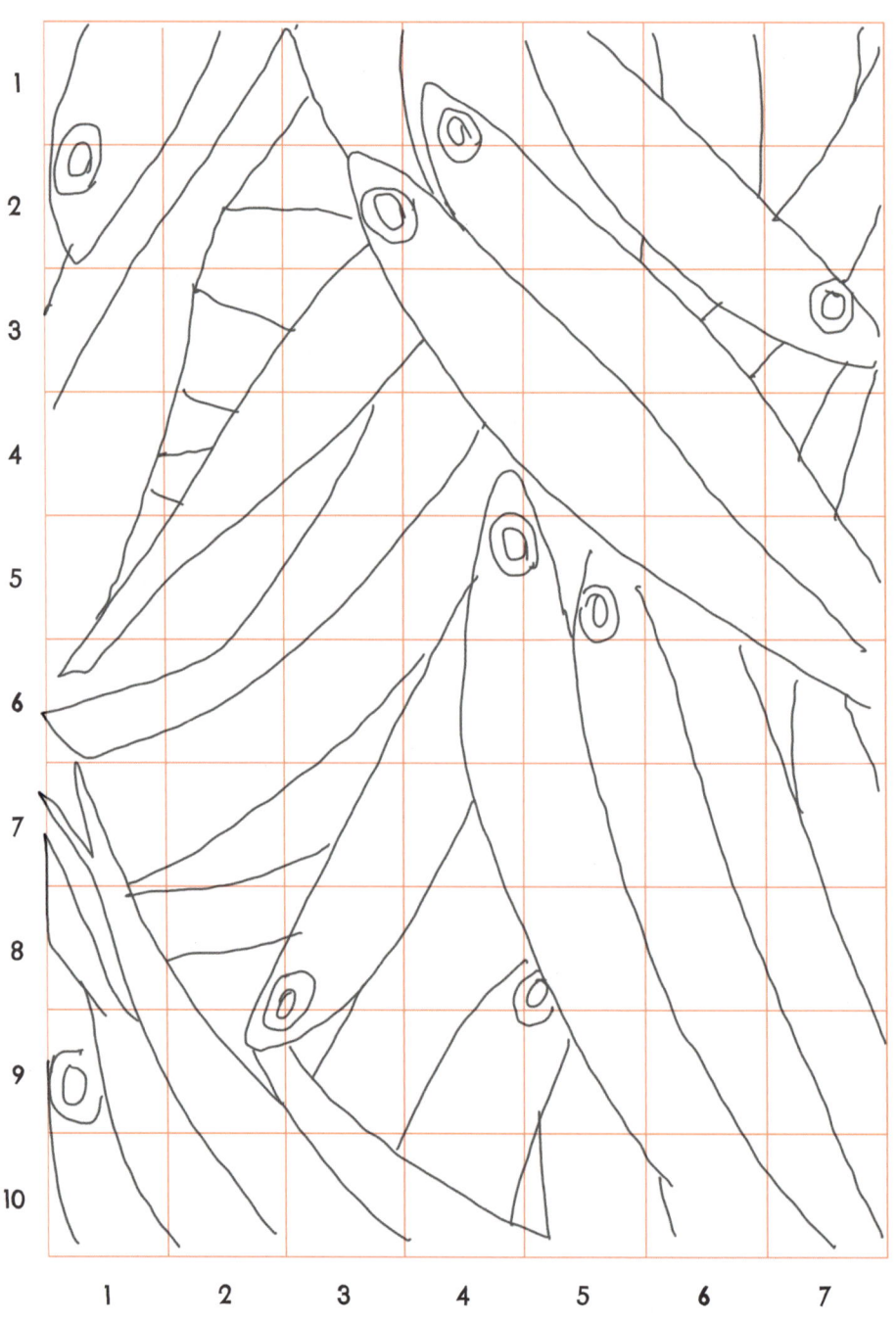

Try different types of strokes until you find the one you're most comfortable with.

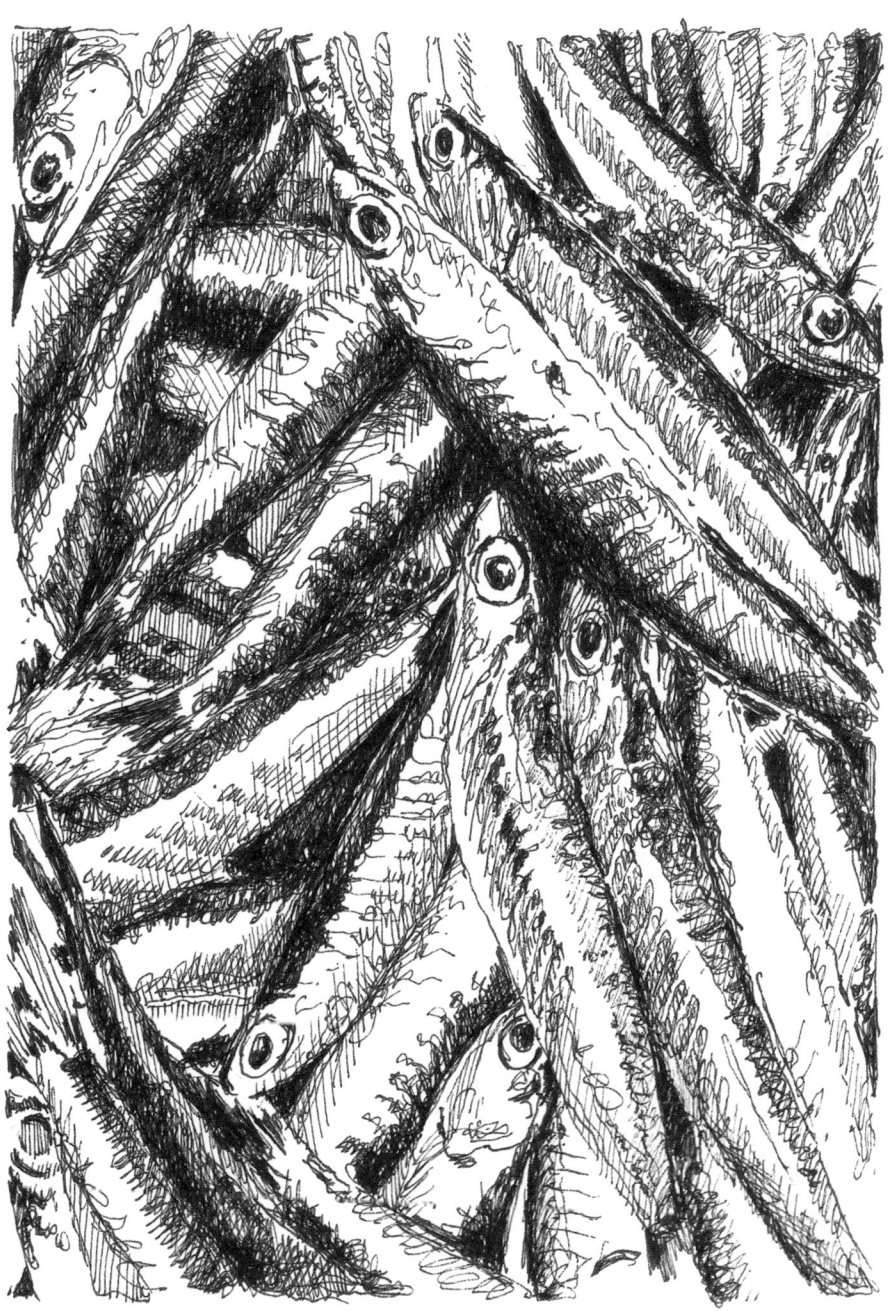

Technique used: Scribbling
Supplies: 0.05 fineliner

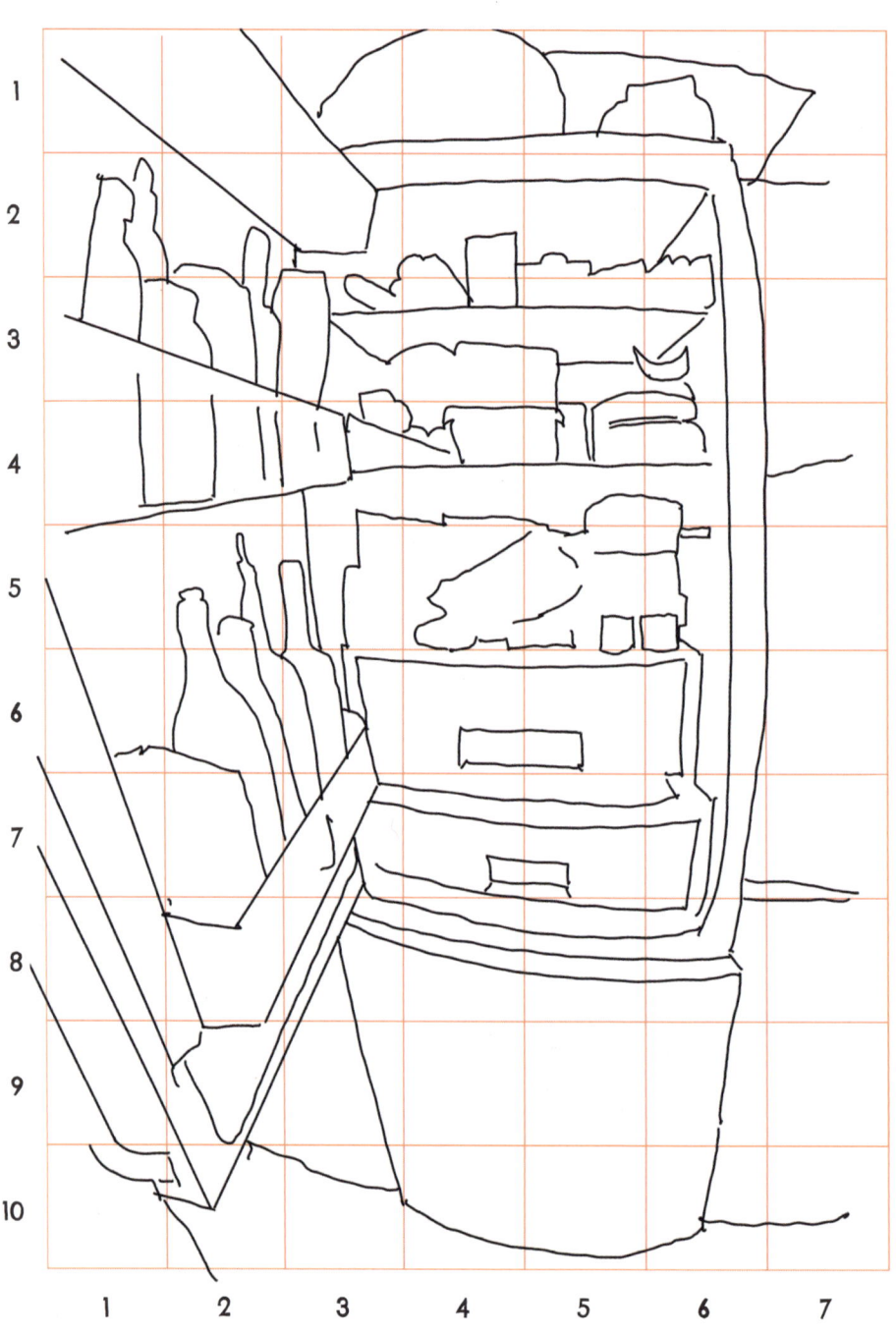

Notice that most of the values are achieved with cross hatching. Slowly, layer upon layer, you can achieve the necessary depths. Don't detail objects inside, just suggest them.

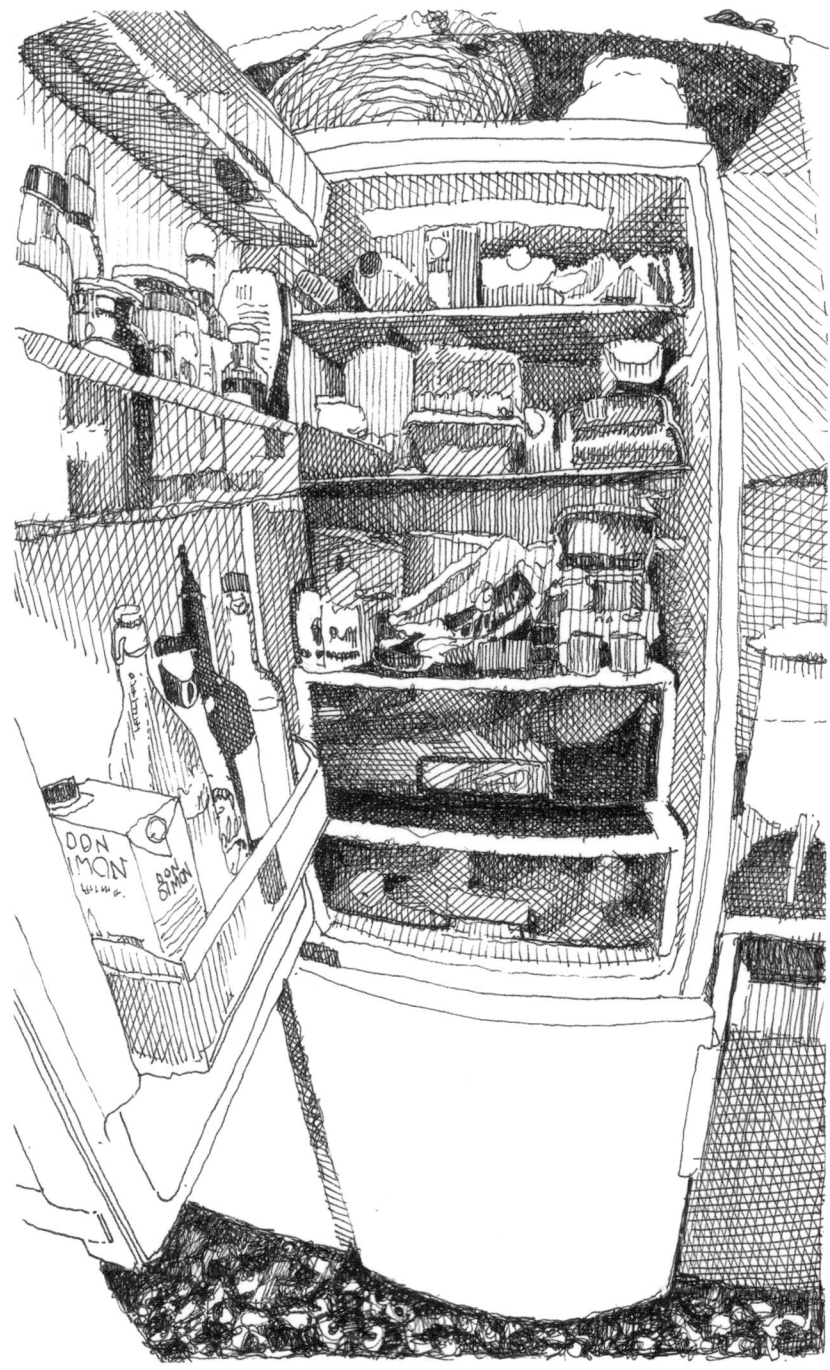

Technique used: Cross hatching and scribbling
Supplies: 0.05 fineliner

Prompts

Using verbal prompts to draw can be a powerful tool to find inspiration, refine textures, explore compositions and experiment with different techniques. This is the moment to challenge your creativity in a different way. I invite you to draw the following prompts in the panel below, interpreting them in whichever way you desire, and using the techniques and supplies of your choice.

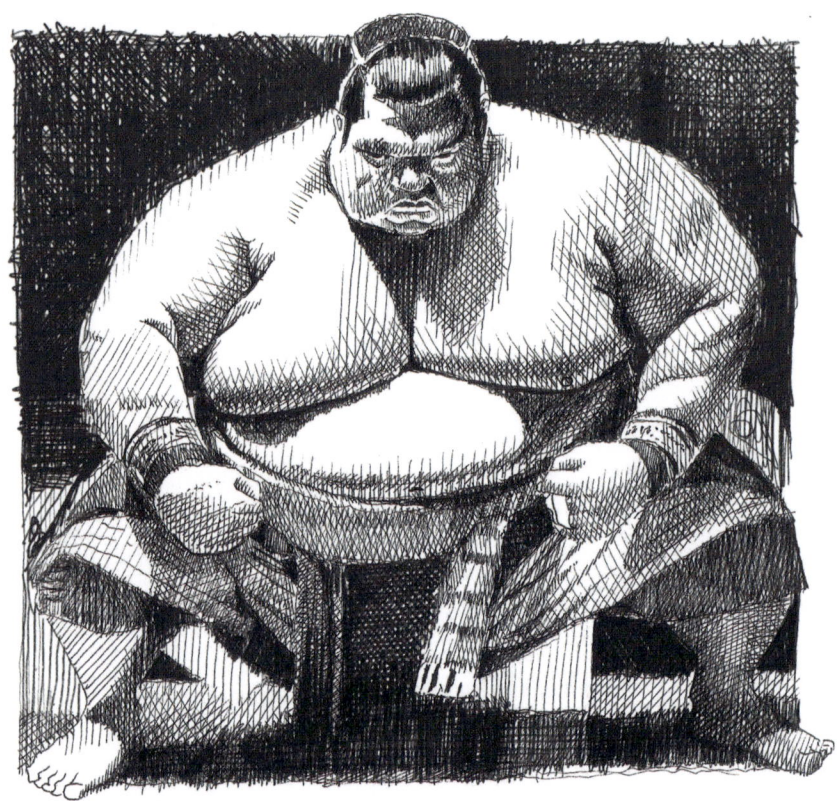

This sumo wrestler is inspired by the prompt 'strength' and the drawing of Wellington boots on the opposite page is an interpretation of 'shallow'.

Acid	Pilot	Wood	Antique
Yoga	Love	Music	Mouse
Fast	Pillow	Chandelier	Sport
Exciting	Fan	Textile	Chick
Massive	Swing	Field	Pot
Bull	Catch	Cook	Strength

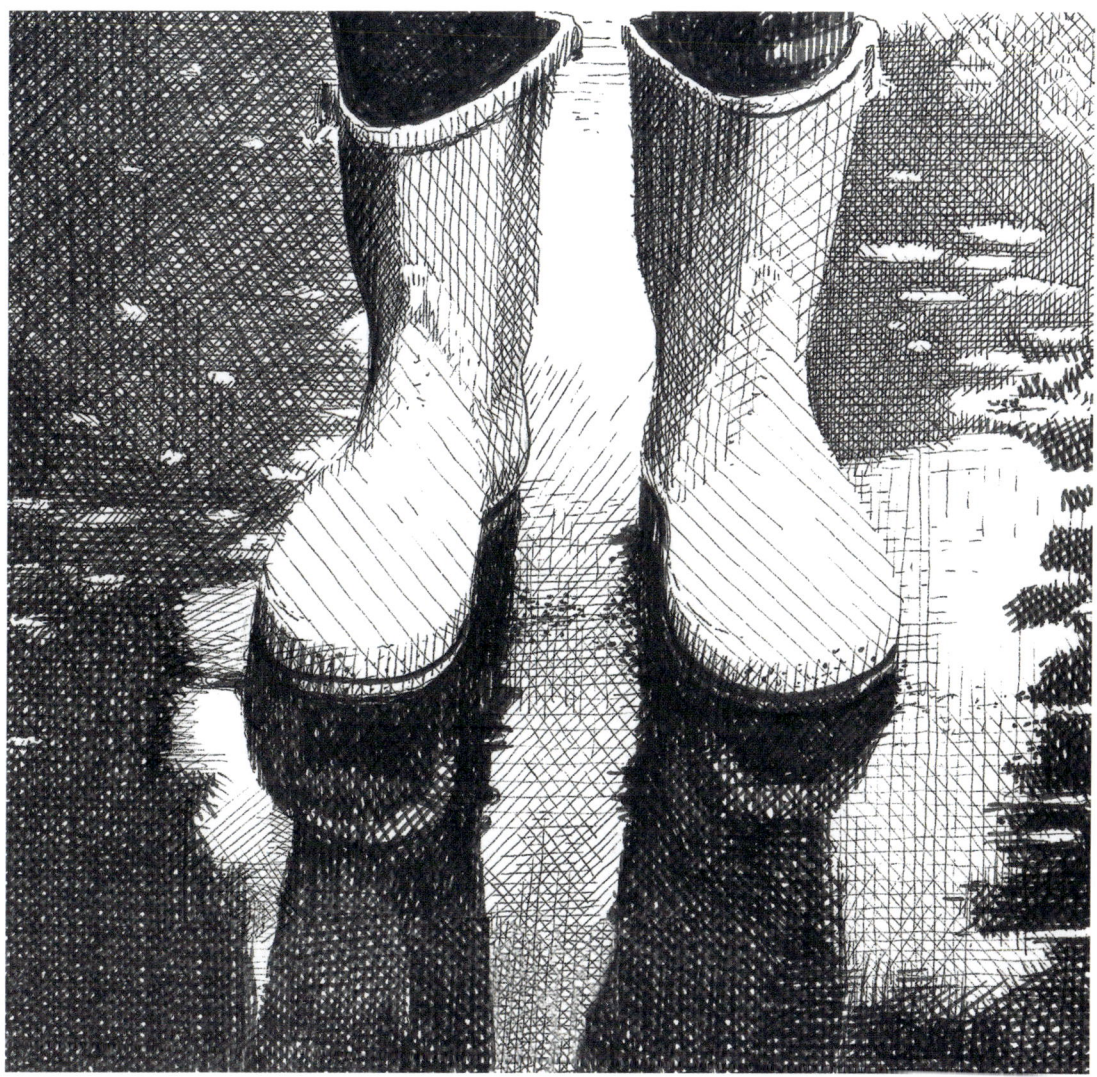

Feel free to approach the prompts in the way that inspires you the most, interpreting each image in whatever manner comes to mind.

Dark	Husky	Hat	Water
Gas	Burger	Packet	Flower
Enormous	Pastry	Stone	Fragile
Dessert	Shop	Shallow	Milk
Wild	Snake	Leather	Horn
Sushi	Chocolate	Snow	Coat

Index

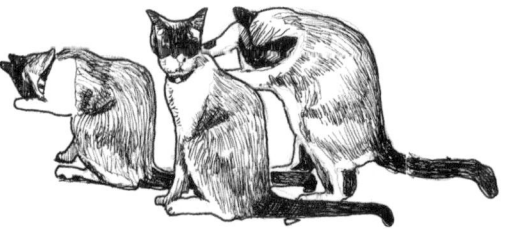

Acknowledgements

To María José, undoubtedly my biggest fan, for
supporting me and being understanding of the time
I dedicate to drawing.

To Marcel and Andrés, for putting up with all the times
I have drawn you poorly. Without you, the journey of
daily drawing practice wouldn't be the same.

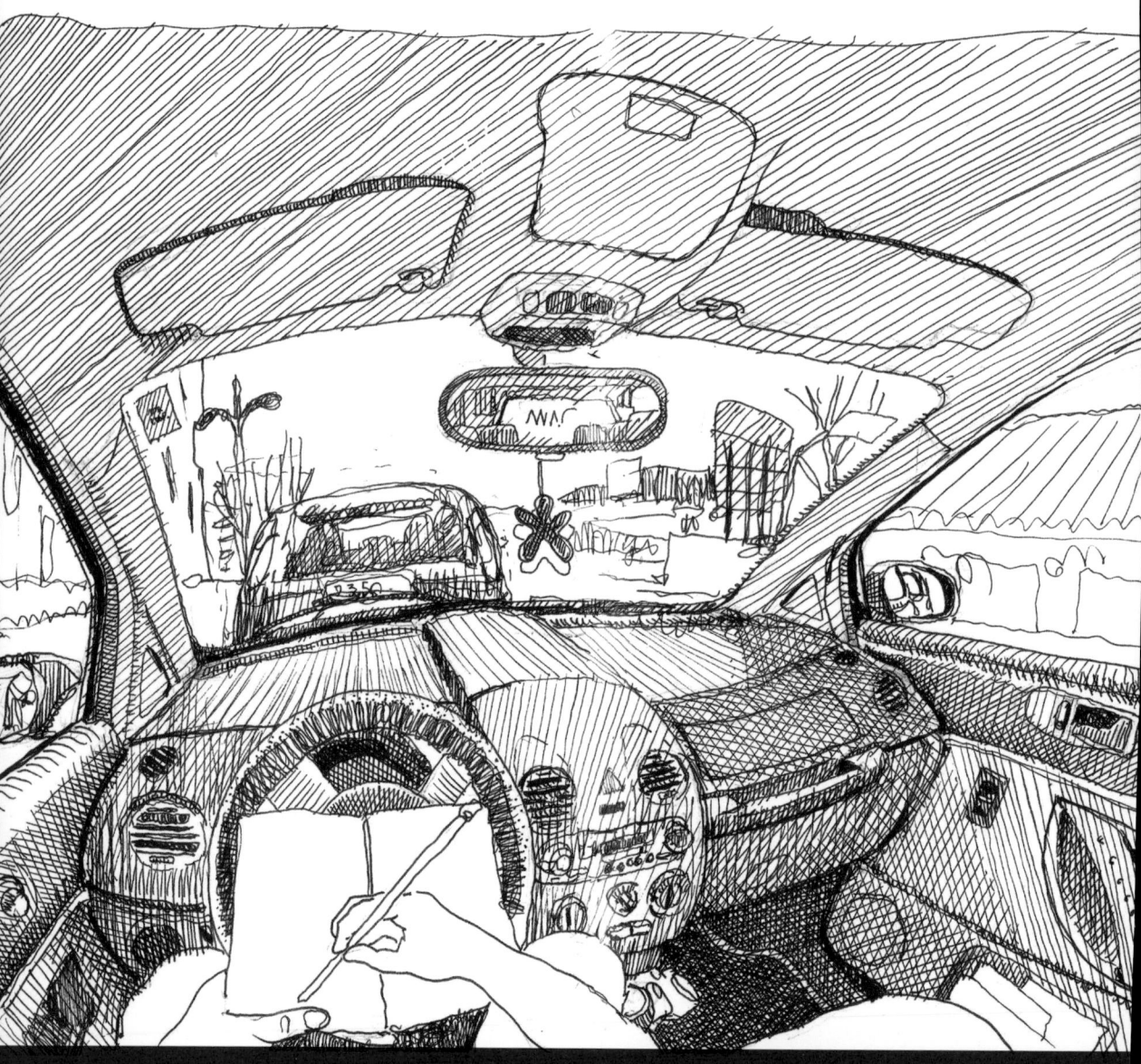